The Visual

Marketing

Revolution

26 Rules to Help Social Media Marketers Connect the Dots

D1456442

STEPHANIE DIAMOND

QUE®

800 East 96th Street, Indianapolis, Indiana 46240 USA

THE VISUAL MARKETING REVOLUTION

TRADEMARKS

All terms mentioned in this book that are known to be trademarks or service marks have been appropriately capitalized. Que Publishing cannot attest to the accuracy of this information. Use of a term in this book should not be regarded as affecting the validity of any trademark or service mark.

WARNING AND DISCLAIMER

Every effort has been made to make this book as complete and as accurate as possible, but no warranty or fitness is implied. The information provided is on an "as is" basis. The author and the publisher shall have neither liability nor responsibility to any person or entity with respect to any loss or damages arising from the information contained in this book or from the use of the programs accompanying it.

BULK SALES

Que Publishing offers excellent discounts on this book when ordered in quantity for bulk purchases or special sales. For more information, please contact

U.S. Corporate and Government Sales
1-800-382-3419
corpsales@pearsontechgroup.com

For sales outside of the U.S., please contact

International Sales
international@pearson.com

EDITOR-IN-CHIEF
Greg Wiegand

ACQUISITIONS EDITOR
Michelle Newcomb

DEVELOPMENT EDITOR
Ginny Bess Munroe

MANAGING EDITOR
Kristy Hart

PROJECT EDITOR
Andy Beaster

COPY EDITOR
Cheri Clark

INDEXER
Rebecca Salerno

PROOFREADER
Debbie Williams

TECHNICAL EDITOR
Michael Brito

PUBLISHING COORDINATOR
Cindy Teeters

COVER DESIGNER
Anne Jones

COMPOSITOR
Nonie Ratcliff

CONTENTS AT A GLANCE

Part IV: Tactics For Social Media Platforms

TABLE OF CONTENTS

Part III: Content to Get Customer Attention

PART IV: Tactics for Social Media Platforms

ABOUT THE AUTHOR

Stephanie Diamond is a thought leader and management marketing professional with 20-plus years of experience in building profits in more than 75 different industries. She has worked with solopreneurs, small-business owners, and multibillion-dollar corporations. As a best-selling author, she has written six business books, including *Social Media Marketing for Dummies* and *Social CRM for Dummies*.

She worked for eight years as a Marketing Director at AOL. When she joined, there were fewer than 1 million subscribers. When she left in 2002, there were 36 million. While at AOL, she developed a highly successful line of multimedia products that brought in an annual $40 million in incremental revenue.

In 2002, Stephanie founded Digital Media Works, Inc. (DigMediaWorks.com), an online marketing company that helps business owners discover the hidden profits in their businesses. She is passionate about guiding online companies to successfully generate more revenue and find their real value.

As a strategic thinker, Stephanie uses all the current visual thinking techniques and brain research to help companies get to the essence of their brands. She continues to focus on helping companies understand and communicate their value to customers.

Stephanie received a BA in Psychology from Hofstra University and an MSW and MPH from the University of Hawaii. She lives in New York with her husband and Maltese named Colby.

DEDICATION

To Barry, who makes all things possible.
To my family, for their encouragement and love.

ACKNOWLEDGMENTS

It is my great privilege to write a book about visual marketing. I want to offer great thanks to Pearson Publishing, Inc., for letting me present my ideas about why visual marketing is an important concept that will influence marketing for years to come.

The following people were especially important in creating this book, and I offer very sincere thanks:

- To the wonderfully creative Michelle Newcomb at Pearson, who helped me realize my vision for this book.

- To the editors at Pearson—Development Editor Ginny Bess Munroe, Project Editor Andy Beaster, and Copy Editor Cheri Clark for their dedicated work to make this book as clear and useful as possible.

- To Michael Brito for his excellent savvy advice and technical edits.

- To Matt Wagner, my agent at Fresh Books, for his continued support and hard work on my behalf.

- To the very talented and wise thought leaders who influence my ideas on visual thinking including Michael Deutch, Derek Franklin, and Chuck Frey.

Finally, to the smart readers who will take this book and extend it far beyond my thinking to find greater uses for online marketers.

WE WANT TO HEAR FROM YOU!

As the reader of this book, *you* are our most important critic and commentator. We value your opinion and want to know what we're doing right, what we could do better, what areas you'd like to see us publish in, and any other words of wisdom you're willing to pass our way.

We welcome your comments. You can email or write to let us know what you did or didn't like about this book—as well as what we can do to make our books better.

Please note that we cannot help you with technical problems related to the topic of this book.

When you write, please be sure to include this book's title and author as well as your name and email address. We will carefully review your comments and share them with the author and editors who worked on the book.

Email: feedback@quepublishing.com

Mail: Que Publishing
           ATTN: Reader Feedback
           800 East 96th Street
           Indianapolis, IN 46240 USA

READER SERVICES

Visit our website and register this book at quepublishing.com/register for convenient access to any updates, downloads, or errata that might be available for this book.

INTRODUCTION

"The Revolution won't be televised; it will be Instagrammed."
–Steve Rubel, EVP/Global Strategy and Insights for Edelman PR,
Ad Age Digital, 7/24/12

Ref: http://adage.com/article/steve-rubel/
revolution-televised-instagrammed/236266/

The prophetic quote above by Steve Rubel, EVP/Global Strategy and Insights for Edelman, harkens back to a 1970 song by Gil Scott-Heron called "The Revolution Will Not Be Televised." Rubel's article says that unlike in the past, everything we do today (including wars) can be captured by a smartphone or camera and shared online.

With the introduction of the graphical interface by Apple in the 1980s, Internet users began seeing their text information presented in a more visual way. Over time, they became accustomed to seeing information presented this way. In 2012, visual displays reached a tipping point when services like Pinterest, Tumblr, and Instagram became major social media sites in record time.

In this book, we look at some of the physical (brain) and psychological reasons everyone loves visuals. At its most basic level it's the fact that people consume information that's easy to understand. Visuals are novel and can usually be consumed with a glance. In addition, given advances in technology, people can play with those images and make new ones. Tools like Instagram filters make novice photographers feel empowered.

ABOUT THIS BOOK

The purpose of the book is to give you ideas about how you can marry the very best social media methods with the power of visuals to reach your customers and rapidly grow your business. It doesn't cover everything you need to know about this topic, just what you need to know to take meaningful action.

This book focuses on not only things you can do to make visual marketing easier for you, but also your staff and your customers. Included are methods and tools that will help you connect the dots between social media and visuals.

Whenever possible, we leave out long explanations and present a method for you to try. The tools selected were chosen because they are easy. Of course, there are many others you can use—new ones are created every day. The tools in this book were selected to help you get a fast start.

Throughout the book, when I use the word *visuals* I refer to a wide variety of formats that include the following:

- Diagrams
- Templates
- Checklists
- Flowcharts
- Mind maps
- Pie charts
- Storyboards
- Bull's-eye targets
- Hub-and-spoke graphics

I hope you'll explore how to make visuals work for your marketing efforts. It's easy to fall back on using the same two or three formats for everything we do.

ORGANIZATION OF THE BOOK

The book content is presented in the form of 26 Rules. In each rule you will find a mix of the following topics:

- **Method:** The method refers to the action step you can take using the information in that rule.

- **Tools provided:** These are tools you can try with the method that will make the rule easier to implement.

- **Tools to consider:** This refers to additional tools that are available online, mostly free, that you can also consider as you explore.

- **Ideas to use:** This section summarizes some of the ideas presented in the rule so that you can quickly refer to the main points.

- **Idea map:** At the end of each chapter, there is an idea map (a form of mind map) of the rule. To get the most from it, you can add your own notes and comments. Your own notes are always the most valuable part of any exercise.

To organize the book's content, there are four distinct types of information presented in this order: rules, tools, content, and tactics.

This book is divided into four parts:

- **Part I: Rules for Social Media Marketers**

  This part looks at the process you as a social media marketer can follow to lay the foundation for effective marketing. It includes a discussion of visual persuasion and the use of storytelling.

- **Part II: Tools to Help You Create Your Visual Marketing**

  In this part, we look at readily available visual tools you can use to empower yourself and your team. We include the use of mind maps and graphic organizers.

- **Part III: Content to Get Customer Attention**

  This part looks at the kinds of content you should consider creating for your customers. We look at such things as infographics and eBooks.

- **Part IV: Tactics for Social Media Platforms**

  In this part, we look at the tactics you can use to reach your customers by putting the rules into practice. We cover most of the major social media platforms and demonstrate some ways to build relationships with your customers.

My goal for the book is to equip you with the knowledge you need to tackle visual marketing. I hope I've connected the dots and shown you a roadmap to enhance your own marketing efforts.

Part I

RULES FOR SOCIAL MEDIA MARKETERS

RECOGNIZE THE POWER OF VISUAL PERSUASION

In Rule 1 we look at how visuals unconsciously affect our behavior. By looking at images, we can draw conclusions that might or might not be intended. Those conclusions are why images are so vital to your business. You'll learn how to recognize the power of visual persuasion. We include a template to help you analyze your online presence.

WHAT YOU NEED TO KNOW

Let's start with a rule that is critical to your understanding of why visuals are so powerful. Visuals persuade. It's a subtle process of which we are generally unaware.

Our brain processes language visually. When we see something, we create a visual representation of it and store it in our mind. When we call it up, we see it as a visual representation. You never see a word in your mind; you see a picture. Yet you are not aware of the process. In fact, educational researchers at the Department of Labor tell us that over 83% of our learning happens visually.

Traditionally, educators pay little attention to the part visuals play in our ability to learn. But we all start out using visuals as a way to navigate our world.

We learn to take our first steps and avoid disasters by watching others. We watch the reactions of our parents' faces when we fall. If they look frightened, we cry. If they laugh and encourage us, we try again. We don't need anyone to instruct us; we simply watch. If there were no formal education available, the method of watching and copying would continue into adulthood.

The same cannot be said for text. We need to be taught to read and write so we are trained to focus on words. We are taught how to write so that we can spend all our time learning through text. As we progress through school, our interest in visuals is discouraged and we rarely use it as a tool.

To help you understand visual thinking, here are some facts about how your brain processes visuals that will help you communicate with others:

> Educational researchers at the Department of Labor tell us that over 83% of our learning happens visually.

- **Understand how we see:** Rather than learning the clinical explanation of how we see, you are better served by understanding how you see information and how marketers use it to persuade you.

  Here's how it works: Your eyes take in small chunks and process them as images and then move to the next chunk. You think you are taking in a large amount of information at once, but that's because your eye keeps moving. Remember this when you present information.

  Start with a small piece of content and gradually add. Don't expect someone to look at a complicated visual and understand it immediately. Too much visual information at once causes a person to look away. They need time to process it, literally.

  That means that the best marketing visual is one that has limited information and which can be understood with a quick glance. Think about eliminating unnecessary elements whenever possible. Your audience will thank you.

- **Visualize with your mind's eye:** Your brain makes a visual representation of whatever word or concept you are thinking about. Your brain allows you to "see" it with your mind's eye so that you can use it. The trick with visual thinking is to make what is in your mind understandable to others (and sometimes yourself).

- **Create representations of ideas:** As you struggle to make your thinking visual, you should be aware that your audience is seeking to find patterns and make associations with things it already knows. If you think about showing visuals from that perspective, you can help your audience make connections more quickly. We talk about this in Rule 9, "Make Ideas Tangible."

TIP   When you are creating presentation visuals, ask yourself, "What is this concept like?" and "How is it different from something people already know about?"

- **Understand that maps have important functions:** Maps have several different meanings when we talk about the brain. Typically, when we think about the value of maps, we usually think about using them to get from one place to another that is unfamiliar to us.

  That is exactly what maps do in our brains as well. For you to move from the desk to the door, your brain analyzes and creates a map of your environment for you to navigate. If you also think about maps this way, you will be more likely to use them to show people ways to "navigate" from one idea to another.

- **Help your left and right brain work together:** Through current major advances in brain science, we know that different parts of our brains have very specific functions. There has recently been some disagreement about whether we could literally separate our brain into right and left functions. It appears to be more complicated than that.

  But what most neuroscientists agree about is that some part of the brain (we'll call it left) handles such things as logic and speech distinctly from the (right) part that handles creativity and emotion.

  When you employ thinking tasks that use both "sides" at the same time, you are maximizing your brain's functioning. An example is using a mind map for brainstorming. A mind map uses both the left and the right side of the brain at the same time. We look at mind mapping in detail in Rule 10, "Use Diagrams and Data Visualization Tools to Explain Marketing Ideas."

- **Be aware that colors affect shopping behavior:** An infographic by KISSmetrics called "How do colors affect purchases?" reports that 1% of shoppers are affected by sound and smell, 6% by texture, and 93% by visual appearance. As a marketer, you can't ignore the impact of visuals like color. (To see the infographic, go to http://blog.kissmetrics.com/color-psychology/?wide=1.)

DO YOU SEE WHAT I SEE?

The most important thing to know about how we see is that not everyone sees the same thing. This is not a function of eyesight, but one of culture and experience. In her book *Now You See It: How the Brain Science of Attention Will Transform the Way We Live, Work and Learn*, Cathy Davidson talks about a brain-science concept called "attention blindness." Attention blindness refers to the fact that people see what they expect to see based on their experience and cultural upbringing. "We think we see the whole world, but we actually see a very particular part of it....We're not really as smart as we think we are." As a marketer, you need to be aware that your visual content might not hit the target for all customers because they don't see what you think they see.

THE POWER OF VISUALS AND TEXT

By using both visuals and text, you enhance the power of each to communicate your message. As we noted, using your full range of brain functions helps you maximize your understanding of something and aids your customer too.

For example, here's an easy one. Good design dictates that whenever you use a photo, you put a caption along with it. Research shows that most people will read the caption after looking at a photo. Visual conventions like this were created to support understanding. The more familiar you are with them, the more you can enhance your ability to communicate your message.

Another example is the use of visuals with a blog post. Most good blog posts include a graphic and when possible a video. Visuals break up the monotony of a text block and set the tone for the post. If the picture is humorous or emotional, we know what to expect. If the text matches the picture, we feel that the expectation has been met. If a video accompanies the post, most people will at least begin to watch it. For example, see Rule 12, "Use Visual Presentations to Connect with an Audience," for a discussion that includes how adding images to updates draws a much deeper level of engagement than those without images.

A study by John Doherty called "What Kind of Content Gets Links in 2012?" for SEOMOZ, 2012 found that posts with text, images, and video had the most links to them.

TIP Want more proof about the value of pictures with text? According to John Medina, author of *Brain Rules*, "If information is presented orally, people remember about 10%, tested 72 hours after exposure. That figure goes up to 65% if you add a picture."

EVALUATE YOUR ONLINE ABILITY TO PERSUADE

Because the Web places such a strong emphasis on visuals, it's important for you as a social media marketer to learn how to look at your own sites, other businesses' websites and blogs, and so on and be able to extract the information that helps you understand how they win new customers.

If you feel confident analyzing and making improvements to your online channels, you will function at a much higher level when you make choices about what tactics to use. Whenever you're not clear about what to do you should go back and look at your overall strategy.

Determining what to change is the key to the process. You can make big changes that have little or no effect, or small ones that produce great results. You need to be able to distinguish which ones have the most impact.

So what's the best way to do that? You can start with information that is critical to your success online. Its validity has been tested and proven. I've taken a set of principles developed by Psychology Professor Robert B. Cialdini and I've added five more principles to create a visual method for you to evaluate any online site. The first set of rules was formulated by Cialdini and outlined in his classic book *Influence: The Psychology of Persuasion*. In it, he outlines the six key ways people are persuaded.

He uncovered these principles by conducting experiments and by talking to the people who are in the business of persuasion—advertisers, marketers, fundraisers, and so on. We'll look at how to test these rules against your online sites to make sure you present your product or service in the most effective way.

TIP Don't worry about creating "undue" influence. No one is going to purchase and keep a really bad or defective product. We assume that what you are selling merits consumer attention. Even if you persuade someone to make a poor impulse buy, the buyer will inevitably develop buyer's remorse and then return it, never buy from you again, or both. So don't worry about manipulation. You are giving your brand a chance to be heard. The rest depends on quality, value, and delivery. Nothing can change that.

First let's get an overview of the principles, or key ways people are persuaded, and then we'll see how to apply them. I'm sure you'll recognize several of them—direct mail and web marketers have applied these rules to great effect for years.

- **Reciprocity:** This is the quid pro quo ("this for that"). To keep the scales of our interactions balanced, we strive to make sure that we are not taking more from someone that we're giving in return. If someone is constantly doing favors for us, we feel uncomfortable and move to stop them and balance out the scoreboard.

  In some cases, we might even move to sever ties with the person because we can't keep the scales balanced. This mostly applies to behaviors, not goods.

  How this applies to your online marketing: Remember to offer as much or more than your customer does. If customers supply contact information, you send them a valuable report or something else they value. It is always a good idea to overdeliver. This can motivate a buyer to buy from you in the future, keeping the scales balanced.

- **Social proof:** People want to see other people doing something before they try it. This reminds me of a famous quote by Yogi Berra, Yankees manager: "That restaurant is so crowded that no one goes there anymore." Obviously, he meant that because of the crowds, *he* didn't go there anymore. But the idea of a restaurant with a waiting line brings in the crowds. Everyone thinks that someone knows more than they do about a situation.

How this applies to your online marketing: People want proof that you are a known quantity. Other people need to be seen endorsing your product or service so that they can feel confident that they are getting a good deal. If they don't see testimonials, it might make them wonder.

- **Liking:** The common refrain on the Web is that you want to do business with people you "know, like, and trust." That's an easy way to remember that if you are seen as difficult to deal with or untrustworthy, your business will vanish. The importance of trust is driven home by the results of the Edelman Trust Barometer Study 2013 (http://trust.edelman.com). The survey measured trust in institutions, industries, leaders and the impact of recent crises in the banking and financial service sectors. The survey population was drawn from the global population and found that there is varying distrust in institutions and businesses around the globe.

How this applies to your online marketing: Author Rohit Bhargava wrote about this extensively in his book, *Likeonomics*. If a person instinctively doesn't like you, that person just won't do business with you. Make it a point to share who you are. At the very least, make sure there are pictures on your site of actual employees. If I don't see a picture of the person in charge, I wonder why.

- **Authority:** People trust those who have attained some status. We trust doctors, people with fancy titles, and those who have great wealth. We confer special status on them for obtaining something we haven't gotten.

How this applies to your online marketing: This is why celebrity marketing is so popular. If you like a famous singer and she likes widgets, then you must like widgets. This is also why experts are tapped to introduce products. People assume that the expert wouldn't endorse it if it was bad. As we know, people are emotional buyers.

- **Scarcity:** This is a tricky one. People fear missing out on something that someone else will get. If you convince people that your product is in limited supply or will be going away soon, you get their attention. It signals to them that the product must be valuable.

How this applies to your website: If your product is not truly in demand or in limited supply, it might be hard to use this tactic. You don't want to be seen as sleazy.

- **Commitment and consistency:** People perceive themselves to be rational beings. If they think they are acting irrationally, they will try to change their behavior. They also like to think that they keep their word.

How this applies to your online channels: If you get a commitment from someone to buy at a later date, the person will feel compelled to think hard about it if she doesn't. It will make her uncomfortable. If the person believes that her decision isn't rational, that will also trouble her. If your customer believes that she has committed to buy and that it was a rational decision, she will be more than happy to comply.

In addition to these rules, I want to add five other crucial items to your list. I have been talking about them since I started working online in 1994, but they are particularly important for social media:

- **The use of stories:** Robert McKee, the great screenwriter, calls story "the uniting of an idea with an emotion." That's what makes it so powerful. We'll be looking at the use of stories in greater detail in Rule 3, "Social Media Is Storytelling, So Tell Stories." When you are analyzing online sites or offers of any kind, it's a must to look at the stories presented and assess their power.

- **WIIFM:** Or "what's in it for me?" Everyone asks this question and your online marketing needs to answer it in a very obvious way. Forget subtlety—no one has the time to search for what the payoff will be.

- **Relationship building:** This is where social media networking is key. Customers want to see who you are as a person and see how you are like them. People want to do business with people who have the same values they do.

- **Toe in the water:** This is the way for customers to make a very small commitment to spend money with you and see whether they will spend more. They might go from a $5 purchase to a $200 one, or go from a free offer to a purchase that costs thousands. It depends on where they are in the buying cycle and whether you meet their needs.

- **Commitment to being "green" or part of the larger community:** If you hold your products to high green standards, people will feel good about doing business with you. If this is not directly applicable, people want to see you contributing to your community or undertaking charitable endeavors.

 ## A VISUAL MARKETING METHOD

Method: How to use the Six + Five Principles of Persuasion to analyze whether your online sites are as persuasive as they can be.

Tools: Mind-map template; marked-up website example

Now let's look at how we can apply these principles to analyzing any online site.

Figure 1.1 shows a mind-map template I created for you to use to analyze online sites. Pick and choose the items as they relate to the specific type of site. Just try to include as many principles as you can so you understand how well the site does the job.

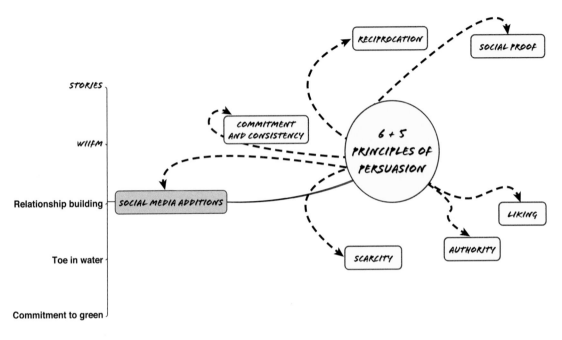

FIGURE 1.1

Six + Five Principles of Persuasion.

With the mind-map template in front of you, look at the website to see whether you find evidence of each concept. Make notes on the template, if you want, to help you remember your thoughts. Also, you can mark up the site image. I used Snagit. After you complete the markup, you will be able to see how effective the site is in using all the principles.

Figure 1.2 shows the sample website I marked up from the template. It is an image of the website for Peet's Coffee and Tea. Alfred Peet emigrated from Holland in 1966 to start Peet's Coffee in Berkeley, California.

Until his death, he devoted 43 years of his life to coffee. Everyone who works for Peet's cares about creating the best coffee possible and the customers know it. They have devoted coffee roasters who train for 10 years before they earn their certification as a roaster for Peet's.

Their customers have formed a real bond. If you were going to compete with Peet's (and I wouldn't recommend it), you'd have to focus on creating your own unique story. But what would you look at to see how Peet's serves its constituency and what its strengths are?

Let's examine the image shown in Figure 1.2 while looking at the mind-map template. We'll start at the upper right and go clockwise.

FIGURE 1.2

Peet's Coffee website.

RELATIONSHIP BUILDING

In the upper right, you'll notice that Peet's has a My Account area where you store your ordering and account information. This is key to making sure that it's easy for the customer to keep reordering. Customers can also see a record of everything they've ordered to date. It discourages them from starting over somewhere else. If you have any kind of reorder process, you need this. In addition, it encourages people to return to the site and once there they see the latest offers and community activity.

SCARCITY

Next we see scarcity in the form of "Limited Availability Online & In Retail Stores." This does several things, establishing scarcity being the first thing. But it also causes the customer to come back often to see what he might be missing and what's exclusive for people who are "smart enough" to be Peet's customers.

BANNER WITH STORY AND GRAPHICS

If you look at the banner graphics, you see the power of pictures that suggest a story. The site references the Elkhill Estate in India where Peet's gets some of its beans. Also we see the

Who We Are section, where more of these stories can be found. These help the customer to trust and identify with Peet's. This section talks about the founder and gives you an online tour. In the various sections you see a great deal of this kind of content, which shows that Peet's pays attention to the customers.

GREEN ATTITUDE

Also in the Who We Are section you'll see information about Peet's sustainability efforts, their care for their growers, and the community programs they conduct.

WORD OF MOUTH FOR MORE SOCIAL PROOF

Peet's used to have a way to "invite a friend" but now uses the more popular social method of inviting reviews (in the shop section) and blogging. You'll also find local store reviews on places like Yelp.com.

LIKING, BELONGING, AND LISTENING TO FEEDBACK

At the bottom of the home page, you see both Twitter and Facebook links. This shows that Peet's interacts with customers and wants to hear what they are thinking. It's also a great way to try out new offers and promote exclusives.

RECIPROCITY

Reciprocity is next. Peet's has a link that enables customers to exchange an email address for the newsletter and special offers. It's a quid pro quo. I hope you're already using this. It's a great way to grow your list.

TOE IN THE WATER

Next is toe in the water. That's what I call the sampling of products and services to see whether customers would consider doing further business. Peet's showcases its best coffees in samplers to entice the customer to find something they like.

SOCIAL PROOF

Social proof here is represented by the section on "Peetniks," whom the company describes as their best loyal customers. This is where you can set up recurring delivery. The implication is that there are lots of people who have remained satisfied Peet's users.

Use the template to evaluate your sites and see how you can improve what you're doing by adding, modifying, or removing content.

WIIFM

"What's in it for me?" Answer this question for the customer by analyzing how many things you can spot on the home page that show value. For example, on the home page we see the online account storage, the Peetniks areas, stories about iced drinks, and so on.

AUTHORITY

This is an interesting one. Peet's isn't using celebrities, but if you look in the Grocery area, you see that Peet's products are carried in major supermarkets, which are the celebrities of this industry.

 ## TOOLS TO CONSIDER

Snagit (http://Snagit.com) is what I used to mark up the website shown in Figure 1.2.

 ## IDEAS TO USE

A visual analysis of your online presence using the template will help you enhance your own site and evaluate your competition.

When you are creating presentation visuals, ask yourself, "What is this concept like?" and "How is it different from something people already know about?"

The best marketing idea is that which can be understood with a quick glance.

If you also think about maps as having a function related to brain activity, you will be more likely to use them to show people ways to "navigate" from one idea to another.

IDEA MAP

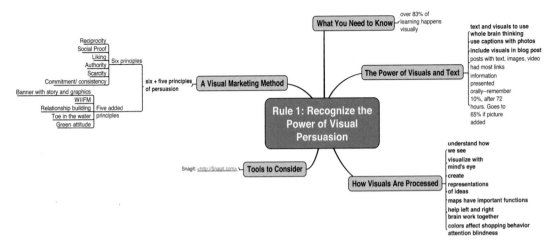

Idea Map for Rule 1

ENDNOTES

Doherty, John. "What Kind of Content Gets Links in 2012?", SEOMOZ blog http://www.seomoz.org/blog/what-kind-of-content-gets-links-in-2012

Bhargava, Rohit. *Likeonomics: The Unexpected Truth Behind Earning Trust, Influencing Behavior and Inspiring Action.* Wiley, 2012.

Cialdini, Robert B. *Influence: The Psychology of Persuasion.* Harper Business, 2006.

Davidson, Cathy. *Now You See It: How the Brain Science of Attention Will Transform the Way We Live, Work and Learn.* Viking, 2011.

CREATE PERSONAS TO UNDERSTAND YOUR CUSTOMERS

In Rule 2 we look at how using a tool like a persona helps you more effectively target your customer. It helps you stay focused on messages that resonate with them and cause them to buy from you rather than a competitor. We give you a visual persona template to help you get started.

DISCOVERING PERSONAS

The term *persona* was coined by Alan Cooper in his 1999 book, *The Inmates Are Running the Asylum*. In it he says, "Personas are not real people, but they represent them throughout the design process. They are hypothetical archetypes of actual users....We don't so much make up our personas as discover them as a by-product of the investigation process."

Remember that personas represent actual people. Developing personas happens through discovery. You can't make one up out of whole cloth just to satisfy your need to segment your audience. Personas must represent a group of real customers who have the same goals for purchasing your product. You need to understand their motivations and needs. Personas are used to help you make marketing decisions. If you use them in that way, you'll reap big benefits.

WHAT YOU NEED TO KNOW

Every business has three things it can do to increase sales:

- Increase prices

- Increase the amount each person buys

- Increase the number of customers

To do any one of these things effectively, you need to know your customer. As a social media marketer, you probably spend your time (or your staff spends their time) on social platforms looking at what people are saying about you. You respond by tweeting, pinning on Pinterest, encouraging likes on Facebook, and a whole lot more. But unless you know who you're talking to and what they want, you won't be able to do any of the previous three things to increase sales.

Your marketing message on social media is powerful only if it hits the right target. If you haven't determined the right message based on your unique customer, you've wasted your time. It won't be heard.

So what can you do to understand your customer better? You need to constantly focus on providing value. This includes monitoring their conversation, providing helpful content and excellent customer support.

By doing this you will also uncover the niches that are the most profitable for you. After you determine what these niches are, you can create personas that represent each niche.

> If you haven't determined the right message based on your unique customer, you've wasted your time. It won't be heard.

UNDERSTAND YOUR NICHE

Picking the right customer niche(s) is critical to a successful business. But, zeroing in on who you should sell to can often engender fear. What kind of fear?

- Fear of leaving out an important target by mistake

- Fear of picking the wrong target

- Fear of making a bad choice

When I started my online marketing agency, I was faced with the same question you might be asking yourself: "Just who is my customer and how can I reach them?" This question can't be answered overnight, but you need to start making decisions. A message that is aimed at everyone reaches no one.

The good news is that when you take the time to fully identify a niche and see how much easier it is to develop marketing campaigns, your fear will disappear.

If you already have niches identified, you might feel that either your knowledge about them is insufficient or that maybe you've targeted the wrong audience. If that's the case, you'll really benefit from the persona template we'll discuss.

So let's dig into the concept of niches. What is a niche? A niche is a narrowly defined segment of an audience that is uniquely in need of your product or service. For example, you could focus selling to "online business owners who need copywriting services." But it would be even better to identify a niche segment of "female online business owners over 50 who need ongoing copy written for their online business sites."

Don't worry if you don't have that description worked out on day one. Identifying niche audiences is an iterative process. But even at the start, you can begin to identify the key characteristics of your audience. Most good niche segments include demographics, psychographics (how people feel), and a host of detailed information about their preferences.

Let's look at a few ways you as a social media marketer can gather information about your customers to determine a niche. You are lucky that you are doing this at a time in history when your ability to reach customers is unparalleled. At no other time could you have been able to speak so directly to your customers on a global scale.

The old general store was a place for people to gather and express their opinions and make specific requests, but geography was the gating factor. With the Internet, you can find profitable niches made up of people from around the world.

Consider these options when you are trying to collect information about your customers:

- **Searches on social media:**

  Do the obvious searches on Facebook, Twitter, LinkedIn, and YouTube for your business names—products, brand, personnel, etc. Then search topics your products encompass to find more hits. For example, if you sell granola, type in words like *cereal* and *breakfast* to see what people are saying. Check back and see what keywords you are already using that could be used as a search.

  Set up a Google alert (http://www.google.com/alerts) for any keyword topic that interests you. After you set it up, you will get an email when new information about that keyword is available.

  Check tools such as BuzzFeed (http://BuzzFeed.com), Social Mention (http://socialmention.com), Topsy (http://topsy.com) and Nielsen Online (http://www.nielsen-online.com) to see what has buzz in your topic area.

To search blogs, use sites like Technorati (http://Technorati.com) and Google Blogsearch (http://Blogsearch.google.com).

Use tools such as Quantcast (http://Quantcast.com) to find trends and audience demographics.

Enterprise users can check out some paid tools like Sysomos (http://www.sysomos.com), Salesforce Marketing Cloud, formerly Radian6 (http://www.salesforcemarketingcloud.com), and Trackur (www.trackur.com) to collect social media intelligence and brand mentions.

- **Direct one-to-one with customers:** Can you get on the phone and chat with customers when they call in for support? Most marketers shy away from direct phone contact with customers, but when they call you, they are in a talkative mood. You can learn something about why they bought your product. If you are afraid that this only puts you in touch with people who have a "problem," think how valuable that can be for finding out the important information.

- **Analyzing competitors' products:** This one can be valuable if you do it right. What this means is that you should widen your understanding of who your competitor is. You might have tunnel vision and see only the "deep pockets" competitor you fight at every turn. Your customers are not locked into that. They consider a whole range of options you might dismiss. For example, if you sell a productivity tool, think about what tools your customers might pick if they didn't know about your product. Would they try books? Would they try free apps that approximate what they want? Broaden your concepts and you might find some interesting data or an idea for a new product.

- **Surveys:** This is one of the tried-and-true methods that marketers usually use at some point. It is more valuable when you have at least a hundred people so that you can get more than a handful of responses. But any data can be helpful. Try zoomerang.com or surveymonkey.com. If the survey is very small, be careful about jumping to any conclusions.

- **Comments on your blog:** Look for anything that resonates with customers. Are there areas of interest you haven't created content for? Do people respond to the same content over and over? Note what questions they are asking and create content to address it. Investigate what's there. Also look at comments on your competitors' blogs to see what your potential customers are saying.

- **Keywords:** You must be using the right keywords. If you haven't developed a list, start today. When you know what keywords your customers are using to find companies like you, you can create content they want and help them find you.

- **Analytics data from your website or blog:** Obviously, this can be very helpful if you take the time to look through the data.

- **Questions your staff wants to ask:** To get a full picture of your customer, you need to involve all your departments. Ask them to tell you what questions they want answers to. For example, ask your customer service department what they want to know. Then go to your billing department and ask them. Each one of the departments will have a different perspective and can open the discussion to a wider understanding of issues. Great conversations about customers can happen when you hear a question you didn't expect. You can then follow up and see what you can learn.

SPEAK THE LANGUAGE OF YOUR BUYERS

One of the key things you want to do when learning about your market is to get to know the language of your customers. The best way to do this is to listen to them on social media. Monitor their comments, read their posts and exchanges on social media. Never assume that you know what they want until you've actually listened to them.

Have you ever noticed that when you get together with friends you use many of the same words and phrases to describe things? The same goes for your customers. They use certain words and phrases that are part of their understanding of your product's topic.

For example, if you ask someone whether they are a numismatist, they will look at you like you're crazy unless they are coin collectors. How about people who love embroidery? Should you inquire about the size of the hoop they use? That's perfectly acceptable.

The reason language is so important for social media marketers is that unless you know the keywords that customers use to find you, you won't be able to help them locate you. You need to focus on giving them everything they need to make a buying decision.

How do you do this? One of the best ways is to find the keywords used by your customers. This does two things. It enables you to communicate with individual customers more effectively and it improves your search engine optimization (SEO) rankings.

For those who are new to SEO, it refers to providing online content on your websites and other channels that search engines display. Let's use Google as an example. Google has paid advertisements using keywords on the right side of the page. Advertisers pay to be listed in the right column (as close to the top as possible).

It has what it calls 'organic' ranking on the left side. They use the term organic because the content is ranked 'naturally' based on how many people search it. The more people search for content, the higher it shows up in the left column. Obviously, you want your content to rank highly on the left so you don't have to pay for people to find it.

You do that by making sure that your content contains the words and phrases that are searched by Google users.

TIP Another way to familiarize yourself with how your customers speak is to use a tool like Followerwonk (http://followerwonk.com). This tool enables you to analyze your Twitter followers in a great many ways. You can look at the competition and see who their followers are and learn their demographics. You can generate reports that are highly visual and easy to use. It also gives you information about your follower's followers so that you can determine their level of influence. Followerwonk has free and pro accounts.

USE PERSONAS TO CLARIFY YOUR TARGET MARKET

Creating personas to represent customers is a technique that has been used by software designers for a decade. It has recently gained favor among marketers who see the value of being able to segment their audience in a unique way.

I want you to think about the personas you create as part of the storytelling you will do for social media. Personas are the characters you are creating your stories for. They can show up in many ways. It all depends on the stories you want to tell.

Remember that you can't have a real person represent a persona. The persona is a representation of a well-defined group. Using a real person defeats the purpose of creating personas. You can't limit yourself to the actual needs and desires of only one customer.

Creating personas will help you do the following:

- **Tell your best stories.** When you create personas that really reflect your customers and then create the stories targeted to them, you will solve the ongoing problem of "how do I figure out what content to create?"

- **Focus your marketing efforts on an ongoing basis.** Many of us have been in meetings where the discussion veers off the topic because someone is genuinely excited by a new idea. They see a great new angle to apply to the latest social media marketing campaign.

But who is the target? If it's "a 30-something interested in experimental music sites" it's clearly not one of the personas you are targeting…! It may be a great idea, but if it's not one of your personas you need to pass on it.

When you have clearly defined personas, you can ask the staffer to clarify which persona the idea is targeted at. This usually results in a swift return to reality. It saves time and money and keeps everyone focused on what matters. That alone makes it worth doing.

- **Decide which audience to target for each campaign and specifically what content and message you need to create for them.** It's easy to lose sight of and neglect your constituencies. By reviewing all your personas each time you start a campaign, you will be sure to include content for the right ones. Not every persona will be targeted every time.

- **Decide where to invest your marketing dollars.** You can determine which of your personas is more likely to respond first to new products and services and can spend your marketing budget there.

- **Use a common language with your staff to talk about customers.** When you invoke the name of a designated persona, everyone will understand the reference.

OVERCOMING OBSTACLES

I believe that there are two main reasons (among other, lesser reasons) that might make people dislike the use of personas.

The first reason is the name *persona*. Calling a tactic a persona makes it sound as if it's a complex idea. We know that's an instant way to turn off the creative brain. No one uses the term *persona* in everyday life. If you think you'll hit some resistance, give each persona a name and use it. Calling a persona Henry Johnson is so much friendlier than Persona #1.

The second reason marketers might not like personas is the use of persona documents. Most persona documents are dull. They often include large blocks of text with only a picture (sometimes) to break up the tedium. We take a different tack with our worksheet to help you be more creative.

We try to mix some fun into the topic with the use of our persona "pie" worksheet that is discussed next. The pie is made with all the ingredients that make up your unique customer.

 ## A VISUAL MARKETING METHOD

The exercise discussed in this section shows you how to use personas to clarify your target market.

Tools provided: Persona pie worksheet

Creating personas takes time. I've supplied a persona pie worksheet in Figure 2.1 to help you create your first persona.

As you look at the worksheet you see that there are two sections. The upper section is where you put in the demographic information for your persona and the lower section where you enter psychographics like key motivators and buying triggers.

TIP
Take some time to collect the information you'll need in order to fill in this worksheet. It should be revised over time to keep it current with the marketplace. If anyone in the group gets impatient because you don't have a persona completed immediately, let him know that "baking" real insights about customers takes time.

Persona Pie Template

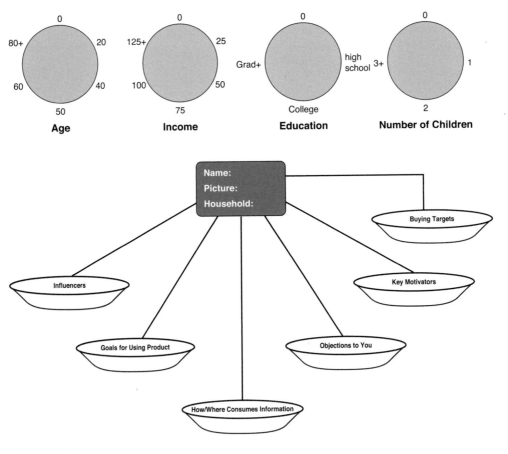

FIGURE 2.1

Persona pie template.

1. At the top there are four "pies," representing the demographics of the customer:

   Age

   Income

   Education

Number of Children

On each of the pies labeled above fill in the data ascribed to that persona. If the persona is aged 20, shade in that section. Do that for each of the four pies.

The purpose of using pie charts is so that you can glance at the persona to remind yourself where that persona falls demographically for each of the measures. For example, if you put each of the personas worksheets next to one another you can see that by looking at the pies side by side, one is 20 and one is 60. As you use the personas to develop campaigns you can glance at the worksheets to quickly see the differences.

You may only have one persona when you begin using them. In that case you'll use one worksheet and fill in all the information you know. Then as you gather more information, come back to the worksheet and fill it in.

When you add another persona, add a new worksheet. Keep each persona worksheet prominently displayed so that everyone references the same information.

2. Next is the center of the worksheet with the person's name, picture, and household status (that is, single, married, and so on). You can use an image or draw one that is representative.

3. Below that are the "plates," filled with the information you want to capture about your customers:

- **Influencers:** Who do your personas listen to and admire? Do they have role models? Knowing who they respect is a good clue to what they value.

- **Goals for using the product:** What do these personas want to get from using your product? Does it save them time or money?

- **How/where do these personas consume their information:** You want to know this because it will tell you where you should be. If they primarily use email, you'll want to create a newsletter. If they are always on Facebook, you need to concentrate your efforts there.

  You probably won't be able to fill in all the information at once. It will take time. As you continue to add information, you learn about your personas, the more effective they will be.

- **Objections to your company or product:** This refers to any negatives the persona might associate with your company or product. Do they think your product is cheaply made? Do they think your tech support is expensive? Ferret out these things so that you can counter them in your content.

- **Key motivators:** This relates to the persona's personal life. Do they want to help a specific charity? What money worries do they have? Are they working to put their kids through college? Do they have to care for elderly parents? Try to find out any information about what motivates them.

- **Buying triggers:** What compels your persona to consider buying your product? Is it triggered by a celebration, an emergency, or a life status change (such as wedding, divorce, and so on)?

In Figure 2.2 a sample worksheet shows you how a completed one might look.

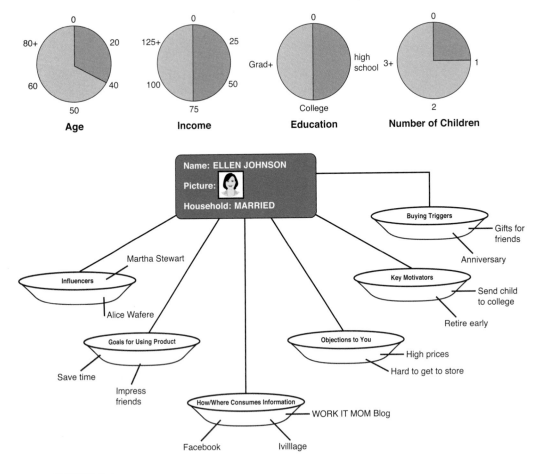

FIGURE 2.2

Persona pie template in progress.

We see on the filled-in form that our persona is Ellen Johnson and she has the following characteristics:

Married

Age: 40

Income: $75K

Education: College

Number of Children: 1

Influencers: Martha Stewart

Goals for using the product: Save time; impress friends

How/where consumes information: iVillage.com; Facebook; Work it Mom! Blog

Objections to your company: High prices, hard to get to store

Key motivators: Send child to college; retire early

Buying targets: Anniversaries and gifts for friends

 ## IDEAS TO USE

You need to clearly identify your niche before you start creating personas.

Remember to target specific keywords to your personas so that when you create a story you have everything you need to get traffic.

Creating personas will help you identify the right messages that will resonate with your customers instead of using a hit-or-miss scheme.

Know the precise words your customers use so that you can speak as one of them.

IDEA MAP

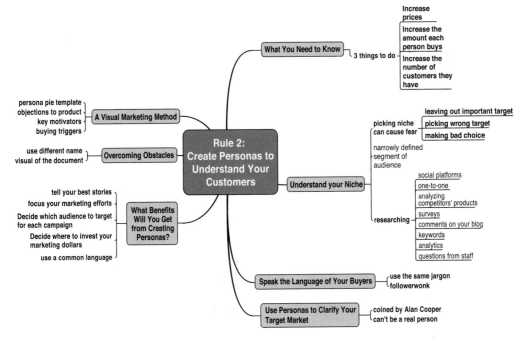

Idea Map for Rule 2

ENDNOTES

Cooper, Alan. *The Inmates Are Running the Asylum.* Indianapolis: Sams, 1999.

SOCIAL MEDIA IS STORYTELLING, SO TELL STORIES

In Rule 3 we look at how you can combine your personas with your storytelling to create powerful stories for your social media marketing and community engagement. We offer a structure and a way to capture your stories.

WHAT YOU NEED TO KNOW

Along with our unending thirst for visuals, our brains are hard-wired to pay attention to and enjoy stories. If you can turn raw business information into visual story form, you are helping your message be heard.

There are many reasons why our brains love stories:

- Because we can relate to stories, they often give us ideas about how to handle situations we might face.

- Stories engage our emotions, and therefore they can help us cope with emotions that we are unable to express ourselves.

- Stories give us heroes to emulate.

- Stories often motivate, inspire, or strengthen us.

- Stories can persuade others.

Stories engage both sides of our brain, mixing information with emotion. As we discussed in Rule 1 "Recognize the Power of Visual Persuasion," engaging both sides of the brain is the most powerful way for you to reach your audience.

But, for marketers, the essence of storytelling can be deceptive. A lot of things we call stories are details of larger narratives that relate to branding. If we forget to help the customer link these details up to that larger narrative, we fail to engage the customer in the long term.

For example the brand idea for Apple is that you "Think differently" if you use Mac products. A piece of this narrative might be used in a market campaign introducing a new feature to the iPad. You link the idea that Apple is taking a different approach to this feature because they are the company that causes you to "Think differently."

To understand how our brains receive stories, we need to look briefly at the construction of the brain. Neuroscientists tell us that we've made major breakthroughs in the past 10 years in our quest to understand the brain. They have discovered that our brains have three distinct "brains." They are the cortex, the mid-brain, and what is often called the lizard brain:

- The cortex is where we reason and solve problems.

- The mid-brain is where we deal with our emotions.

- The lizard brain is the one that reacts without thought. It helps you decide whether danger is coming.

As a marketer, you first encounter the lizard brain—the one that reacts with fear to the unknown and threats of harm called the "fight or flight" response. Your first goal in any story you tell is to make sure that the lizard brain does not perceive a threat.

TIP You might hear the sales refrain "A confused mind always says no." Another variation on this could be "A frightened lizard brain always says no." If the buyer's lizard brain senses harm (in this case, let's say that the beginning of your story stated the high cost of the product), he will try to escape the situation as soon as possible. This explains why many marketers withhold the price until the end of a presentation.

One way to avoid engendering fear in the lizard brain is to slowly present a story with details and visuals so you don't evoke the "fight or flight" response. The visuals help the brain process information ahead of the words.

THE BIGGER PICTURE

Customers are thoroughly engaged with companies when they share a context about the brand with others in the community. The rise of customer communities can be explained in part by looking at an article called "In Search of Charisma," by Alexander Haslam and

Stephen D. Reicher, in *Scientific American Mind*. Haslam and Reicher discuss the work of social psychologist John C. Turner, who defined the term "social identity." According to Turner, social identity causes us to act in specific ways when we identify with a group or community.

For example, we exert influence on each another, we define ourselves as having an "us-ness," and we believe that members of the group are more helpful in advancing the group interests than those outside the group.

This is how customer communities play their part in social media. People who are following companies and consider themselves fans are part of the "us."

These customers check in frequently on the company's social channels like Facebook to see what's happening and try to participate. They become part of the community who understands the context for the brand's actions. They relate and share experiences that bring them closer.

> **TIP**
>
> Don't forget that part of the story on social media platforms is "we give our loyal customers discounts and extras." You need to make that part of the narrative. Several studies show that one common reason most customers engage on social media platforms is to get discounts.

One of the most obvious examples of an "us" community is the group of Apple fans who support and identify as Mac users.

CUSTOMERS GET SWEPT UP

So what's the real secret to persuasion by story? It's getting the viewer completely caught up in what's going on. In effect, the viewer persuades herself by undergoing the transformation with the protagonist in the story.

This effect can be explained by a psychological construct called "narrative transport." This concept is discussed in a September 18, 2008, article in *Scientific American* by Jeremy Hsu, a science and tech journalist, called "The Secrets of Storytelling: Why We Love a Good Yarn."

As Hsu discusses, narrative transport refers to the state of complete immersion in a story. The reader or viewer is swept away to the point where he is lifted out of reality and into the story itself. In doing so, he can identify with the hero and imagine that he is part of the story.

Narrative transport refers to the state of complete immersion in a story. The reader or viewer is swept away to the point where he is lifted out of reality and into the story itself.

So what does this mean for your social media marketing? Can you hope to engage your customer to the point where he becomes sold? Perhaps.

Studies have been done that compare different advertisements to determine which one is more effective in creating narrative transport. One study by Jennifer Edson Escalas, Associate Professor of Marketing at Vanderbilt University, shows that creating a narrative for an advertisement for running shoes and adding strong arguments about the value of the product is more effective than the analytical pitches she created.

What worked? Here's some of the copy:

> "Imagine yourself running through this park. Your feet feel remarkably light. You look down and see a pair of Westerly running shoes on your feet. They weigh only 10 oz. You notice a spring in your step. Westerly running shoes provide strong support with their advance stability system. Westerly's cushioning system spreads shock, reducing injury. Imagine yourself in Westerly running shoes to improve the comfort and quality of your morning run…"

You can see what is happening to the readers/viewers as they follow the story. They are imagining themselves running and being delighted with the lightweight shoes on their feet. They feel as though they've experienced something positive and want to repeat that feeling the next time they run. This motivates them to buy the shoes.

 TIP Think about how you can inject this vicarious feeling into the stories you write and send out via social media platforms. Try to develop one by starting with the prompt "Imagine yourself…."

WHY ARE BUSINESS STORIES DIFFICULT TO GET RIGHT?

Business stories can be powerful. But stories created by companies can miss the big picture.

The key to a good story is to take the protagonist through a "trial by fire" and have her come out the other side a changed individual. The journey of that trip is the story. The problem with ineffective business stories is that companies create stories where nothing transpires and no one is different at the end.

So, what kind of stories are we talking about? One of the reasons it is difficult to create a business story is the fact that people are unclear about what a business story is. You know which stories are "regular" stories to you. You think of your favorite movies or the anecdotes you hear from your family at the dinner table and you're not confused. Those are stories.

But what kind of story would you tell your customers to develop your relationship with them? There are several categories you can mine for these stories:

- **Stories customers tell:** You want to tell stories that reflect the voice of the community. As part of the group that identifies themselves as customers and fans of your company, you want to make sure to reinforce the "us-ness" factor. Stories that customers tell are, of course, the backbone of social media. But you need to take an active role in scooping up those stories and making them part of your brand. You want to make sure that you display and retell their stories because they are the most authentic.

- **Stories about the company:** These stories are a little harder to develop because they aren't about how great you are. Those types of stories are floating around on your website and promotional material and are rarely believed by customers. Those are not the stories you want to tell. The stories you want to capture are those that tell how the company serves the customer.

  For example, tell the story of how the founders overcame great odds to start a company that would make something people really needed. How they struggled to find the right materials to make them environmentally safe.

  Anything that is self-serving is a waste of time. The old-style marketing that includes details about more revenue and higher profits should be saved for the stockholders. You want to let your customer know what you've done for them lately.

- **Stories about the industry and people in it:** Most industries have stories of exciting trends and ideas that explain what they do. It's important to connect with current topics and relate them to what you are doing.

- **Stories from inspirational leaders and mentors:** Sometimes the best stories come from your mentors who inspire you. Write down the stories they've told you and see whether you can apply them to what you are doing. You should also mine for stories from the great leaders of the industry and cite them where appropriate—for example, stories about how Steve Jobs came up with his ideas and developed his products.

TIP

When capturing stories, don't forget to collect metaphors that are used by your staff and customers. When you're telling stories, metaphors can help drive the point home. The great thing about metaphors is that they are visual language. For example, when you say someone is a "writing machine," people understand that you are likening that person to something powerful that runs without stopping. They will also visualize a machine that writes!

THE STORY STRUCTURE

To construct business stories, you will find several variations on the "Hero's Journey" first identified by Joseph Campbell. Campbell documented a narrative that is found in stories throughout history. It consists of several documented steps that the hero goes through in a typical narrative. I think that's a bit too complicated when you are trying to create business stories that need to be short and to the point.

One excellent structure created by The Actor's Institute Group (TAI Group) (http://theTAIgroup.com) is detailed in an article by Kaihan Krippendorff, innovator and author of "Outthink the Competition." The article in *Fast Company* (March of 2012) is called "Using Great Storytelling to Grow Your Business."

In the article, Krippendorff identifies what the TAI Group calls a story spine as shown in Figure 3.1, which lays out a useful structure to tell a business story:

1. Introduction of the current reality: What is the time, place, and the people in the scene?

2. Conflict arrives: What problem interrupts the calm scene?

3. A struggle ensues: What do the characters do to resolve the problem?

4. The conflict is resolved: How is it resolved?

5. A new reality exists: How have the characters changed as a result of the action?

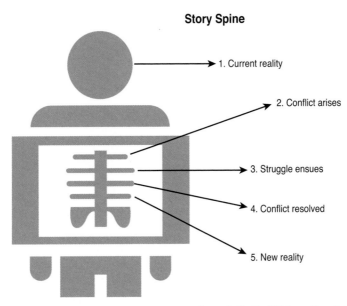

Suggested by the TAI Group Story Spine

FIGURE 3.1

Story spine.

It's important to follow each step in sequence. It takes you from the opening of the story which shows the status quo to the end where a new reality is now in place. It's very important to have a structure like this to follow when constructing a story. It helps you identify the actions that must take place to move the story along.

One of the big mistakes that people make when creating stories is that they don't show action. It's not enough to show a sequence of details. You have to show that each of the steps leads to changes and problems the hero must solve. The excitement in the story is watching what decisions the hero makes and whether they help him reach his goal or not.

A VISUAL MARKETING METHOD

With the story-spine structure as a backdrop, let's look at a way that can help you start the process.

CAPTURING EXISTING STORIES

There are two important things to do in order to capture good stories. The first is to capture them when they happen, and the second is to extract the most important information so that you can create an engaging story.

The blank worksheet shown in Figure 3.2 can be used to do both.

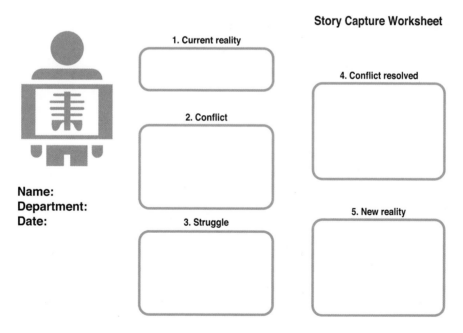

FIGURE 3.2

Story capture worksheet.

Here are steps to take to capture your story:

1. Make sure that you give the story spine diagram to anyone who will be collecting information, and explain what each section means.

2. Give these people the template and tell them that for some part of a day (this can be repeated in small chunks of time or whole days as feasible) you want them to document the stories that they hear about from customers.

3. Distribute the capture screen template to all appropriate groups, customer service, sales, shipping, bloggers, tweeters, etc. You want a diverse set of information.

After the collection process, do the following:

1. Begin to analyze patterns and develop themes. You'll start to see common items. Collect enough so that you have a good sample.

2. Match the themes to your personas and keywords so that the stories you craft clearly have a real target with actual keywords.

3. After you've created the stories, test each to see whether it resonates on a tool like Storify.com (see "Tools to Consider").

4. If a story tests well, figure out what content you need to create to make the story come to life: visuals, text, video, and so on. Then you can invest in the content knowing that you've got something worth amplifying. Figure 3.3 shows a sample template that has been filled in.

Here is an example of how the most important information is extracted:

1. **Introduction of the current reality:** The company is a high-end housewares store. The customer orders the crystal vase at the last minute for her mother's 80th birthday. She is assured it will arrive on time.

2. **Conflict arrives:** The vase arrives and although it's heavily wrapped inside, she finds it has been cracked. She's in a panic because her mother's birthday party at a hotel ballroom is in two days.

3. **A struggle ensues:** She takes out a trouble ticket but needs to hear back right away. She's not sure what to do and complains to her friend. Her friend, who is more tech savvy, gets on Twitter and tweets about the incident to the company Twitter account asking for immediate help.

4. **The conflict is resolved:** A company rep calls the customer and arranges to have the vase delivered to the party with a big bouquet inside it.

5. **A new reality exists:** The bouquet and vase make a big splash and everyone is pleased with the great service. The rep saves an account.

Story Capture Worksheet

Name:
Department:
Date:

1. Current reality

Customer buys vase for mother's 80th birthday.

2. Conflict

Vase arrives cracked two days before the party.

3. Struggle

Customer doesn't hear back from trouble ticket. Friend contacts rep on company Twitter account.

4. Conflict resolved

Rep arranges to have vase with beautiful bouquet delivered to the party. Everyone is impressed.

5. New reality

Rep saves the account. Customer sends video of her mother thanking company.

FIGURE 3.3

Story capture worksheet in progress.

With this story you have the opportunity to get photos of the birthday girl and her bouquet and the happy customer. Perhaps you can get a video or an audio that you can pair with a photo. You can also get a screenshot of the tweets.

 ## TOOLS TO CONSIDER

Storify.com (http://storify.com) is an interesting tool that enables you to create a story line from your social media. You collect items from places like Facebook, Twitter, and visual sources like YouTube, Flickr, and Instagram to narrate your own story. For an example of how Storify and other social platforms can be used to document a story, look at the section, "A Healthcare Company Educating People Around the World" in Rule 21, "Instagram is Great for Quick Visuals From Your Mobile.

 ## IDEAS TO USE

Try to sweep your readers/viewers into the story so that they become part of the journey. (See the section above on "How customers get swept up" for more on narrative transport.)

Stories are the best way to engage both sides of the brain by mixing information with emotion.

Use a story structure to give your story the best chance at succeeding with an audience.

IDEA MAP

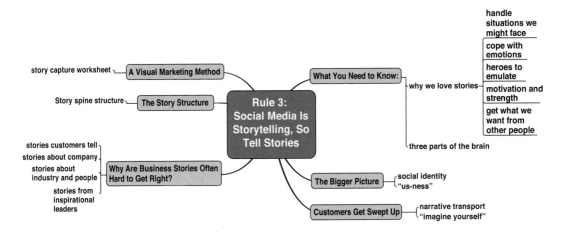

Idea Map for Rule 3

ENDNOTES

Escalas, Jennifer Edson. "Self Referencing and Persuasion: Narrative Transportation Versus Analytical Elaboration." *Journal of Consumer Research*: 2007.

Haslam, Alexander, and Stephen D. Reicher. "In Search of Charisma." *Scientific American Mind*: July/August 2012.

Hsu, Jeremy. "The Secrets of Storytelling: Why We Love a Good Yarn." *Scientific American*: September 18, 2008.

Krippendorff, Kaihan. "Using Great Storytelling to Grow Your Business." *Fast Company*: March 2012.

UNDERSTAND HOW YOUR CONTENT SUPPORTS YOUR BUSINESS

In Rule 4 we look at understanding how important your content (visual and otherwise) is to the growth of your business. It can't be an afterthought. We show you a tool you can use to determine where you are in reaching your business targets.

WHAT YOU NEED TO KNOW

Content is one of the foundations of your business. All products and services need to be surrounded with the information that helps customers use and enjoy them. So what is content? It's all the information you provide about your products and services. It can be in visual form like an infographic or video or text. It includes such things as press releases, blog posts, product manuals, search ads, Tweets and Pins. If you're supplying the right content, i.e. the information your customers value, there can never be enough.

Businesspeople are now more accustomed to considering content a necessary part of the conversion process. It wasn't always so for my clients. Previously, they would balk at the idea that their product manual (usually unusable) wasn't all that was needed.

In fact, it was often the case that the inadequate amount of information on how to use and enjoy a product created returns. Buyers would get frustrated

trying to put something together or trying to understand the functions. They often shipped products back.

Not only did customers return merchandise, but they also would not likely buy again. Business buyers were no different. They would complain to their colleagues about the lack of value and reputations would be dented.

It's important to remember that information of another kind is also created. It's in the form of opinions from customers. With the advent of social media, marketers began to understand that people would be reviewing, rating, and commenting on every part of their business. That was the wake-up call.

They realized that it's imperative that customers have access to the best content to support them at every phase of the process. If a quick-start guide or diagram isn't easy to use, the business hears about it.

If a business doesn't offer adequate support on multiple channels, it loses customers to companies that do. For example, many businesses now offer customer support on Twitter. Customers take note of those who don't and in some cases switch to the competitor that does.

The ability to hear from customers is a two-edged sword. One tweet from a dissatisfied customer can go viral and impact a business overnight. For example, in 2010 comedian-director Kevin Smith was kicked off a Southwest Airlines plane for not purchasing two seats.

> Content is one of the foundations of your business. All products and services need to be surrounded with the information that helps customers use and enjoy them.

He had already purchased two seats for a later flight but was able to get on an earlier flight with only one seat but off he went. Smith alerted his huge twitter following to the situation along with humorous photos he labeled, "too fat to fly." This got him a tremendous amount of attention and press. Southwest offered him an apology and a $100 voucher. Needless to say he didn't take it and milked the comedy for several days. Clearly, Southwest didn't benefit from the publicity.

HOW CONTENT FITS IN

Let's look at some of the possible online business models you can employ and see what kind of content would fit in:

- **Selling information:** This one is the most obvious. If you sell information as your product, you need to be clear about what has value to your clients and be able to charge for it.

Visual content needed: Because information is your product, you need to provide supplementary videos, images and visual infographics, and free reports with graphics that demonstrate that your content is worth the cost. You can also point to good customer testimonials as proof of value.

- **Selling a shippable product:** When you sell a shippable product, you have to make sure that you do everything you can to simulate the "feel of the product in your hand." Studies show that a person is more likely to buy a product if he holds it in his hand.

  Visual content needed: Here is where visual content really makes a big difference. You can use product shots, images of people using the product, and anything else that makes the customer imagine how the product would feel.

- **Selling a service:** The goal here is to provide as much visual proof as possible that other customers are satisfied with the service and would recommend it.

  Visual content needed: You'll want to have photos or videos of your customers extolling the virtues of the service. If you can, offer a free consultation or a quiz that gets people thinking about how your services would make a difference to their specific business.

- **Selling an online application:** The goal here is to make sure that the customer can evaluate the product and integrate it into her work.

  Visual content needed: In this case you'll want to provide a free trial or free version if at all possible. You'll also want to have training videos, visual learning content, and photos with customer endorsements. *For example,* one company that provides great training videos is Nuance (http://www.nuance.com) They have several versions of voice recognition products under the Dragon NaturallySpeaking umbrella. The software allows users to dictate text rather than type. They provide their customers with training videos on every topic but also do weekly webinars to discuss the finer points of the products. They also run a user community where users share their knowledge.

THE POWER OF GREAT CONTENT

Good content ultimately does several things for your potential and current customers. Can your content pass this test?

It should do the following:

- **Educate:** It teaches the customer what he needs to know about the product and how to use it.

- **Entertain:** It presents the information in a way that is fun and appealing.

  Visuals used here help the customer get beyond any fear she might have about the difficulty or usefulness of the product.

- **Persuade:** It helps the customer get over any objections he might have and therefore buy the product.

  Visuals used here help the customer see the actual benefits of owning the product. For example, they could show people who look more successful, who look smarter, or who appear to be part of the in-crowd.

- **Tell a story:** It presents the information in a format that makes the customer personalize it.

  Visuals here engage the customer's imagination and help them feel the emotions you want to engender.

- **Share:** One of the ultimate tests of good content is to see whether it gets shared. When people send your content to their trusted circle, you have hit the mark. They have chosen to be an advocate for your idea or product.

- **Find:** Customers who want this information should be able to find it based on the search engine optimization (SEO) you have done.

  For more discussion about content, check out Rule 7, "Know Your Content."

SNACKABLE VISUAL CONTENT

When we look specifically at visual content, it's important to remember that less is more. Most often, you should create visual content that supports your ideas and simplifies them.

In an article from the Content Marketing Institute by Clare McDermott, called "Infographics are a Full Meal," Leslie Bradshaw, co-founder of JESS3 (http://jess3.com), talks about snackable content. She defines snackable content as content that can be shared in smaller bites.

Not all visual content must be like an infographic that serves up a lot of information in one visual. Infographics are wildly popular and have a place. But you also need to provide content that's easy to share on platforms such as Facebook, Twitter, and Pinterest. Thus, smaller bites. Bradshaw calls these pieces of smaller content data graphics.

Figure 4.1 shows an example of a data graphic produced by JESS3. It is displayed on the company's Pinterest account. You'll notice that they're providing a small amount of information that can be quickly digested and shared.

MAKE A COMMITMENT

Most businesses that don't make a real commitment to create great content won't achieve the success they envision for themselves. They remain puzzled, when the answer is right in front of them. As discussed in Rule 1, "Recognize the Power of Visual Persuasion," people are persuaded visually.

FIGURE 4.1

JESS3 and Eloqua infographic.

The Web has trained customers to expect a certain level of visual professionalism. If they don't find it they won't choose you.

So what does it mean to make a commitment to good content? You need to do the following:

- **Understand what great content looks like:** To get ideas, look at successful examples around the Web. Many large companies (as well as small) are creating impressive examples. (For examples and a discussion of great content check out Rule 16, "Digital Publishing and eBooks Are Here Now—Use Them.")

- **Develop a budget to support the effort:** It's important to realize that content creation should be supported by an actual budget. How large a budget it should be depends on the size of the effort required. You need to hire or outsource people with the right skills and you need to let them devote time to creating good stuff. This doesn't mean that you need to keep a design house on retainer. But it does mean that graphic designers, videographers, and others will be needed.

TIP Don't decide you can't afford to get something professionally done until you look around at what's available. There are many sites like elance.com or odesk.com where you can find people willing to work at different rates. Also, if you are a small company, see whether someone you partner with has a designer who might want to treat the two of you as one project. That will increase the designer's productivity. If you can assure her a set number of hours over time, you might get a better rate.

- **Continue to experiment and revise:** Content styles and types are constantly in flux. Two years ago, infographics weren't the enormous hit they are today. Keep your eyes open and make sure you see what trends are erupting.

- **Keep an inventory of everything you have:** One of the keys to having great content is to know you have it. An inventory of what you have (see Rule 7, "Know Your Content" for information on how to create a Topic Inventory) ensures that you will use it to the fullest. You want to repurpose items and make sure that everything that can be used or refreshed is available. Repurposing helps get you that all-important Return on Investment (ROI) you crave.

- **Make SEO a priority:** SEO must be part of your commitment to content. As previously discussed, if your content can't be found, it won't support your business goals. Keywords need to be present in text and attached to everything you produce. Depending on your budget you could hire a company or a freelance resource to get you started developing keywords.

  In its most basic form you want to at least pick words that help people search for your business and make sure to add them to the content you create.

TIP Remember that in order to be found you need to tag your images for search engines. This is key. You need alt tags and title attributes. Ask your webmaster to make sure that these are always present.

A great example of a company that produces content as part of its business plan is HubSpot (http://www.hubspot.com) Figure 4.2 shows all the resources the company provides free of charge.

 ## A VISUAL MARKETING METHOD

Method: A quick method to help you figure out the current state of your business to determine what you need to work on.

Tools provided: Bull's-eye assessment template

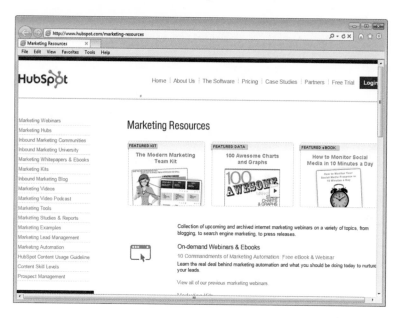

FIGURE 4.2

HubSpot marketing resources.

I created this template to help my clients quickly figure out where their focus needs to be to get the most traction. When you are close to a situation, sometimes it's hard to figure out what should be done next.

HERE I AM, STUCK IN THE MIDDLE WITH YOU

My favorite quote about process is from Rosabeth Moss Kanter at the Harvard Business School. It's called "Kanter's Law" and it states, "Everything can look like a failure in the middle." The wisdom of this law points out that when you are in the middle of any project, you don't have the optimism you started with. The bright, shiny idea you were so confident about has crashed and burned. The end is nowhere in sight, so you can't judge whether the actions you took to overcome the problem will work. You're in the middle with all the chaos that naturally occurs in any undertaking. Luckily, you are not reacting to anything but fear. The truth is that if you saw something that needed correction, you would take that action, so this reaction is simply emotion. When you realize that, it makes things easier.

Figure 4.3 shows a template I created in the form of a bull's-eye.

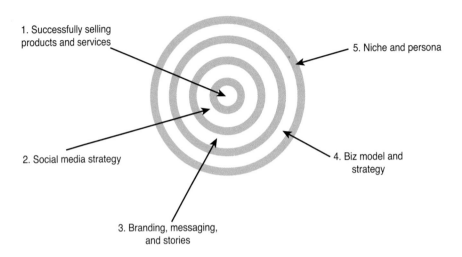

FIGURE 4.3

Bull's-eye assessment.

To start the assessment, you begin at the outer ring and look at the numbers. They go from 5 to 1. If your business is at its optimum place, you would be at number 1—the center of the bull's-eye.

How to assess the current state of your business:

Start at the outermost ring. It's number 5, customer niche. If you have your customer niche and personas figured out to your satisfaction, you can move to the next ring.

The next ring is number 4, business model for revenue and overall strategy done. If you believe that you understand your business model and know how you are generating revenue, you can move to the next ring.

The next ring is number 3, branding, messaging, and stories. If you believe that you have your branding in place, have solidified your messaging, and have created powerful stories matched to personas and keywords, move to the next ring.

The next ring is number 2, social media strategy. If you believe, based on your branding, messaging, and stories created in the previous ring, that you have developed your social media strategy, move to the next ring.

The final ring is number 1, successfully selling and marketing your products and services. If you're here, you've hit the target! You can enjoy your success and continue to revise and improve all the things that got you there.

If you were stopped at any ring, start there. Work on developing or creating whatever needs to be done to move to the next ring. If you don't, you will never progress to where you want to be.

IDEAS TO USE

Visual content should educate, entertain, and persuade, and should be shareable and findable.

Visual content shouldn't overwhelm the viewer. Keep it simple.

If you don't make a commitment to creating great content, you will severely handicap your business, regardless of industry.

IDEA MAP

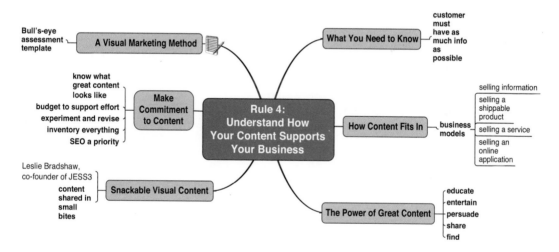

Idea Map for Rule 4

ENDNOTES

To create a visual business plan, check out *Business Model Generation,* by Alexander Osterwalder and Yves Pigneur, Wiley, 2010.

McDermott, Clare. "Infographics are a Full Meal; Consumer Audiences Need Snackable Content." Content Marketing Institute. http://www.contentmarketinginstitute.com/2012/08/consumer-audiences-need-snackable-content.

TAKE BUYERS ON A JOURNEY

In Rule 5 we look at how customers buy online and what you need to do to capture their interest. We examine a new process and demonstrate a way for you to analyze your customer's buying journey content.

WHAT YOU NEED TO KNOW

When you look at the buyer's journey today, you see a process that bears no resemblance to online purchasing in the twentieth century. I was at AOL in 1994 when users began to learn how to buy online. It was an exciting and challenging time. Everything was new and no one could predict how the process would unfold. Here are a few examples of the growing pains:

People were reluctant to put their credit card numbers online (with good reason)

Users didn't understand how shopping carts worked and couldn't buy

Buyers would call on the phone to make sure their purchase went through even if they got a confirmation.

So what happened? As we know, technology dramatically changed the buyer's journey. Not only can a buyer look at comparison sites, but they can take their mobile devices with them when they shop to get the best deals.

New technology enables buyers to blaze their own trails and find out exactly what they want to know before they make a purchase. They don't have to step foot in a showroom unless they want to. Or they can go to a showroom and then buy online. Retailers can't control the process. They can only use every tactic available to encourage the shopper to buy from them.

Buyers no longer follow a linear process where they decide to look at a product, seek out a salesperson to get information, and then buy. Now they skip around or skip steps completely. Perhaps they will try the demo and then buy. Or they might read consumer comments and just buy the one that gets the highest rating. They're more likely to make decisions without consulting a salesperson but rather after listening to other buyers.

> Buyers no longer follow a linear process where they would decide to look at a product, seek out a salesperson to get information, and then buy. Now they skip around or skip steps completely.

An infographic by Orangecollarmedia.com (http://www.orangecollarmedia.com/) titled "Buying on the Internet" offers these statistics:

- 74% of the U.S. population is on the Internet.

- Of that 74% of the population, 81% researches products online.

- 66% of Internet users have purchased an online product.

If you are a marketer who feels comfortable with the old process of just putting information on your website and expecting buyers to find you, you won't last long.

HOW WE BUY ONLINE

The buyer's journey that I detail here is a changeable process. The key is to provide the right answers to buyers' questions by anticipating what they will want to know at each stage of the buying process and then let them chose the order in which they collect that information.

Let's begin by looking at the things a buyer wants to know before making a purchase, as shown in Figure 5.1. The journey is depicted as a puzzle in the shape of a cross.

The key to understanding the buyer's journey is that it is not a flowchart. (See Rule 10, "Use Diagrams and Other Data Visualization Tools to Explain Marketing Ideas," for more on flowcharts.) There are no prescribed steps, and these are general guidelines. Buyers will choose their own path depending on what they are buying and how important it is to them. For this reason, consider the buyer's journey "cross puzzle," as shown in Figure 5.1, as a checklist of things to cover.

Buyer's Journey

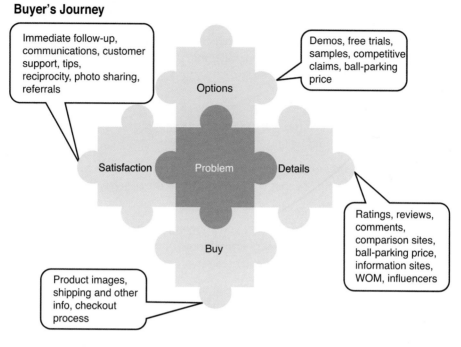

> Immediate follow-up, communications, customer support, tips, reciprocity, photo sharing, referrals

> Demos, free trials, samples, competitive claims, ball-parking price

Options

Satisfaction   Problem   Details

Buy

> Ratings, reviews, comments, comparison sites, ball-parking price, information sites, WOM, influencers

> Product images, shipping and other info, checkout process

FIGURE 5.1

Buyer's journey.

TIP

As you follow along, you'll notice that I am not talking about the format, meaning how the content is delivered. I am talking about the information that must be present in several formats to provide buyers with the information they need to make a decision. There is no way to know exactly how your customers want to receive the information. That's what you need to determine using your persona template.

PROBLEM

We start by looking at the center of the image, which is labeled Problem. This is where the buyer starts. The customer needs to buy something because of some problem she wants to solve. It could be something big, such as the need for a new car to get the customer to work. Or it could be something simple, such as the need for a better vacuum cleaner because of a new dog. It could also be the need for a service provider, such as a gardener, dentist, or business coach.

PERSONAS

This is where you use the information you collected about your personas to provide information to solve the problems of your customers. You should take each of your personas and walk them through purchase scenarios.

Look at factors such as these:

- **Demographics:** Your personas will have the demographic makeup of your customer so you know who you should be targeting.

- **Buying Triggers:** For you as a marketer, it is important to analyze what triggers the need for your product so that you can anticipate the urgency with which your customer will act.

  For example, if you sell birthday cakes, you know that there will be a group of people who rush in at the last minute to buy something. You need to think through all the information such people will need and create a procedure that accommodates this.

  If you are a dentist, you know that there will be dental emergencies that require special handling. If you are selling cars, an emergency purchase is less likely, but it could happen.

  Your priorities should be dictated by the triggers your customers face. Another way to look at triggers is to think about them as a way to create a need. For example, Hallmark did not create Mother's Day, but it seized the opportunity to make it a trigger to buy greeting cards. Perhaps you can think of something that ties your product to an event or idea.

- **Key motivators:** These are the underlying things that motivate the buyer, such as getting promoted at work or retiring early. If your product doesn't inhibit larger goals, they can go on to consider it. For example, suppose a customer is putting money away every month in an early retirement fund. If your product costs so much that it prevents them from putting money in their retirement fund that month, you are not a viable choice for them at this time.

- **Objections to you:** Your credibility is made up of many different elements. These include what your customers say on review sites, comments on your blog, comments made to customer service people, and so on. A first-class website goes a long way toward establishing your credibility. Make sure that your design and content are up to the standards your customers expect.

Questions to be answered in the Personas section include these:

- Are your personas up-to-date?

- Do you know what the motivation and triggers are for your customer?

- Are you aware of the objections raised by your potential customers?

Next we look at the categories in the buyer's journey by going clockwise around the image. Remember that I am not suggesting that your customer will follow this path from options to details in the same order. That's why it's not depicted as a flowchart. This chart is constructed to help you make sure you hit customers at every point in the buying process. Obviously, after they have purchased, you move to the satisfaction arm of the cross puzzle.

OPTIONS

Options refer to the *who* and the *what*—customers start by asking, "Who is selling the product and what should I know about it?" They cast a wide net to see what kinds of solutions are available to them. One of their main goals is to eliminate products or services that don't meet their needs.

Typically, someone who is looking at options will be looking for such things as these:

- **Demos and free trials:** This is obviously the domain of software and application providers, but if you can figure out a way to make this work for your product or service, by all means do so. It includes such things as free consultations for service providers.

- **Samples:** This refers to ways to get the physical product into the hands of your customer. Studies show that if a customer holds your product in his hands, he will be more likely to buy it. If you can supply a coupon or arrange to give your customer a sample, it can be worth your time.

- **Competitive claims:** Customers see who the competitors are and they actually look at ads that catch their attention.

- **Price:** Customers estimate the price to see what's available.

Questions to be answered in this section include these:

- Have you provided all possible demos, free trials, and samples, as well as a way to convert these trials to a purchase?

- Do you know what your competitors offer and what is the same or different about their offers?

- Are you aware of all possible prices for your type of product or service and where your product falls in this price range?

DETAILS

When buyers look for specifics, they test their choices against the opinions of others. Some people might jump to this as their first step to identify what's popular. Others might start at options. That's why it's critical that you provide information that suits both of these buying styles. That's also why I include price ball-parking here too.

You want to make sure that you look at the details as your customer would. This is where influencers and blogs play a part. It is likely that your customer follows certain influencers and reads blogs that relate to your topic. You will want to identify and read these as well. You should do everything you can to understand what influences your buyers. You should also try to engage the influencers to see if they will let you do a guest post to otherwise present to their audience.

The key is that you always need to know what impacts your customer's decisions. That is why I always recommend that you keep in touch with popular culture. There might be memes or other events that change the way your customer views your products or services. If you're in the dark, you can't react.

TIP The use of the term 'meme' was coined in 1976 by biologist Richard Dawkins but has gained favor online. It refers to a cultural idea that gets spread virally.

As part of your persona analysis, you looked at where your customers go to find information. As you analyze the information available to your customers on the Web, you need to visit these platforms and sites. For example, if you know that your customers spend time on Facebook, you should do research about your product there and see what your customers searching on Facebook will find about you.

One way to do this is to research all the places where people discuss your products. These include places where you find:

- **Ratings, reviews, comments:** These can be found at places like Amazon (http://amazon.com), Epinions (http://epinions.com), and Zagat (http://zagat.com).

- **Comparison sites and ball-park pricing:** Bizrate (http://www.bizrate.com) and Nextag (http://www.nextag.com).

- **Online business information sites:** Mashable (http://mashable.com) and TechCrunch (http://techcrunch.com).

- **Word of Mouth (WOM):** Social platforms are where many people discuss brands and products with their "friends." You should be sure to cover Facebook, Twitter, YouTube, Google+, and LinkedIn.

- **Influencers:** Find influential blogs in your topic area. You can do this by searching the blog directories Alltop (http://alltop.com) and Technorati (http://technorati.com).

Questions to be answered in this section include these:

- Do you know where your customers go to consume information?

- Have you looked at your ratings, reviews, and comments and responded to them?

- Do you know who the influencers are in your topic area?

BUY

Next up on the journey diagram is the "Buy" area. This is where the shopper has decided which option he wants and is getting down to the final details. Price is finalized here. The buyer knows what he wants to spend.

These include customer service issues such as the following:

- **Visual depiction of the product:** This refers to the visuals you use to display your product or service. If the product is an eBook, does it have an attractive cover? If the purchase includes a service, does it have a name and clear description? Apple, the master of design, shows you exactly what you'll get and when you'll get it, and Apple customers are probably as impressed with the packaging as they are with the gadgets.

- **Shipping and other information:** Before customers finalize their decision, make sure that you have covered all the questions they might have about how the product or service is delivered. If you don't, they will either leave without purchasing or call customer service. Both options are expensive.

- **Shopping cart/checkout process:** As users are homing in on their purchase, they enter the shopping cart process. Shopping cart abandonment (when the user leaves before completing a purchase) is still a huge problem. You might take it for granted that your process is easy, but be sure to confirm that by taking the trip through the process yourself.

Questions to be answered in this section include these:

- Have you taken the time to create the visual product images you need to sell and do promotions?

- Did you provide all the information about shipping, delivery, and other such information? Is it easy to find?

- Have you done a walk-through of buying the product to make sure that the process is easy to complete?

SATISFACTION

As a social media marketer, you know that ongoing satisfaction is one of the most important things you need to attend to with your customers. This is where the relationship with your customer can deepen. If your customers are satisfied, you hope they will let the people of their networks know.

These are the kinds of things you should be paying attention to here:

- **Immediate follow-up:** Make sure that you have an autoresponder or some other mechanism that sends a thank-you to your new customer along with any receipts or other payment documents. This is the time when buyer's remorse could set in. Welcome customers into the community and help them find their way around your website or other major sites. Invite them into the community.

- **Ongoing communication:** Be sure to establish a newsletter or weekly email that customers can opt into. They keep you in contact with customers. Don't just show up when you have something to sell.

- **Support on social networks:** Be prepared to offer support on a social network or a community building tool such as Get Satisfaction (https://getsatisfaction.com). If customers can't find you, they will forget you the next time they shop.

- **Tips and tricks:** If appropriate, have a training area with tips and training for your product. Also, make sure your help documents and FAQs are helpful. In my experience, they can fall short.

- **Maintaining reciprocity:** We have specifically talked about the importance of reciprocity in Rule 1, "Recognize the Power of Visual Persuasion," and Rule 18, "Landing Pages Won't Perform Without Visuals." It's always a factor. Make sure that you're giving value as time goes on.

- **Visual sharing:** Photos of your staff and events should always be included. Make sure you have plenty of customer photos to help connect real people with one another.

- **Referrals:** This is where the customer becomes your most treasured sales rep. Make it easy for customers to share your story, and then reward them.

Questions to be answered in this section include these:

- Are all your mechanisms in place to stay in constant contact with your customer?

- Are you sending visual reminders such as photos of events to your customers to remind them that you are on the job?

- Do you make sure to provide ongoing value and free content?

 ## A VISUAL MARKETING METHOD

Method: How to analyze your content for your buyer's journey.

After you have answered all the questions in the previous sections and created your content using the cross-style buyer's journey template, you will want to create some buying scenarios to test the material. This means that you have to take various paths that the customer takes to see whether you have created all the content you need.

For example, take your first persona and walk through the process of researching and buying your product. Set up an actual path that suits your particular needs.

Here's one possible general scenario template:

Your persona named _____ wants to research buying your product or service. The problem she is solving is _____.

She will do the following before purchasing:

- She will likely look at these specific influential sites online: _____.

- She will examine offerings from the following competitors: _____.

- She will determine the estimated price range for the product or service, and that range is _____.

- She will look for free samples or trials to try. She will find the following: _____.

- She will look at ratings, comments, reviews, comparison sites, and online business information sites. Here's what she will find: _____.

- She will listen to friends and word-of-mouth information on social platforms. Here's what she will see: _____.

- She will look at packaging, offers, and ads. Here are examples: _____.

- She will try to find information about delivery issues after she has made her decision.

- She will use the shopping cart to check out and go through the entire buying process. If it is satisfactory, she will complete the purchase.

Remember to revise this template to suit your particular needs. Then, if you have walked all your personas through this process and you haven't found any gaps, you can begin testing your offers.

IDEAS TO USE

Buyers follow their own path, so you need to provide information for every step they take.

The personas you create will help you target the right messages on the buying journey.

Be sure to walk through the process that your customer will take to buy to ensure that it doesn't cause cart abandonment.

IDEA MAP

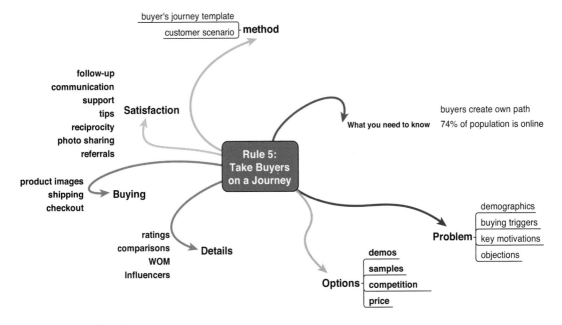

Idea Map for Rule 5

Rule 6

CONNECT USING COLLABORATION'S MANY FORMS

In Rule 6 we look at how different forms of collaboration can help you reach your business goals and bring you closer to your customers. We show you the benefits of using the different forms so you can choose what's best for you.

WHAT YOU NEED TO KNOW

We all know that the Internet has had a dramatic impact on the way people work together. They are no longer locked into time zones and snail mail. What's most interesting is that now that people have had the opportunity to collaborate online, a host of new styles of collaboration have sprung up.

As a social media marketer, you should consider using as many forms of collaboration as you can. Right now, you probably are in touch with your customers via Facebook, Twitter, and so on. It's also likely that your employees collaborate online using workflow tools.

> What's most interesting is that now that people have had the opportunity to collaborate online, a host of new styles of collaboration have sprung up.

Small companies use tools such as Basecamp.com (where employees can upload and share their work documents to be more productive) or Yammer (where a private network is established so that staff can easily share documents and access information), and enterprises use tools such as Salesforce.com (a system that enables staff in enterprises to have access to customer information).

But have you considered co-creation, crowdsourcing, or crowd funding? Depending on your circumstances, you might find that these strategies offer your company unexpected benefits. In this rule we discuss the characteristics of each type: In-house, co-creation, crowdsourcing and crowd fuding.

In the book *Getting Results from Crowds* authors Ross Dawson and Steve Bynghall suggest three key questions you should ask yourself before you decide whether to crowdsource:

- **Inside or outside?** You need to decide whether the task involves proprietary information or patents that can't be shared. If your challenge can be understood only by an insider, the choice is easy.

- **Local or global?** Should the source of your talent be confined to your geographical area? Will you get a better return by opening up the job to people anywhere?

- **Commodity or talent?** You need to determine whether you want to pay people by the hour for specific tasks or hire top-notch professionals who cost significantly more.

FORMS OF COLLABORATION

After you have the answers to these questions, you can determine which type of collaboration is right for you.

To present the benefits of each type of collaboration, I divided the activity into four types: in-house, co-creation, crowdsourcing, and crowd funding as shown in Table 6.1. You see the type of collaboration, the people involved, and an example of each type.

Table 6.1   Types of Collaboration

Type	Source	Company Example
In-house	Employee to employee	N/A
Co-creation	Employee to customers	Napkin Labs
Crowdsourcing	Company to "experts"	iStockphoto
Crowd funding	Experts to customers	Kickstarter

Each of the types of collaboration is discussed in more detail in the following sections.

IN-HOUSE COLLABORATION (EMPLOYEE TO EMPLOYEE)

This type of collaboration refers to the act of working together with fellow employees to develop and complete products, projects, and other activities. With the growth of social customer relationship management (CRM) systems, the ability of employees to integrate their knowledge and projects with one another has taken a great leap forward. In addition, videoconferencing has become much more affordable.

Benefits to employees include

- Increased understanding of other employees

- Ability to innovate

- Increased productivity

- Opportunity to learn new skills

Benefits to the company include

- Development of valuable knowledge bases as in-house assets

- Increased cost savings from productivity and innovation

- Potential for increased profits from innovated products

- **Major downside:** No opportunity to expose internal ideas to the wider pool of new ideas.

- **Company example:** Conceptboard (http://conceptboard.com)

    Using Conceptboard as shown in Figure 6.1, you can create several visual boards (depending on your subscription) that you can work on with your invited guests.

CO-CREATION (EMPLOYEE TO CUSTOMERS)

This type of collaboration refers to the act of working with customers to create, refine, and get ongoing feedback about products. The distinction here is that the focus of the activity is on company products and services. People are asked for their input.

Benefits to customers include

- Improvement of the product

- Increased recognition among other customers

- Acquisition of special perks from the company

FIGURE 6.1

Conceptboard.

Benefits to the company include

- Increased word of mouth about process and products

- Customers' perceived ownership of the product

- Increased revenue from participants

- Customer input at the beginning, which helps prevent missteps

- Gathering of more in-depth knowledge of the customer

- Uncovering of new strategies, trends, or business models

- **Major downside:** Overly vocal customers can hijack the process and intimidate others.

- **Company example:** Napkin Labs (http://napkinlabs.com)

  Napkin Labs, as shown in Figure 6.2, provides tools to help companies listen to the comments of their customers on social media platforms.

FIGURE 6.2

Napkin Labs.

CROWDSOURCING (COMPANY TO EXPERTS)

This type of collaboration refers to the use of people, not employed by a company, who are given the opportunity to work on a project or problem. The solution doesn't have to be related to current products. Jeff Howe, journalist and a contributing editor at *Wired Magazine*, coined the term *crowdsourcing* in a 2006 *Wired* article, "The Rise of Crowdsourcing."

Benefits to customers include

- Incentives, such as cash prizes, a form of payment

- Recognition among peers and/or a larger audience of experts

Benefits to the company include

- Easy access to various experts

- Less expensive than employees

- Publicity for the company

- **Major downside:** Unless you choose projects well, you could put a halt to company progress by having to wait for the project to finish.

- **Company example:** InnoCentive (http://www.innocentive.com/)

 InnoCentive, as shown in Figure 6.3, provides companies access to a network of interested people who compete to provide solutions to these companies.

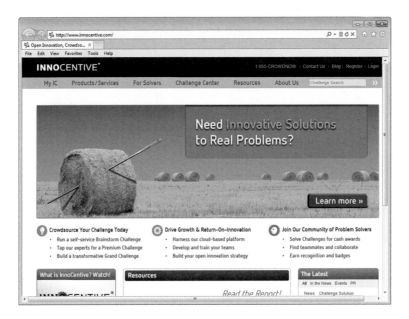

FIGURE 6.3

InnoCentive.

CROWD FUNDING (EXPERTS TO CUSTOMERS)

Crowd funding is the act of putting out new product ideas to be funded by anyone who believes in the product and wants to support it.

Benefits to participants include

- Opportunity to align themselves with a worthy cause

- Ability to support creative ideas that might not have high revenue potential

- Opportunity to join a new community of people who support the cause or idea

Benefits to the company include

- Investment to make production possible

- Publicity for the creators and the product itself

- Opportunity to showcase work to large investors

- Ability to fund an idea with great social impact

- **Major downside:** You might expose your effort to legal or other unwanted scrutiny.

- **Company example:** Kickstarter (http://kickstarter.com)

Kickstarter, as shown in Figure 6.4, provides a platform for entrepreneurs who want to get funding for their new products.

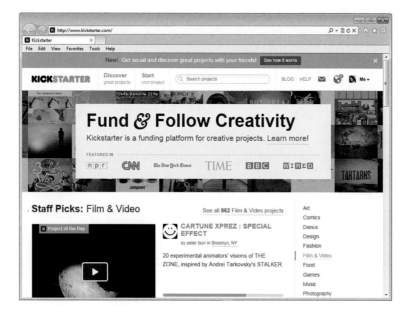

FIGURE 6.4

Kickstarter.

IDEAS TO USE

Consider using as many forms of collaboration as you can after you have carefully evaluated them.

Co-creation gives customers a stake in promoting the completed product.

If you have proprietary material, it might not be a good idea to use crowdsourcing.

IDEA MAP

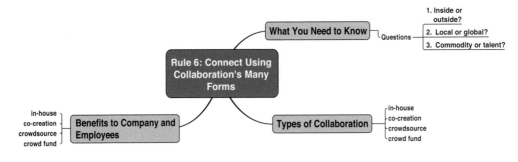

Idea Map for Rule 6.

ENDNOTES

Dawson, Ross, and Steve Bynghall. *Getting Results from Crowds: The Definitive Guide to Using Crowdsourcing to Grow Your Business.* Advanced Human Technologies, 2011.

KNOW YOUR CONTENT

In Rule 7 we look at how to assess the content you already have in order to determine what you need to create. We give you a tool you can use to develop the inventory.

WHAT YOU NEED TO KNOW

Your online content doesn't provide enough visual persuasion. You might be wondering how I know. Am I clairvoyant? Not really.

Most online sites still don't take advantage of the visual potential of the Web. If you are reading this book, you probably agree and want to do something about it.

As we've discussed, the use of online visuals has exploded. Sites like Pinterest have grown by leaps and bounds, and we know that the capability to share visual content is what makes it so popular.

What we don't see is the increased use of visuals on ordinary websites or blogs unless they are hosted on a blog site such as Tumblr, which was created to host multimedia.

Is the lack of pictures because it's hard to manipulate visuals? Evidence doesn't support that. We've all seen more cat pictures than we ever thought possible. Sites like Flickr, Facebook, and Instagram are overflowing with photos of all kinds.

What's more likely is that it's a function of several things. It could be a lack of one or more of the following:

- **A budget to upgrade your total visual image:** Your website was probably designed more than two years ago and you don't want to change it until it's absolutely necessary. Whether your business is large or small, you want to use your funds elsewhere.

  For this reason you continue to use the same colors, fonts, and visual direction you chose several years ago. Much has probably changed since then but you don't have an inexpensive way to make that change.

- **Understanding of the power of visuals to sell and persuade (see Rule 1):** Many people discount the impact that visuals have on persuasion, yet we know that when a photo is placed next to product information, the user studies the photo to get clues about the product or service. We know that when a user sees a video, she is likely to watch it and respond. Visuals and other factors persuade us in ways we are unaware of.

> Most online sites don't take advantage of the visual potential of the Web. If you are reading this book, you probably agree and want to do something about it.

FIRST TELL ME THE PRICE

Several experiments have been done with wine drinkers that indicate that if they either do a blind taste test or are told that the wines are a higher price, people will choose what they believe to be the higher-priced wines regardless of taste. In an April 26, 2011, article in *Wired Magazine* by Jonah Lehrer called "Should We Buy Expensive Wines?" he details several of these studies. One such study conducted by psychologist Richard Wiseman found that there was no real correlation between price and taste. He writes, "The 600 plus participants could only pick the more expensive wine 53 percent of the time, which is basically random chance." This clearly shows that there is more to persuasion than we believe.

- **Knowledge about what makes a good visual for your online sites:** Wooden people in stock photos are not the best choice. You have the option of choosing from so many visual possibilities—don't limit yourself. Something eye-catching or even quirky might be more attention getting. Just don't get too abstract.

You might not have the time to devote to the study of visuals, but you can evaluate the images you already have. Following are six quick guidelines to consider:

- **Understand the mission of the image, video, and other visual elements:** Is it supporting text or standing on its own? It shouldn't be there just because it's pretty. People read in all sorts of information from images. Test the image by asking others what it means to them in relation to the page.

- **Make it simple:** Don't overwhelm the viewer. Cut to the chase and say what you need to say with the visual content. You're not running an art museum. If you have created an illustration to show a process, include plenty of white space.

- **Make it real:** Avoid stock images that look nice but don't really relate to the authenticity or personality of your company.

- **Don't reinvent the wheel:** Use symbols and images that everyone will understand. If people have to spend too much time figuring out what you mean, they will skip the content completely—so much for creative drawing. See Rule 9, "Make Ideas Tangible" for more on this topic.

- **Present a professional image:** People will judge—that's a sad fact. This book talks about the power of visuals to persuade people. If you have an amateurish look, people will assume you don't know any better or don't care and they won't choose you. Use a template and modify it or get professional help to establish an overall design.

- **Use suitable fonts:** Mix fonts and sizes at your own peril. Never let a web page look like a ransom note.

TOPIC INVENTORY

To figure out what content needs to be created, you need to take an inventory of what you already have. This advice can be a bitter pill to swallow. The last thing you want to do (or have staff do) is spend time looking at what you've already published. But you'll never get a handle on telling your story if you haven't documented your existing content and tested it against your social media conversations.

Most content professionals recommend that you create an inventory of your content. What this entails is going to every page of content you have on the Web and making an inventory of everything on it.

For example, you would go to each section on your website—such as press releases, articles, and products—and inventory each image, each section of text, or whatever you find there. When it's complete, you have a full accounting for all your content and will be able to start to repurpose and create new content. If you have a content management system (CMS), you might be lucky enough to produce your content inventory from that.

TIP Much of the literature on content inventories suggests that you do an inventory when you are moving to a CMS or redesigning your website. If you wait for that, you are hurting your business. Do it as soon as you can.

You may not be able to tackle a complete inventory project immediately because your content collection it is too large and complex. There is an alternative you can consider in the interim that lets you take a smaller bite. It's called a topic inventory.

A topic inventory consists of documenting all the specific topics that you consider core to your business. The purpose of doing this is to be able to see all the information you have on those topics and then be able to repurpose them into other formats. For example, if you have a blog post on a topic you could turn it into an audio or video.

Let's drill down further. If you are a software developer a core topic would be "features of the product." You would want to collect all the material in your collection that discussed product features. You would then break that down into each individual feature. You would then document each type of information you have for each feature including videos, web pages, blog posts, etc.

The downside to creating a topic inventory instead of inventorying everything as a whole is that you might miss items that you can repurpose. For example, you might have a collection of videos whose titles are not documented. If you were going through all your content, you would find these and be able to add them to the inventory. But because you are only going through your collection to find specific topics like "product features" as in the example above, you would miss them. But if your alternative is no inventory versus a topic inventory, I suggest you do a topic inventory.

 A VISUAL MARKETING METHOD

Method: How to create a topic inventory.

Figure 7.1 shows a template you can use to create your first topic inventory.

The fields are as listed here:

- **Topic:** This is the topic you will select by looking at your story lines, blog categories, website navigation, social media platform topics, landing pages, and so on.

- **Title:** This is the tile of your article or other written text.

- **Keywords:** These are the keywords that match the content you have selected.

- **Personas:** These are the personas that are targeted for the specific content.

- **URL:** This is where your content can be found.

- **Images:** These are the images that support the content.

- **Video:** These are the videos that can be found with the content.

- **Time sensitive:** This refers to the shelf life of the content. If it is specific to a time-limited campaign or sale, note that.

Topic Inventory Template

	Topic	Title	Keywords	Personas	URL	Images	Video	Time sensitive?
Topic:								
Topic:								
Topic:								
Topic:								

FIGURE 7.1

Topic inventory template.

> **TIP** I didn't add traffic stats to this list, but if you can get them, you should certainly add them. If you know that the content is popular, you can plan to repurpose it and create more like it.

Let's create a topic inventory for a housewares store.

Figure 7.2 shows an example of a Topic inventory in progress.

Topic Inventory Template

Topic	Title	Keywords	Personas	URL	Images	Video	Time sensitive?
Topic: Customer service							
	Delivering velvet sofas in a thunderstorm	customer service, tech support, outlet, sale	Ellen Johnson, Mrs. Winthrop	furnwidgets.com/testimonials/400	colllins.jpg Blakely_sofa.jpg	collins.mp4	no
							no
	Picking gifts for the hostess	customer service, gift services	Mrs. Winthrop, Bob Flint	furnwidgets.com/faq/291	Gift_registry.jpg	Picking_gifts.mp4	no
Topic: Storage solutions							
	How to organize your kitchen storage	storage solutions, sale, containers	Ellen Johnson, Mrs. Winthrop	furnwidgets.com/storage/221	green_containers.jpg	Organizing_kitchen.mp4	no

FIGURE 7.2

Topic inventory in progress.

To get started, you should pick five to seven of the most important topics to inventory.

The first topic might be "Amazing customer service stories." If you look at the template example, the topic should be parsed this way:

Topic: Amazing customer service stories

Title: Delivering velvet sofas in a thunderstorm

Keywords: customer service, tech support, outlet, sale

Video: Video named Collins.mp4

Images: Collins.jpg, Blakely_sofa.jpg

An example of another topic might be storage solutions. The content should be parsed this way:

Title: How to organize your kitchen storage

Keywords: storage solutions, sale, containers

Video: Organizing_kitchen.mp4

Images: green_containers.jpg

You should continue to fill out the spreadsheet template until you have collected the inventory around those topics. Then you evaluate based on what you have, and what needs to be created to fill out those topics. Couple this with the template in Rule 9, "Make Ideas Tangible."

 ## IDEAS TO USE

It's critical that you take some kind of a content inventory as soon as possible so that you know what you have and what you need to create.

Be sure to fill out the template with all the media formats you have—videos, images, and so on.

Evaluate your visuals carefully so that you don't wind up with styles you consider obsolete.

IDEA MAP

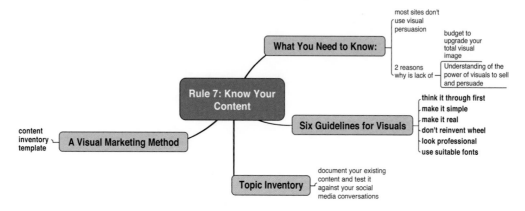

Idea Map for Rule 7

ENDNOTES

Lehrer, Jonah. "Should We Buy Expensive Wines?" *Wired Magazine*. April 26, 2011.

Part II

TOOLS TO HELP YOU CREATE YOUR VISUAL MARKETING

Rule 8

USE MIND MAPS TO SEE WHAT YOU'RE THINKING

In Rule 8 we look at how using a technique called mind maps helps you clarify your thinking and improve the ideas you generate. We show you a mind map you can use to generate more ideas for blogging.

WHAT YOU NEED TO KNOW

When it comes to using visual techniques that can serve to clarify communication for your customers, your staff, and yourself, consider creating mind maps. I have included a form of mind map called an idea map at the end of each rule. They show you the big picture and the details on the same map. Another example is the "Persona pie template" in Rule 2, "Personas are the Key to Understanding Your Customers."

I started using them well before mapping software became available. Back then, I used paper and colored pencils or pens to make my maps. Sometimes you'd need to erase a lot or completely start over. Regardless of the implements you use, mind maps are an important tool that you need to have in your business kit.

Tony Buzan, the well-respected author, educator, and trainer, is credited with naming and popularizing the concept of mind maps in the U.K. in the 1960s.

He developed them to help students memorize their lessons. They proved to be an effective way for students to learn faster, retain information, and raise their grades.

Soon businesspeople began using them and they have steadily grown in popularity. With the emphasis on visual thinking and planning, and the development of cutting-edge mapping software, mind maps have become even more popular. Both major corporations and small business owners use them to assist with various functions including marketing, human resources, information technology, and consulting.

One of the main reasons mind maps have endured is that they help both individuals and groups do their best work. Using a mind map levels the playing field for "solopreneurs" and small business owners. Mind maps multiply brain power. You can figure out your strategy and develop campaigns that rival those of large enterprises. When enterprises use maps, they help make sense of multiple ideas and opinions.

WHY MIND MAPS INTIMIDATE SOME PEOPLE

In working on maps with clients over the years, I've found that most people fall into one of two camps: They love them or they hate them. I think there are several reasons for this that have nothing to do with the technique itself. The people who say they dislike mind maps generally fear the following:

- They think they are not a visual learner and believe that they won't be able to create their own maps.

- They fear that they won't understand them well enough to create one properly and will then appear foolish in front of their colleagues.

- They think that they will need a long time to learn the process and they don't want to spend the time.

- They fear that mind maps are only for creative types and don't have any real value for logically minded thinkers.

None of these assumptions happens to be true, but they are commonplace responses. You won't need artistic talent and it won't take a long time to learn the process. Mind maps work like our brains do. They help you make connections and they don't require linear thinking like an outline does.

In fact, fancy artwork can impede the progress of mind maps. If the recorder drew complex drawings on the map, that would slow down the process. Most graphic facilitators work quickly and use instantly recognizable things such as icons and shapes. Speed is a necessary

> In working on maps with clients over the years, I've found that most people fall into one of two camps: They love them or they hate them.

component of documenting ideas on mind maps because the ideas don't wait for the recorder to finish.

When you are introducing the process to an individual or a group, it's good to start by working the map by yourself. This shows off the technique and demonstrates how easy it is to jump right in. After a small piece of the map is done, ask the group to join in. Someone will always jump in and you're off and running. Not everyone will love using the maps, but people might warm up to them over time. It all depends on how valuable the information is to them.

I AM SHOCKED, SHOCKED!

Because of all the complex maps and data we are presented with today, an interesting phenomenon has been identified by Don Dansereau, Professor of Psychology at Texas Christian University.

He coined the term "map shock" to refer to the response a person has when he looks at a complex map or chart and is unable to make sense of it. Such a person is completely bewildered.

Perhaps some people who dislike mind maps have had this experience upon seeing their first map.

PRINCIPLES OF GOOD MIND MAPS

Tony Buzan created a list of mind map "laws" to follow when creating a map. Although many people who create them have never heard of these principles, I think it's valuable to record at least some of them here because they represent best practices.

Included in his principles are the following:

- Always use a central image and images throughout your maps.
- Use variations of size of printing line and image.
- Use colors throughout the map.
- Use only one keyword per line.
- Print all words.
- Make the central lines thicker.
- Develop a personal style.
- Use a hierarchy.
- Use numerical order.
- Keep your paper placed horizontally (in landscape mode) in front of you.

TIP I've seen mind maps with several more keywords (or a phrase) per line than one. The reason to use only one keyword per line is so that it's easy to remember. When you use a very long sentence, you can't glance at it and instantly recognize the concept. Remember that your eyes are taking in small chunks of information at one time and connecting them to a visual representation in your brain. You defeat your ability to recognize the keyword if it's too long to take in with one look.

USING MIND MAPS FOR ONLINE MARKETING

Let's look at how mind maps can help you with online marketing.

You could use a map to

- Brainstorm a website redesign
- Create a marketing campaign
- Develop a blogging calendar (we do this one below)
- Write a blog post (you'll find more on a visual blogging tool in Rule 12, "Use Visual Presentations to Connect with an Audience ")
- Uncover new ideas for stories on your website
- Create a map of evergreen tweets (information that doesn't go out of date) on topics or quotes to use over time

The reason mind maps work with all kinds of marketing tasks is that they provide a way for you to do the following:

- **Do a brain dump of ideas:** You have the opportunity to get everything you are thinking out of your head and onto the page.
- **Break tasks into small workable pieces:** After you get the major topics solidified, you can then begin to separate them into steps you can take in the order in which you need to take them.
- **See the big picture and the details at the same time:** When you look at your map, you can see the big picture by looking at the main topics. You can then drill down to the ideas that radiate out from them to see the detail of each. You can continually add more detail as you go and still have a big-picture view.

In the later section "A Visual Marketing Method," we illustrate these three points to create a map.

MIND MAPS ARE USEFUL FOR WORK GROUPS

We know that mind maps make ideas tangible, and that in itself helps people work together. Here are some other reasons to try it at work:

- Everyone has a chance to contribute. There is no hierarchy to the participation; anyone with a good idea can throw it into the mix. That means the boss and the staff members' ideas are weighted equally on the map.

- At the end of the session, you can get everyone to sign off on the ideas. This means they can't say later that they didn't know about them.

- Mind maps show the big idea and the details so that everyone can get specific "marching orders" at the same time. This also means that everyone knows what everyone else is doing.

To get the most from a mind-mapping session on a group project, be sure to follow the sequence that Buzan and other mind-map experts always suggest in writing about mind maps:

1. **Fast start:** When you start, quickly get everyone to call out ideas that come to mind. This helps them get out the "low-hanging fruit." The low-hanging fruit, in this case, are the ideas that come quickly to mind and need to be recorded first.

2. **Revise:** After a substantial map has been created, the group should evaluate it to see whether they want to change anything before they stop for the day.

3. **Incubate:** Next comes an incubation period during which your mind works on the map without any conscious input from you. This enables the group to come back to the map with "fresh eyes."

4. **Revise again:** The group comes together again to revisit the map and make adjustments.

5. **Final version:** Remember that a mind map is organic and should grow and change with the life of the project so it's never really final. Revisions and additions can be made to the map as often as the group feels is necessary.

TIP Never delete earlier versions of a mind map. Keep them as a digital file or a paper document. You don't want to lose the historical data that can give you clues about what the group was thinking and where decisions came from.

A VISUAL MARKETING METHOD

Method: How to map out blog articles using your blog structure.

Tools provided: Blog wonder wheel template (a form of mind map); example with blog ideas

Figure 8.1 shows the wonder wheel worksheet.

Wonder Wheel Worksheet

Categories

Personas

Types

Image Renar SC, from the Noun Project

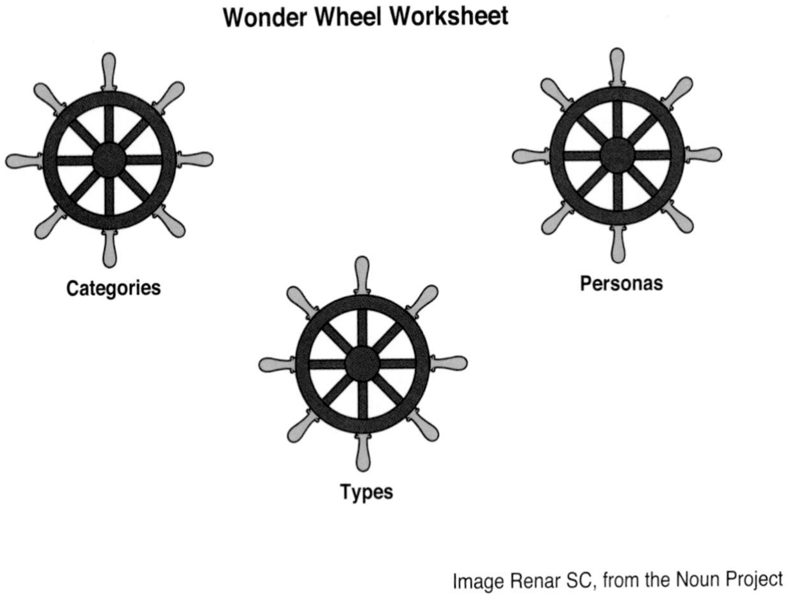

FIGURE 8.1
Wonder wheel worksheet.

When you look at the wonder wheel worksheet, you see three different wheels that will lead you to your editorial calendar:

- The first wheel is the Categories wheel. You should put your own categories in there so I left them blank. In the example I provided (Figure 8.2), I filled in some of the marketing section.

TIP If you want to modify the worksheet to include more than just articles, you can add media categories such as podcast, video, and audio.

- The second wheel (Figure 8.2) is the Types wheel, and it has the types of blog posts you should consider using. For each of those types, you see several headline suggestions. In the sample (Figure 8.2) I filled in some that I like.

- The third wheel is the Personas wheel. You need to add all your personas on the wheel so that they are visible and won't be overlooked.

Wonder Wheel Worksheet

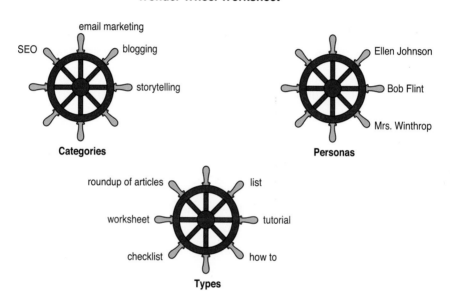

Image Renar SC, from the Noun Project

FIGURE 8.2

Wonder wheel in progress.

The choices from these wheels lead to your editorial calendar. An editorial calendar is a form of calendar which bloggers, magazine editors, and others involved in publishing use to plan out their content. For example, as a blogger you may choose to make May the month you publish content about niche marketing. This means that you would put all the new posts you have written on this topic to be published in May.

I chose not to create a wheel for the calendar because you most likely have a calendar of some sort to put them on. If you don't, you can certainly add another wheel with months on it. I would break them up into quarters so that the sheets are easy to read.

TIP If you're looking for an application to put your team's assignments on, you might want to consider workflow tools like DivvyHQ or Kapost.

Figure 8.2 shows the example in progress.

How to fill in the wonder wheel template:

1. To complete the plan, start by picking a category from the Categories wheel. You might have many categories that you rotate through in a month, or you might have just a few. You choose what works for you. For our example I'm choosing storytelling.

2. From the Types wheel first pick a style of blog post. For our example I'm picking list.

3. To recap, I chose storytelling and list. Now I need to create my headline using these elements. So for a headline I'm picking "Top 5 ways to find interesting business stories."

4. Next, decide which persona(s) are targeted in this article. I'm targeting Ellen Johnson.

5. Finally, choose when you will publish the post and list the publication date on your calendar. Repeat this for as many posts as you need to fill up your schedule.

You might find that when it comes time to write the post, you want to change to another topic based on what's pertinent to you at the moment. That's fine; just put the original post somewhere else on the schedule and write the one you want to write. The idea is to have a backlog of ideas you can use.

TOOLS TO CONSIDER

Following are some tools you might want to try:

Mind maps:

Mindjet: http://mindjet.com

Bubbl.us: https://bubbl.us

TIP You can find lots of great examples of maps from sources like Biggerplate, at http://www.biggerplate.com/, and the Mind Mapping Blog at http://mindmappingsoftwareblog.com/

Idea tools:

Alltop: http://alltop.com

Soovle: http://www.soovle.com/

BuzzFeed: http://buzzfeed.com

Social Mention: http://socialmention.com

Images:

Topsy: http://topsy.com/ For everything, photos, video, etc.

Zemanta: http://www.zemanta.com/

Flickr: http://flickr.com

Morguefile: http://morguefile.com

Calendar tools:

DivvyHQ: http://www.divvyhq.com/

Kapost: http://kapost.com/

Contently https://contently.com/

Writing tools:

InboundWriter: http://inboundwriter.com

Scribe: http://scribeseo.com/

 ## IDEAS TO USE

Mind maps should not be limited to idea generation. Use it for all your daily business activities, such as planning and writing.

Mind maps help you compete with much larger enterprises by multiplying brain power.

Use the established principles of mind mapping whenever possible.

 IDEA MAP

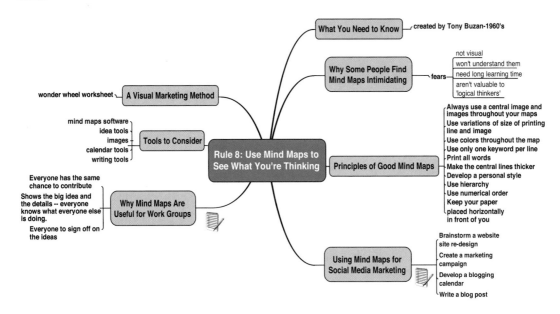

Idea Map for Rule 8

ENDNOTES

Buzan, Tony, and Barry Buzan. *The Mind Map Book: How to Use Radiant Thinking to Maximize Your Brain's Untapped Potential.* Plume, 1996.

MAKE IDEAS TANGIBLE

In Rule 9 we look at how to take the ideas that are swirling around in your head and bring them out into the open to examine and discuss with others.

WHAT YOU NEED TO KNOW

Communicating ideas is probably one of the most difficult things people have to do, both at work and at home. Ideas can be so clear in our minds yet so hard to communicate.

I'm sure this has happened to you. You explain an idea and think that people know exactly what you mean, when, in fact, they don't. We think that our frame of reference is the same as everyone else's so that what we see is obvious to them.

Being able to communicate our ideas helps us solve problems, make decisions, and be more productive. For this reason, making ideas visible is now a priority for many businesspeople.

It is our job, as social media marketers, to try to understand how our customers think and to present them with solutions to their problems. Not only do we need to understand how customers use the product, but we also need to know what needs it satisfies.

Obviously, this is not an easy task. You've seen all sorts of misses when it comes to product marketing. One of the main reasons why marketers fail is that they can't communicate their ideas in a way that makes the customer recognize it as an answer to their particular problem.

When we expose our thinking methods, we help others understand how we arrived at our conclusions. It also makes everything we discuss visible.

This begs the question, "With all the technology available to us today, should we use old-school tools such as paper and pen to get our ideas across to our colleagues?"

An article in *The Wall Street Journal*, "Doodling for Dollars" by Rachel Emma Silverman, the Management/Workplace editor, discusses the fact that major corporations and small businesses alike are encouraging their employees to use visual note taking.

Instead of employees being tethered to their gadgets, they are encouraged to use tactics such as sketching to explain their ideas. Some companies like Facebook are pushing the use of whiteboards, while others are hiring graphic facilitators to document meetings.

Citrix Systems' Catherine Courage, VP of Product Design, talks about a "design collaboration workspace" the company created at their headquarters. Silverman describes the workspace in the following way: "Whiteboards cover almost every wall and table. Markers, sticky notes, and construction paper are readily available." The workspace is used by "gadget obsessed engineers and other employees to let loose and sketch ideas" says Courage.

If major tech companies are using these tools, shouldn't you consider them?

> This begs the question, "With all the technology available to us today, should we use old-school tools like paper and pen to get our ideas across to our colleagues?"

OLD-SCHOOL TOOLS?

I have long been an advocate of the benefits of making ideas tangible. When I started researching this book, I wanted to know whether neuroscience had uncovered any answers relating to the benefits.

Is the use of physical items like pens and paper more or less beneficial than using digital tools when one is developing ideas? Some evidence suggests that for learning, using a pen and paper trumps the keyboard and screen.

In an article by Kathy Laurenhue, a well-respected writer, trainer, and curriculum developer, called "Sharpening Your Memory with a Pen," she cites a study done by Dr. Anne Mangen, professor at the University of Stavangers Reading Centre in Stavanger, Norway and Jean-Luc Velay of the University of Marseille which concluded that students who used paper and pen rather than keyboard and screen were able to learn the material more effectively.

Laurenhue says, "The act of handwriting—literally the feeling of touching a pen to paper—appears to imprint a 'motor memory' in the sensorimotor region of the brain." She notes that no such activity is found in that region when a keyboard is used. So if you prefer to use physical tools when you're generating ideas, it might be because you feel you're getting more traction. This, of course, doesn't negate the value of using digital tools. It's wise to use both.

CREATE ARTIFACTS

We communicate all sorts of things when we take an idea and create artifacts to represent it. For example, if you lay out your idea as a flowchart of stickies, you've instantly communicated several things to your audience:

- **Sequence:** The choice of a flowchart to depict your idea indicates that there is an ordered sequence. You've chosen a deliberate style of diagram to communicate how the idea works. You should also be aware that how you position objects has meaning for the brain. For example, a view out a window impacts the feeling a person has in the space he occupies. It gives context to the space.

- **Media:** Choosing to use stickies rather than one large sheet of paper might mean that you are encouraging others to change the order in which they are displayed. That's because each sticky can be removed and modified. Of course, you can scratch out ideas on sheets of paper, but if you really want to encourage movement, you would choose something like stickies that can be repositioned. Your brain takes note of movement as novelty, so you add value by doing that.

- **Color:** If you chose to color-code your stickies or use a specific color of ink to indicate something, you are able to communicate pattern groupings.

- **Size:** If your stickies are different sizes, you can communicate a hierarchy. The bigger the sticky, the more important or closer it is to something.

You can communicate all this information with just a few stickies! That's why it's so valuable to make your thinking visible to yourself and others.

BENEFITS OF TANGIBLE IDEAS

What are some of the benefits of making ideas tangible? When we can see ideas they do the following:

- **Help us comprehend more quickly:** Since we know that our brains recognize visuals faster, we can make ideas easier to understand.

- **Help us focus:** People are able to focus and direct their thinking. One of the challenges of working with ideas is that you need to narrow down the scope of your discussion to the things that matter. When ideas are tangible, we know what to focus on.

- **Provide a common language:** When you work together on the same content, the group names concepts using a common language and stays consistent.

- **Create documentation:** By making ideas tangible, you create a record of your thinking. It becomes a snapshot in time. Then you have the ability to go back and review your assumptions.

- **Propel us forward:** You are able to get off to a faster start instead of working with a computer application that might require a learning curve.

- **Allow for portability:** If you use portable tools to document ideas, they can go anywhere you go. Many people carry around a small notebook in which they can write down their ideas so that they won't lose them.

MAKING YOUR IDEAS VISIBLE

Let's look at some of the ways you can make your ideas viewable to others:

- **Symbols:** Using symbols is a common way to communicate information. It can be something as simple as a dollar sign ($) or as complicated as a scientific formula, such as $E=MC^2$.

- **Pictures:** Pictures are a primary way the brain understands information.

- **Color:** The choice of color can communicate such things as mood and importance. For example, if we highlight a word in yellow, we imply that it is worth noting.

- **Shape:** Shape communicates such things as how something should be used. If you see a spoon—a handle and a bowl shape—you understand that the bowl shape can hold something in it and that you can grasp the handle.

- **Size:** Size can convey importance or magnitude. If you have two items next to one another on a chart, it is likely that the larger item is bigger or more important than the smaller one.

PRETTY PICTURES DON'T LIE, DO THEY?

Discover Magazine published an article in 2012 called, "True or False: Illustrations Make Information More Believable," by Sophie Bushwick. In it, Bushwick discusses a study which finds that "people are more likely to believe a statement is true when it is accompanied by a picture—any old picture—or verbal description." The researchers attributed this to our brain's ability to create "pseudoevidence."

Pseudoevidence is factual information we make up to support information with visuals if we have no evidence to the contrary. This explains why people are likely to believe information about celebrities in glossy magazines. They have no evidence to support an alternative conclusion.

This should cause you to think about using visuals to support information you discuss. Hopefully, you are publishing something that's true.

PHYSICAL TOOLS THAT MAKE IDEAS VISIBLE

Let's start by looking at some tools you can use to make your ideas come to life.

Write on the following:

> Sticky notes
>
> Whiteboards/electronic whiteboards
>
> Paper walls/ flip charts
>
> Idea paint (makes any surface a dry-erase board)
>
> Hand-drawn maps
>
> Sketchnotes
>
> Variety of paper stock
>
> Notebooks
>
> iPad (see Rule 25, "Mobile Apps Provide Visual Opportunities," for more on this topic)

Write with the following:

> Colored pens, pencils
>
> Ink
>
> Chalk
>
> Markers
>
> Stylus

Present digital ideas with the following:

- **Digital pen:** This is a pen that records what you write and turns it into a digital image. It can also record audio and play that back.

- **Digital camera:** The ubiquity of cameras in phones makes it possible to always have a camera with you.

- **Software:** There are many new software applications (both online and desktop) that can be used to draw and sketch. This category also includes mapping tools and digital diagrams.

TIP

You might want to try a new combination of notebook and digital app created by Evernote and Moleskine, as shown in Figure 9.1. It's called the "Evernote Smart Notebook" by Moleskine. It enables you to write in a paper-based Moleskine notebook that has special paper and stickers. These features enable you to take a picture of your handwritten creation and send it directly to your Evernote account. This seems like a great way to use the benefits of a paper notebook with the value of a digital storage mechanism that can be searched.

FIGURE 9.1

Evernote Smart Notebook.

Finally, let's look at some of the methods marketers use to bring ideas to fruition:

Graphic Facilitation:

- One recent addition to visual note taking is graphic facilitation. Graphic facilitators take visual notes called sketchnotes during speeches, conventions, and other meetings. Most often they are visible to the participants and are worked on a big canvas. Others might create smaller notes depending on the requirements of the meeting.

- Sketchnotes capture the essence of what is being said and make the ideas visual. As we know, this makes the meeting more memorable and helps everyone understand the important ideas. Figure 9.2 shows a sketch from sketchnoter Mike Rohde, who is the author of *The Sketchnote Handbook*.

FIGURE 9.2

Rohdesign.

Storyboards:

- Storyboards have been used by designers and writers for generations. They help storytellers demonstrate how their ideas play out. The storyboard might depict a movie or a commercial for a product. A storyboard can also be used by an interface designer who wants to help solve a problem the user faces.

- The value of using storyboards is that they cause you to think about what will be said and how it will look in order to convey a message.

- As a marketer, you might use storyboards to help you create a marketing video, an ad, a case study, or a game.

Idea Boards:

- Idea boards come in all shapes and sizes. They are like 3D Pinterest boards. You can pin on colors, shapes, inspirational photos, and anything else that helps you be more creative.

- Marketers might use them to help design an application interface or to establish a mood for a design piece by showing colors and fonts. They can also establish the quality and taste of an ad.

NOW TRY THIS!

In her book *Writing for Visual Thinking*, Andrea Marks suggests five exercises you can do to stimulate your ability to move between visuals and text. Try these when you are feeling blocked and unsure about what to do next:

1. **Flip the medium:** Write a description of a piece of artwork as if it were done in a different medium. This gets you to use your visual ability to transform the item and describe it in words.

2. **Go to a familiar place:** Go somewhere familiar and focus on a different sense. For example, note smells instead of visuals.

3. **Make a process book:** Collect different formats and materials for a project you are working on so that you can see what your thinking was at the beginning and how your thoughts have progressed. By scanning the visuals, you can see mood and depth of thought. A process book is a folder or notebook where you collect images, write notes, and compile information. Start one when you begin your project.

4. **Create a DADA grab bag:** Cut 20 images and words out of a newspaper or magazine. Put them in a bag and pull one out and write a 50-word story relating to that item. Dada refers to an art movement (1916-23) that started in Switzerland as a backlash to World War I.

5. **Find the metaphor:** Look at a project you are working on and find a metaphor to describe it. Metaphors help people visualize the concept you are trying to explain.

A great example of a company that is making its ideas tangible and bringing them to market is Quirky.com, shown in Figure 9.3. The owner of the company, 25-year-old Ben Kaufman, says his company is the "Proctor & Gamble of the twenty-first century."

FIGURE 9.3

Quirky.com.

What Quirky does is help people who have good ideas for practical household gadgets present them to a group of interested consumers. Consumers sign up to vote on and improve their favorite ideas. If the product goes to market, they might share in the revenue.

Quirky has a group of in-house designers who help bring the idea to completion. Quirky brings two products a week to market, so they are serious about design and good ideas. What's interesting is that you can watch a product go from a sketch to a full-blown product and perhaps participate in its success. An example of a popular Quirky product is a power strip whose sockets rotate so that big power plugs can fit side by side.

 A VISUAL MARKETING METHOD

Method: How to capture your ideas and develop them.

Tools provided: Template

The idea process shown in Figure 9.4 is one that I use to help me work on ideas and book projects. I hope it will help you get started when you are trying to develop your own ideas.

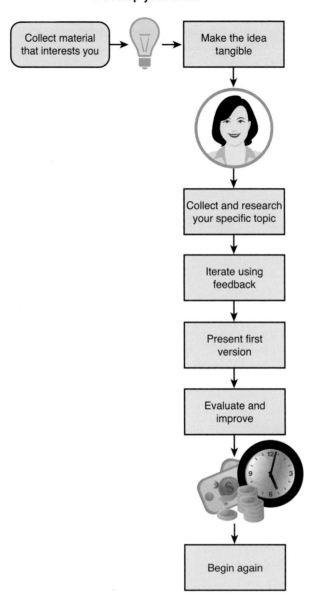

FIGURE 9.4

Develop your ideas.

These are the seven steps for developing your ideas:

1. **Collect material that interests you.**

   If you are a person who needs to come up with new ideas for your job, you are likely one who collects interesting information. Your collection of information can serve as the foundation for new ideas. Read widely and save information in a way that is understandable to you.

2. **Make the idea tangible.**

   When you are ready to use a particular idea for a project and want to expand on it, make it visible to others by using the techniques we talk about in this book. Include diagrams, maps, idea boards, presentations, and so on.

3. **Collect and research your specific topic.**

   Now it's time to research with a purpose. Collect more new information that specifically relates to the project. Now that you're deep into the topic you may find that information you rejected now has a place. Review all the material you've already collected and select the information that adds to the value of your project. Create several iterations of your visuals and add an outline that begins to add order to the chaos.

4. **Develop and iterate from feedback.**

   Show your ideas and get feedback. You want to see what people understand and what confuses them. Also be sure to include any insights that come your way, and update the project.

5. **Present the first version.**

   Show version one to others. This will be your first crack at finalizing the idea.

6. **Evaluate and improve.**

   Again, get more feedback. See what story rings true and who gets the idea.

7. **Begin again to add new things.**

   Use your idea in practice. As you go along, you will learn new things and add to the idea yet again. Don't hesitate to go back to the beginning to see what you were thinking and how your thinking has evolved.

 TOOLS TO CONSIDER

IdeaPaint (http://www.ideapaint.com)

Online boards:

Conceptboard (http://conceptboard.com)

CorkboardMe (http://corkboard.me)

IDEAS TO USE

Physical tools such as pen and paper make a connection with the brain that just doesn't happen with keyboard and screen. Grab a tool such as a pen or marker and express your ideas for others to see.

Making your thinking visible to others helps them to both understand and contribute more quickly.

Graphic facilitation helps meeting attendees grasp the big ideas and remember the content.

Use the Develop your Ideas template to develop your ideas.

IDEA MAP

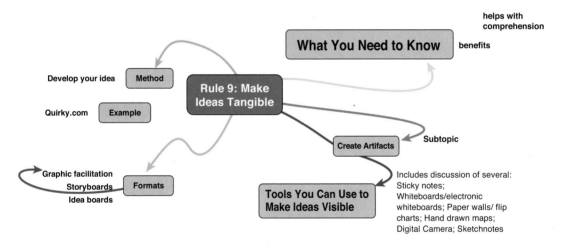

Idea Map for Rule 9

ENDNOTES

Bushwick, Sophie. "True or False: Illustrations Make Information More Believable." *Discover Magazine*, August 13, 2012.

Laurenhue, Kathy. "Sharpening Your Memory with a Pen—Brain Science." 2011. http://mindmusings.com/2011/02/27/sharpening-your-memory-with-a-pen-brain-science/.

Marks, Andrea. *Writing for Visual Thinkers: A Guide for Artists and Designers*. New Riders Press, 2011.

Rohde, Mike. *The Sketchnote Handbook: The Illustrated Guide to Visual Notetaking*. Peachpit Press, 2012.

Silverman, Rachel Emma. "Doodling for Dollars: Firms Try to Get Gadget-Obsessed Workers to Look Up—and Sketch Ideas." *The Wall Street Journal,* April 24, 2012.

Rule 10

USE DIAGRAMS AND OTHER DATA VISUALIZATION TOOLS TO EXPLAIN MARKETING IDEAS

In Rule 10 we look at using diagrams and other graphic organizers to help you explain and display ideas for marketing. We show you some common examples so that you can pick the one that will work best for your specific problem.

WHAT YOU NEED TO KNOW

It's often true that marketers who consider themselves creative people shy away from using diagrams and other visual display tools. After all, they involve math—numbers that mean things! People can also be reluctant to use diagrams because they have seen so many bad examples over the years and are confused about the value of diagrams.

When confronted with a confusing diagram, most people are first inclined to assume that they are not up to the task of understanding it. They puzzle over the diagram and spend time trying to make sense of it. At some point they simply give up. Obviously, this serves no one.

The person who created the diagram was hoping to simplify it. The viewer was hoping that they would be saved from expending the time and effort that goes

into understanding the data. Almost everyone heaves a sigh of relief when they are given a simple diagram that helps them understand the 15-page report attached to it.

In his book *Visual Tools for Constructing Knowledge*, author David Hyerle says that visual tools help us do four things. They help us move back and forth between these thinking modes:

- Text/audio and visual representations: That's reading/hearing vs. seeing
- Linear and nonlinear thinking: That's left vs. right brain thinking
- Disparate facts and interrelationships: That's random vs. connected
- Lists and systems: That's parts vs. the whole

Using visual tools enables us to see how things fit together. We are not locked into one way of approaching a problem. We are easily able to move from one mode of thinking to another.

Throughout this book we look at how visuals help us understand information. In the previous 9 rules as shown in Figure 10.1, we demonstrated the use of visuals to complete marketing tasks.

We have used the following:

- Template mind map to analyze websites (Rule 1)
- Pie chart to understand personas (Rule 2)
- Storyboard to capture customer stories (Rule 3)
- Bull's-eye target to assess your business reality (Rule 4)
- Puzzle cross diagram to follow your buyer's journey (Rule 5)
- Table to look at different forms of collaboration (Rule 6)
- Spreadsheet to conduct an inventory (Rule 7)
- Hub and spoke to develop blog posts (Rule 8)
- Office supplies like stickies as visual aids (Rule 9)

To further discuss the use of data visualization tools, I have chosen several that can help you share your ideas and spread your message. You've seen them before, but after you get over the notion that diagrams are hard to create and understand, you will find that they can be useful to both you and your viewer. The key is to view diagrams first and foremost as pictures.

Almost everyone heaves a sigh of relief when they are given a simple diagram that helps them understand the 15-page report attached to it.

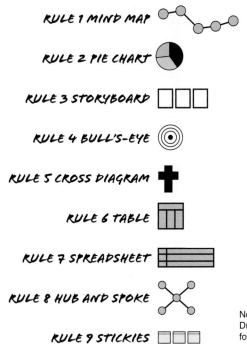

RULE 1 MIND MAP

RULE 2 PIE CHART

RULE 3 STORYBOARD

RULE 4 BULL'S-EYE

RULE 5 CROSS DIAGRAM

RULE 6 TABLE

RULE 7 SPREADSHEET

RULE 8 HUB AND SPOKE

RULE 9 STICKIES

Note:
Drawing depicting all the
formats used in Rules 1-9
on one image

FIGURE 10.1

Visuals used in previous rules.

BENEFITS OF DIAGRAMS

Like all other forms of pictures, diagrams have great benefits. But just because something is put into a diagram, that doesn't mean it's intelligible. You have to strive to make diagrams easy to understand at a glance.

Good diagrams help you do the following:

- Identify patterns
- Organize information effectively
- Communicate your ideas to others

- Make comparisons and classify information
- Make teams more effective
- Save time and money
- Help new employees get acclimated

TYPES OF DIAGRAMS TO CONSIDER

The diagrams we look at here are commonly used for marketing projects. It is by no means a complete list, but it should give you enough ideas to get started adding them to your projects, blog posts, and websites.

TIP The following diagrams deal with problems that have predetermined content. Several of the visual tools we have looked at up to this point are most often used for open-ended responses. For example, a mind map is used for brainstorming—we do not have data previously created that we want to visualize. But, if we want to create a pie chart, we do have the data to plug into it. So remember that's what distinguishes these diagrams from brainstorming tools.

We look at the following five diagram types:

- Flow
- Hierarchy
- Line
- Venn
- Timeline

FLOW DIAGRAMS

You should consider creating a flowchart if you want to show how a process works. Flowcharts can show the steps someone would take to complete an action, or the steps of a computer program.

If you want a customer to learn how to complete a task or take an action, as part of a product sheet you might use a flowchart.

Flowcharts have a few standard symbols you should use:

- An elongated circle designates start or stop.
- Rectangles designate action.
- Diamonds signify decisions.
- Arrows signify direction.

Figure 10.2 shows how these symbols might be depicted in a chart to document a business process such as writing a blog post. It could also be used in a blog post about blogging. Including a chart in a blog post breaks up the tedium of the text and helps explain the concept.

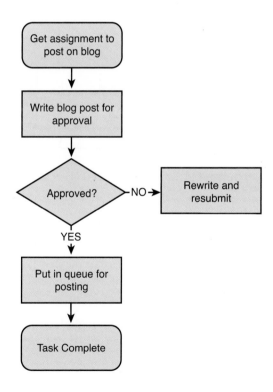

Write and Post to a Blog

FIGURE 10.2

Write and post to a blog.

HIERARCHY DIAGRAMS

Hierarchy diagrams show relationships among the items by classifying them. Most businesspeople are familiar with diagrams that show hierarchy because they have seen organizational charts. These charts might show how a department is staffed by showing the department head at the top and that person's direct reports below. This type of chart might be used in a white paper or case study.

A typical organization chart could look like the one shown in Figure 10.3.

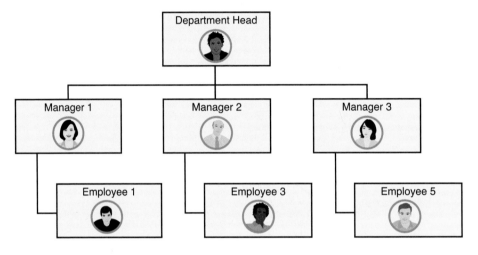

FIGURE 10.3

Organizational chart.

LINE DIAGRAMS

Line charts are generally used to depict changes that happen over a period of time. You can have several lines on the same chart to track changes of different entities. This diagram could be used in a presentation to investors to show the adoption of the product.

A line chart analyzing three marketing campaigns might look like the one shown in Figure 10.4.

VENN DIAGRAMS

Venn diagrams use circles to depict discrete sets of information. The intersection of these data sets is the area that the diagram was created to explain. A Venn diagram explaining the data sets that make up the Visual Marketing Revolution is shown in Figure 10.5.

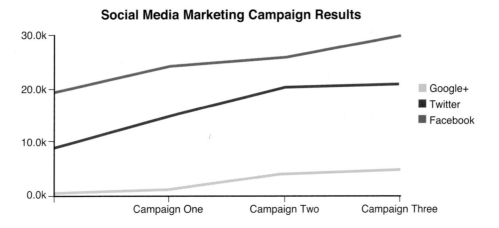

	Begin	Campaign One	Campaign Two	Campaign Three
Google+	0.5k	1.2k	3.8k	5.0k
Twitter	9.0k	15.0k	20.0k	21.0k
Facebook	19.4k	24.4k	26.0k	30.0k

FIGURE 10.4

Fans on social media after marketing campaigns.

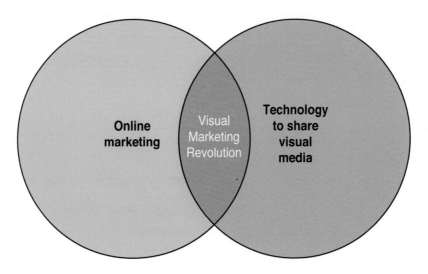

FIGURE 10.5

Visual marketing.

TIMELINE DIAGRAMS

Timelines are used to show the relationship of time to the data depicted. Figure 10.6 shows a timeline for executing a social media marketing campaign.

Timeline for Social Media Marketing Campaign

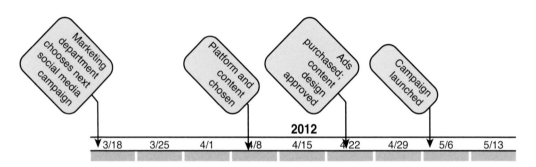

FIGURE 10.6

Timeline for social media marketing campaign.

 TOOLS TO CONSIDER

General diagram programs:

Cacoo.com: https://cacoo.com/

Creately: http://creately.com/

Diagram.ly: http://www.diagram.ly

Diagrammer: http://diagrammer.com

Diagrammr: http://www.diagrammr.com; write sentences that become diagrams

Gliffy: http://www.gliffy.com

MS Office PowerPoint Smart Art: http://office.microsoft.com/en-us/powerpoint/

SimpleDiagrams: http://www.simplediagrams.com/

SmartDraw: http://smartdraw.com

Note: Charts used in this chapter were created with SmartDraw.

Charts:

ChartGizmo: http://chartgizmo.com/

Lucidchart: https://www.lucidchart.com/

Lovely Charts: http://www.lovelycharts.com

Online Chart Tool: http://www.onlinecharttool.com/

Timelines:

Dipity: http://www.dipity.com/

 IDEAS TO USE

Use diagrams to help you recognize patterns that tell the story of the data.

Make sure when you choose a diagram type that you are using it to truly simplify the information. If it's confusing, you will have wasted your time.

There are lots of great online tools to create diagrams, but you might want to start with a paper and pencil to see what fits the data best.

 IDEA MAP

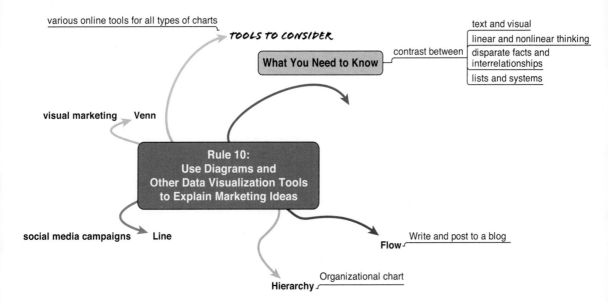

Idea Map for Rule 10

ENDNOTES

Hyerle, David. *Visual Tools for Constructing Knowledge.* Association for Supervision & Curriculum, 1996.

Hyerle, David. *Visual Tools for Transforming Information Into Knowledge.* Corwin Press, 2008.

USE VISUAL GUIDES THAT BUILD ON KNOWLEDGE

In Rule 11 we look at how tools like templates and checklists assist creativity rather than hinder it. We show some examples that can help you and your staff be more innovative and productive.

WHAT YOU NEED TO KNOW

When you think about using a tool such as a template or checklist, do you feel like you're giving up on your own creativity? Does it seem too rigid and exacting? Some people use them only as a last resort. They don't want to put boundaries around their ideas.

The use of popular brainstorming techniques has convinced us that boundaries should be avoided. But there is much evidence to refute this. It has been shown that people who are given no constraints produce less innovative results than those who work to find their way around them.

For example, in Patricia Stokes's book, *Creativity from Constraints: The Psychology of Breakthrough*, she gives example after example of how setting limits and boundaries improved the work of artists, musicians, and other creative individuals.

For the purposes of this rule, we can divide these tools into two distinct types: those that require you to fill in the blanks (templates) and those that require you to check off items (checklists).

If you are willing to use these tools, you will find that you get several benefits, including these:

- **Using the thinking of others:** Templates and checklists reflect the analysis of tasks by others who have previously analyzed the task. Instead of starting with a blank sheet of paper, you start working immediately.

- **Saving time and money:** Using the thinking of others helps you get off to a fast start and a quicker conclusion, saving you time and money. Your results will be better.

- **Offering inspiration:** Rather than squashing your imagination, templates can inspire you to think in a new direction.

- **Adding professional knowledge:** In the case of something like a design template, you benefit from the knowledge of professionals who have studied the problem and can provide you with quality solutions.

> The use of popular brainstorming techniques has convinced people that boundaries should be avoided. But there is much evidence to refute this. People who are given no constraints produce less innovative results than those who work to find their way around them.

TYPES OF TEMPLATES

Templates are all around you if you take the time to notice them. Have you ever created a haiku poem? It has specific rules that must be followed—that's a template. Here are the instructions to create a haiku:

- Line 1 should be written with only 5 syllables.

- Line 2 should be written with only 7 syllables.

- Line 3 should be written with only 5 syllables.

When you think about a poem, does it conjure up a set of rules? Not usually. You think of poets as people who pull ideas out of the air and spin them into lyrical visions.

How about a movie? (We talk about story structure in Rule 3, "Social Media Is Storytelling, So Tell Stories.") Writers adhere to many constraints and can point to specific structures for different genres. Clearly you don't think of writers as uncreative souls, do you?

Templates are in use everywhere. If you feel a resistance to them, it probably stems from a bad experience in school. If you change your mind-set, templates can help you elevate the quality of your marketing and business campaigns.

TIP

Perhaps the resistance you feel about templates can be softened if you use a different name for them. If you look in the Visual Thesaurus (http://www.visualthesaurus.com/), you can find several alternative words for *template*, including these:

> Guidebook
>
> Lead
>
> Steer
>
> Direct
>
> Scout
>
> Pathfinder

When you think about a template as a guide or a pathfinder, it sounds friendlier. So use one of those words instead.

There's a good example of the value of templates in the book *Made to Stick*, by Chip and Dan Heath, who cite studies done by an Israeli research team in 1999 (see "Endnotes").

The researchers used a sample of 200 award-winning advertisements to determine whether they can find commonalities among them. Simply, they wanted to know what made the good ones good.

They found six ideas that they put into "creativity templates." When one group of subjects used the templates to create advertisements, they were able to produce much better results than the two other groups who didn't. Because all the subjects were novices, the use of the templates was the only thing that differentiated the groups.

Why do you suppose the subjects using the templates did so well? One possibility is that templates help us harness the chaos that comes with creativity. We are not being prevented from developing ideas; we are simply organizing them.

I'm sure you're interested to know the structure of the six creativity templates. Complicated names are used for each template, but the ideas behind them are straightforward. Don't be scared off.

They are as listed here:

- **The pictorial analogy template:** A visual/text shows the benefit of the product.

- **Extreme situation template:** A visual/text shows the product overcoming a serious situation.

- **Consequences template:** A visual/text shows the amazing benefit you get if you will only use the product.

- **Competition template:** A visual/text shows the product beating the competition.

- **Interactive experiment template:** A visual/text shows an experiment of the product producing the solution.

- **Dimensionality alteration template:** A visual/text shows what could happen to you in the future if you don't use the product.

You can see that these templates are commonly used. Consider them when you are thinking about your next marketing campaign. You'll see that it's easier to pick from a list than to dream up something with no parameters.

For example, in the Audi commercial for Super Bowl 2012, as shown in Figure 11.1, we see that Audi's headlights are so bright they simulate daylight, which kills all the vampires at the party. This is an example of the extreme situation template. It shows you that if you run into a dangerous situation, your headlights will be bright enough to help you avoid disaster. You get the message, but it's laced with humor.

FIGURE 11.1

Audi 2012 Super Bowl Commercial.

STRUCTURES FOR BUSINESS WRITING

Another way to look at using structure for business applications is the example of writing structures. In his book *Persuasive Writing*, Nick Souter, well know innovator and former National Creative Director of the Leo Burnett offices (major worldwide ad agency) in Australia, outlines different structures you can use for business writing. I've included several in Table 11.1, and I've added a visual column. When you look at each of the examples, think about how they are made stronger by the addition of visuals.

Table 11.1 Writing Structures

Type of Structure	Goal of Writing	Visual
Problem/solution	Recommend	Before and after
Cause/effect	Explain	Analysis of an image
Chronology	To defend/recruit	Timeline
Narrative	Review	Story panels
Process	To instruct	Flow chart
Comparison	To analyze	Side-by-side images
Journalism	To inform	Image of people or place
Q & A	To clarify	Dissection of image

You can see that the addition of images strengthens any argument you make. Imagine trying to describe a problem and its solution without showing before-and-after photos! That's why it's important to add visuals to your marketing whenever possible.

DESIGN TEMPLATES

As the focus of the Web continues to be visual, we've seen the increase in templates that businesses can use to build their online presence. At the beginning of the twenty-first century, companies struggled to develop website designs. The launch of a website could take up to a year to complete. Designs were created from scratch and budgets were large.

In recent years, that problem has been alleviated by the development of templates that can be used by people who have little design training. The most popular of the platforms uses a content management system called WordPress. Companies have sprung up that offer hundreds of themes that can be used with this platform.

Figure 11.2 shows an example of a site with free themes.

FIGURE 11.2

New WordPress Themes website.

WordPress has grown quickly since its launch in 2003. According to W3Techs (World Wide Web Technology Surveys), WordPress has 55% of the market share of content management systems. Prior to its inception, bloggers had to rely on hard to use systems to create posts for their blogs. When I started my blog in 2006, there were very few good options.

One of the most important things that WordPress did was offer a way for businesses to set up a blog or even a small website without needing costly development. You installed it and then uploaded the content into the system.

WordPress managed the way content was handled. As its use burgeoned, designers began offering pre-made templates for blogs or websites that looked like they had been custom designed. Now some enterprises have begun to use WordPress to manage their content online.

CHECKLISTS AS GUIDES

When you think of lists you might think about your grocery list or your list of "to-dos." Lists come in all sizes and shapes. We discuss checklists in this chapter because they create a visual way of presenting information. Information in a checklist has a flow to it. You can start at the top and work your way down. Checklists visually direct your actions.

In this chapter, we look at lists and how they can benefit you. The difference between a list that is a catchall for items to do and a list that dictates a procedure is vast. But both can be visual aids.

Do you think checklists are boring? In 2010, the World Health Organization (WHO) published an article with the following headline, "New Scientific Evidence Supports WHO Findings: A Surgical Safety Checklist Could Save Hundreds of Thousands of Lives." The article discusses studies conducted in medical settings around the world. They demonstrated that the use of a checklist could save a significant number of lives each year. This prompted the WHO to create several standard checklists that aid health workers in performing critical procedures.

In 2011, Atul Gawande, well-respected surgeon and journalist, authored a book called *The Checklist Manifesto* in which he talks about numerous cases in which checklists saved lives. Emergency situations that occur when planes are in the air or someone is wheeled into an emergency room can be made easier with a set of written procedures.

Does this get your attention? Do you need further evidence that checklists and worksheets could be useful to you in your work? It's likely that your daily activity doesn't involve life-and-death decisions, but your daily tasks do matter to you.

The use of checklists can help you and your staff in completing your everyday tasks. Why are checklists so valuable?

They do several things:

- **Organize an emergency procedure when chaos is the norm:** When under stressful situations, people have trouble remembering to complete steps in a procedure.

- **Ensure that no steps are left undone:** Checklists help you go from the first step to the last without missing anything.

- **Help teams coordinate their activities:** When a team works on a checklist together, everyone knows what they are supposed to do and when they should do it.

- **Prevent you from having to rely on your memory:** Everyone's memory is notoriously faulty, especially in an emergency. Checklists remove the need to use your memory.

- **Save time and money:** When a checklist is followed, procedures move more quickly. Fewer errors will be made.

- **Provide consistency in tasks:** Every team that uses a checklist will perform the tasks in the same way.

- **Communicate to your team that the process has been given attention:** When teams use checklists, they know that the procedure has been analyzed and that these are the steps that should be followed to get the desired result.

MAKE CHECKLISTS VALUABLE

In the article "What Makes a Good Checklist," Professor Anne Collins McLaughlin, Ph.D., outlines some important guidelines that can help you create a checklist that is valuable. Obviously, if you are creating a simple list, you would just put tasks down and perhaps cross them off as you do them.

If you are creating a checklist for your team, you'll want to think about what McLaughlin says makes checklists work: knowing the user and knowing the task. Knowing the user involves the following:

- **Making each step explicit:** Detail everything that is not self-explanatory; Make sure that you look at each entry on the list and provide as much detail or steps as needed. For example, here is an example of each type:

  Self-explanatory: Put the scalpel on the table in front of the doctor.

  Needs more detail: Clean the instruments before surgery.

- **Requesting specific outcomes:** If certain steps require things to be written down or noted in some way, make that clear.

- **Identifying conflicts in physical demands:** Remember that if some tasks require you to put down the list and take action, facilitate that action.

- **Considering all possible task scenarios:** Make sure that the list is complete so that nothing unexpected will arrive to dismantle the list.

- **Being realistic about the task:** Be clear about what's required so that you don't make impossible demands on the user.

Knowing the task involves these things:

- **Including pauses:** Give the user some time to complete each task listed before returning to the next item on the list.

- **Using basic usability guidelines:** Take into account readability and scanability. For example, make the type large enough for readers to see without having to use glasses and so forth.

- **Including task possession:** Make it clear who owns each task on the list.

 TOOLS TO CONSIDER

Templates:

Microsoft Office: http://office.microsoft.com/en-us/templates/?CTT=97. Templates for office documents, spreadsheets, and presentations.

WordPress: http://wordpress.org. Free themes for WordPress blogs.

Checklist: http://checklist.com. Checklists templates to use for various topics.

Launchlist: http://launchlist.net. Checklists to use when launching a business.

IDEAS TO USE

When you start a project, never start with a blank sheet of paper. See whether you can find a template or another tool that builds on the thinking that others have done before you. It will enhance your output.

If you feel uncomfortable with the name template, use something that sounds like what it is, a guide or way finder.

Consider looking at the six idea templates that researchers have uncovered to create your next marketing campaign.

IDEA MAP

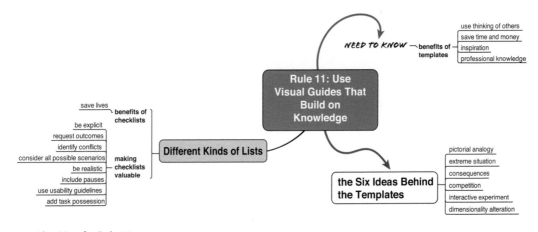

Idea Map for Rule 11

ENDNOTES

Stokes, Patricia. *Creativity from Constraints: The Psychology of Breakthrough*, Springer Publishing Company, 2005

Gawande, Atul. *The Checklist Manifesto: How to Get Things Right*. Picador, 2011.

Heath, Dan and Chip. Template study cited in *Made to Stick* by Random House, 2007: "The Fundamental Templates of Quality Ads" by Jacob Goldenberg, David Mazursky, Sorin Solomon, *Marketing Science* 18 (1999). Link: http://www.cs.uml.edu/radical-design/uploads/Main/Templates.pdf.

McLaughlin, Anne Collins, Ph.D., Assistant Professor, Dept. of Psychology, North Carolina University. "What Makes a Good Checklist." Published by the Agency for Healthcare Research and Quality 2010. http://webmm.ahrq.gov/perspective.aspx?perspectiveID=92#figureback.

Souter, Nick. *Persuasive Writing: How to Make Words Work for You.* Sterling, 2007.

USE VISUAL PRESENTATIONS TO CONNECT WITH AN AUDIENCE

In Rule 12 we look at the things you need to do to step up your presentation game using visuals. We look at a process you can use to develop content for a prezi on Prezi.com.

WHAT YOU NEED TO KNOW

The march toward the visual revolution has changed our expectations about business presentations. Previously, we would sit through a boring slide presentation and assume that this was the best way to communicate information to a group. There were overhead slides and screens with bullets, bullets, and more bullets.

As technology brought us graphical interfaces and smartphones with cameras, people began to use these tools to document and share their lives. They managed to share information that wouldn't put their audiences directly to sleep. So a better way to communicate business messages had arrived!

Enter visual platforms tools such as Pinterest and Instagram. With these, everything changed. In addition, people expected that presentations of all

kinds could be less formal and more visually appealing. Unfortunately, that's easier said than done. We have all been subjected to "death by PowerPoint," but fewer people are watching without complaint. So why do people continue to use it?

Many people who use PowerPoint have spent time learning the tool. Their motivation to try something new is low given all the things they are responsible for in their jobs. If you want to rise above the noise of a slide presentation, you need to take the initiative to try something new.

SMARTER AND BETTER

When trying to initiate something new, you need to keep one major idea in mind as you implement this rule. Kathy Sierra, a well-known writer and learning expert, says that for anything you do, you should try to make "the reader genuinely smarter and better." (See link to blog post in the Conversation Agent Blog by Valeria Maltoni. Conversation Agent has been ranked among the top 30 marketing blogs in the world by AdAge Power150.)

> Previously, we would sit through boring slides and assume that this was the best way to communicate information to a group. There were overhead slides and screens with bullets, bullets, and more bullets.

What she means by this is that you should focus your entire work product on helping your reader accomplish what *he* wants. It's not about your presentation. Of course you want to be acknowledged for your effort, but the real value to the customer is how your presentation helps your audience accomplish, learn, and act better. Sierra's books have remained bestsellers on Amazon because they accomplish this goal.

Many books have been written about how to improve your presentation skills. In this rule, we focus solely on how to create a presentation that uses visual tools and techniques to make a lasting impact.

The benefits to viewers of using visuals in a presentation include these:

- The information is easier to understand quickly.
- Visuals help us retain information.
- Visuals assist in meaningful storytelling.
- Visuals reach our emotions to make the presented information more memorable.
- Visuals help people to connect us with our branding style.

Clearly, visuals need to be an integral part of every presentation you make. Also, remember that if you are presenting on a stage, you are also a visual. People will look at what you are wearing, how you are speaking, and whether you seem nervous or calm. They will draw conclusions based on their own subjective viewpoint.

UNDERSTANDING THE LIZARD BRAIN

In Rule 3, "Social Media Is Storytelling, So Tell Stories," we talked about how the brain is divided into three parts: the cortex, the mid-brain, and the lizard brain (also known as the reptilian brain). The lizard brain is the one that reacts without thought. It has been referred to as the center of the "fight or flight" mechanism. This is the part of the brain that told our ancestors whether to fight an attacker or run away. Today, it is less necessary to fight off threats, but is still operational.

Christophe Morin and Patrick Renvoise at SalesBrain (http://salesbrain.com), a "neuromarketing" agency, also discuss the impact of the lizard brain on presentations. They say there are six stimuli that affect what the brain hears and how it reacts. These six are worth noting when you are considering content for your presentation. The lizard brain has the following characteristics:

- **Self-centered:** It cares only about information that it can use for itself.

  Take action: Make sure your audience knows how they can apply the information to their circumstances. If the info has no connection, they will ignore it. This is commonly known as "what's in it for me?"

- **Contrast:** It notices change. You need to provide something novel. If you don't provide a way for the brain to see differences, it won't act.

  Take action: It's helpful to spell out the differences between issues so that there are clear distinctions.

- **Tangible:** It likes the things it can identify and understand. This is why the simple message works the best.

  Take action: Don't try to present a complex message and hope for the best. You need to break the message into smaller chunks. Try to present the obvious and you'll find it's well received. Most often the obvious is not always apparent.

- **Beginning to end:** It is more likely to remember what it hears first and last.

  Take action: This means you need a great opening and closing. If you have shocking or exciting news, save it for the end.

- **Visual:** It understands and processes visuals, not words. Obviously, it's the quickest way to break through the clutter.

  Take action: Focus time on collecting or creating images that are meaningful. Stock photos are not helpful. You are better off with stick figures that convey the message effectively.

- **Emotional:** It detects basic emotions. Advertisers know that touching emotions is the quickest way to make an impact.

  Take action: Emotions help customers make connections they can remember. Try to inject music, photos, or stories that stir feelings.

LOOK AT EXAMPLES

So how do you go about improving the presentations you are giving now? The first thing you can do is look at popular presentations from all different disciplines. A key to being creative is to adapt ideas used in other disciplines. You'll also want to look at examples of the best commercial ads and podcasts that show you how to present information in an entertaining way. Listen to how the podcaster uses his voice to communicate.

Organizations such as TED (Technology, Entertainment, Design), whose motto is "Ideas worth spreading," have taken an active role in changing the nature of presentations. TED invites leaders from all disciplines to speak about their passion and expertise. They limit their presentations to 20 minutes each and the experience is a rich one.

It's helpful that on the site you can search for talks rated jaw-dropping, persuasive, courageous, ingenious, funny, and so on (see Figure 12.1). This demonstrates the range of speakers and can be instructive.

FIGURE 12.1

TED talks.

TIP One great online resource you should consider using for both displaying and finding great presentations is Slideshare (http://slideshare.com). Using Slideshare you can upload a presentation you have created and it will be displayed as a slide show. You can also search its database to find excellent presentations on a variety of business topics. There are free and fee versions.

"GIVE IT A REST"

Looking for a way to assimilate all the information you gather while working on your presentation? There might be a simple way to fix it in your mind that doesn't involve taking any action. Rick Nauert, Senior Editor on Psych Central, reported on a study by Michaela Dewar, Ph.D. The study says that the best way to retain information is to stop and take a brief rest with your eyes closed. Dr. Dewar says, "Indeed, our work demonstrates that activities that we are engaged in for the first few minutes after learning new information really affect how well we remember this information after a week." This is important. Many of us try to drill exercises with the information by repeating it several times. Perhaps the best way to remember it is much easier. When you are watching and studying information on presentations, just pause and close your eyes!

TOOLS TO CONSIDER

One of the things that you didn't need to think about in years past is where your presentation was built. Now, you have more options. Will it be shown on your mobile device? Do you want to work in the cloud or on your desktop?

Only you can decide what works for you. If you do a lot of work on your mobile device, consider creating a presentation on the iPad or presenting on your smartphone. If you like to work on your desktop, there are choices available. Prevalent tools now allow you to work in the cloud and present with your mobile.

Let's look at some good tools (beyond PowerPoint) you can use in each category:

- **Prezi:** http://prezi.com. Desktop, mobile, cloud, free.

- **SlideRocket:** http://www.sliderocket.com/. Cloud, mobile, free. Tracking analytics are built in. This tool uses templates, as shown in Figure 12.2.

- **Brainshark:** http://brainshark.com. Cloud, mobile, free. Tracking analytics are built in.

- **Haiku Deck app:** http://www.haikudeck.com. iPad only, free. (This cannot display video content.) This app has high-quality graphics, as shown in Figure 12.3.

FIGURE 12.2

SlideRocket.

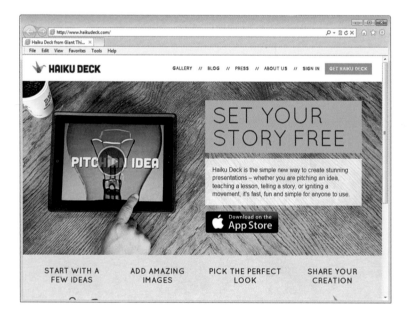

FIGURE 12.3

Haiku Deck.

TIP Depending on the content, you might want to promote your presentation. One of the best ways to do this is to put it on a site like SlideShare (http://www.slideshare.net/) and then provide a link to all your social media channels.

 ## A VISUAL MARKETING METHOD

Method: How to take your next presentation up a notch using Prezi.com, incorporating multimedia content and movement.

If you've decided to create a presentation using Prezi, you're in good company. Major TED speakers from around the world have used it to make stunning presentations.

After you have decided to create a presentation with Prezi, you need to follow the kinds of steps you would take for any project. You want to be clear that you know the topic and understand its purpose.

Don't skip to writing the presentation until you are sure you know why you, instead of another speaker, have been asked to give the presentation. If it's your choice, be clear about your motives.

TIP You can take a PowerPoint presentation you have already created and import it into Prezi. Although this is convenient, you will probably get more mileage out of the presentation if you separate out the content before you use it. In my opinion, importing a presentation directly from PowerPoint might prevent you from using Prezi to its full advantage.

After you are clear about that, you can try this five-step process that specifically relates to creating a prezi:

1. Decide what story to tell.

We've discussed the things you want to keep in mind when you are developing your story. (Read the rules in Part I, "Rules for Social Media Marketers," about storytelling and personas.) Also, you want to present the right stimulus to the lizard brain and to be clear that what you are going to present makes your viewer better in some way.

Take action: With a prezi, you need to decide what words and phrases you will call out to emphasize your story, as shown in Figure 12.4. When you start choose some key words upfront. As you progress, you might want to revise those keywords, but you need to make some choices to begin working.

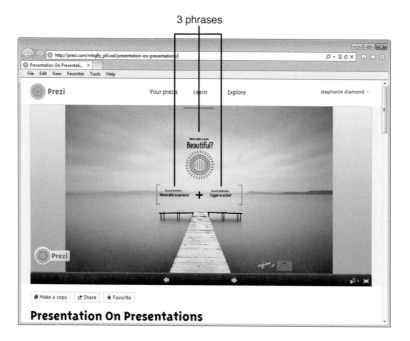

3 phrases

FIGURE 12.4

Prezi.

In Figure 12.4 you see a prezi created by the Prezi team called a "Presentation on Presentations." As you look at the overview, you see three large phrases they have chosen to call out: "Beautiful," "Memorable Experience," and "Trigger an Action." Immediately you know that these are the important components of a presentation.

2. **Parse out the big picture and small details.**

   A prezi lets you show the big picture of everything in the prezi as well as the details that make up the content.

   Take action: It's important to think through the details of the presentation to understand the hierarchy. You want to be clear how the elements relate. Make the more important ones larger, or in some way distinguish them from the smaller items, as shown in Figure 12.5. Here you see the camera as the large big-picture item with the details around it.

3. **Find or create the content elements you'll use.**

   With Prezi, you can include any kind of content that makes sense for your presentation, including video.

   Take action: You can use images, video, sound, PDFs, Excel files, Flash, and PowerPoint. You might consider creating new content because your choices are wide open.

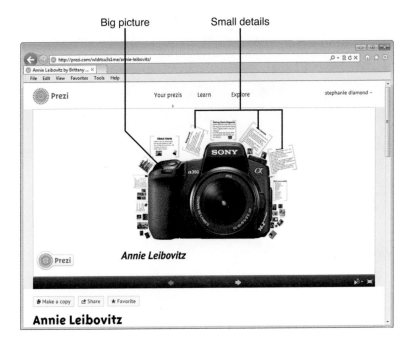

FIGURE 12.5

Prezi about Annie Leibovitz (Prezi credit: Brittany Forsyth).

4. Use movement as a story element.

Prezis are unique in that they appear multilayered instead of flat like most presentations. What this means is that you can move around the canvas and zoom in and out. Used effectively, this movement becomes a vital part of the story.

Take action: To emphasize something, you can zoom right in and move around the content. As part of the application, you also use a feature called a path that is numbered. The numbers tell the application how to navigate the canvas in a step fashion, as shown in Figure 12.6.

5. Present, listen to feedback, and improve.

It is key that you don't stop learning how to improve your presentation. It is an organic entity that can always be improved.

Take action: After you have presented, listen to the feedback you receive and modify the presentation. Even if you have no plans to give the presentation again, the feedback and modifications will teach you how to communicate better with your audience. You will be able to apply that learning to future presentations. It will also give you more ways to learn prezi if you plan to use it again.

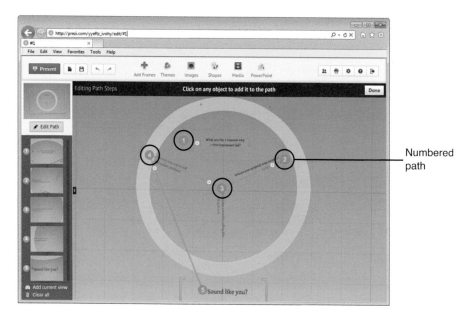

Numbered path

FIGURE 12.6
Editing a path on Prezi.

 # IDEAS TO USE

No matter what your presentation is about, make sure that your focus is on making your viewers better, smarter, more productive, and so on. It's all about what they get out of it, not what you put into it.

Consider using a presentation tool other than PowerPoint to get your viewer's attention. It might take an extra bit of effort, but most of the newer tools are easier than you might think.

Spend considerable time focusing on the visual elements of your presentation. They will give you the biggest ROI.

 IDEA MAP

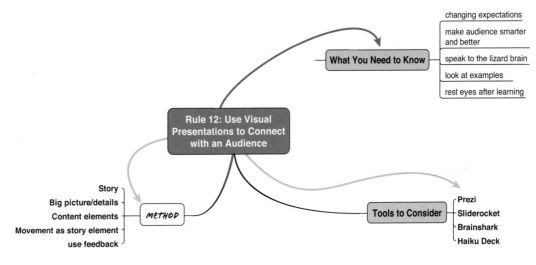

Idea Map for Rule 12

ENDNOTES

"Creating Passionate Users with Kathy Sierra." Blog Interview by Valeria Maltoni of Conversation Agent. http://www.conversationagent.com/2011/03/creating-passionate-users-with-kathy-sierra.html.

Nauert, Rick. "Resting After Learning Aids Memory." Psych Central. http://psychcentral.com/news/2012/07/24/resting-after-learning-aids-memory/42146.html.

Christophe Morin and Patrick Renvoise. "Six Stimuli of the Reptilian Brain." Sales Brain. http://www.salesbrain.com/why-do-you-need-a-neuromap/neuromap-overview/the-6-stimuli/

For more ideas about using Prezi, see Diamond, Stephanie, "Prezi for Dummies" Wiley, 2010.

Part III

CONTENT TO GET CUSTOMER ATTENTION

EMAIL IS STILL A POWERFUL VISUAL MARKETING TOOL

In Rule 13 we look at the visual aspects of email marketing. It's important to choose a tool that makes your email as visually appealing as possible, and we make some suggestions for you to try.

WHAT YOU NEED TO KNOW

As we have discussed throughout the book, your most effective weapon in communicating with the buying brain is to provide a message that includes both text *and* images. This makes email a powerful vehicle for your marketing messages. In this rule, we concentrate more on the visual aspects of email. You'll find lots of books and articles on email best practices.

The goal in this rule is to do the following two things:

- **Help you find a good visual tool to create emails:** Not all email services are created equal. There are some that are less technical that you can run by yourself and others that require a webmaster's assistance. For this method, we choose a tool that is quick and easy.

- **Help you use the right visuals to persuade your customers:** There are lots of ways you can find images for your emails. To find the right image, you must consider two issues: It needs to be a novel image that

strengthens the message you are communicating, and it must be an image to which you have usage rights. You don't want to violate author copyrights. You have to give the proper credit that the creator of the image requires.

Many social media marketers assume that email is a tactic that is losing steam. Because it is one of the oldest tactics, some marketers overlook it in favor of the next bright shiny object. They love the ease of social media platforms that require only a tweet or an update. If this reflects your thinking, you should take another look. Email is still a potent way to reach your customers.

In his article "How to Think Critically About Email Marketing Statistics," Tom Webster, the Vice President of Strategy for Edison Research (the sole provider of U.S. National Election exit polling data), points out that reports trumpeting the demise of email are often misinterpreted. He found that although reports like the Nielsen NetView data seem to say that users are spending less time on email and more time on social media, the report actually says that people are spending more time on mobile devices versus desktops. When you look at how they spend their time on mobile devices, email is the number one activity.

> "Your most effective weapon in communicating with the brain is to provide a message that includes both text and images. This makes email a powerful vehicle for your marketing messages."

That trend is corroborated by reports like those from the Radicati Group, whose "Email Statistics Report, 2012-2016" says:

- Worldwide, in 2012, more than 3 billion email accounts existed and that number is expected to grow to 4.3 billion by 2016.

- Seventy-five percent of those accounts are consumer accounts; 25% are corporate. The number of corporate accounts is expected to increase because more companies around the world are jumping on the email bandwagon.

According to the Email Stat Center, "Email is the preferred method of commercial communication by 74% of all online adults."

TIP One of the challenges when using email is that often the social media manager doesn't own or control the email initiative. For this reason it is important to ask the manager to test a few social media links. Most email programs have tracking capabilities. This means that it tells you such things as how often the social media link was clicked. If the links are successful, the manager will see their value. It may bring him the added engagement from readers that he is looking for.

The reason emails still command customer attention is that they speak directly to customer interests. As Seth Godin, marketing guru who has written eleven best-selling books, prophetically championed in his book *Permission Marketing* in 1999, consumers want control over the messages they receive. You have to ask their permission if you want them to allow you to take up space in their inbox.

This control means even more to consumers than it did at the time of his writing. Advertising messages come at us from every corner of the Web. Being able to screen out the irrelevant ones makes even more sense today. So what are some of the enduring benefits of using email marketing?

Major benefits include the following:

- **Sharing:** Customers are able to share your content on their social channels so that you might be introduced to a new audience. Why go directly to a social platform first when you can get their attention from their inbox?

- **Targeted discounts:** You can send customers specific discounts and tips as one of their preferred brands, so they are more likely to respond.

- **Personalization:** You can send customers personalized messages that request a relationship with them. Of course, this is a mixed blessing if they get messages that say, "Hello [firstname]!" Make sure you have mastered your email tools.

- **Keeping in touch:** If you send a regular email newsletter, you are staying in touch and reminding customers that you are interested in them. It's critical that your newsletter content is not all about you. Ask customers questions and invite their responses. Be sure to encourage them to let you know their likes and dislikes.

TIP   Remember that if you use a tool that supports metrics (which you must—see the "Tools to Consider" section later in this chapter), you can easily segment, test, and track your email messages to learn what resonates with your customers. Being able to experiment at a relatively low cost makes email a perfect tactic for honing your marketing message.

USING QR CODES

One visual tool we haven't discussed thus far is the use Quick Response codes (QR codes). These are visual bar codes, as shown in Figure 13.1, that can be scanned by a mobile device to take the user to a particular link online. This code is easily created by QRstuff (http://www.qrstuff.com/) and takes you to the Amazon link for this book.

FIGURE 13.1

QR code created with QRstuff.

The overall response to QR codes has been lackluster. It's likely because marketers haven't found a killer app for them. Most of the codes link to information that is neither helpful nor novel.

A study by comScore conducted in June of 2011 found that only 6% of the total mobile phone audience has used QR codes. That was about 14 million users at the time of the study. This response hasn't encouraged many more marketers to jump on the bandwagon. In addition, a QR code user most likely is male, is between the ages of 18 and 34, and has an income over $100,000. If that's your audience, don't hesitate to test a QR code.

There is one QR test that I think has some merit, and that is the use of a QR code to take people to a sign-up page for your email list. The key to getting people to sign up is to make it easy. You also want to catch their eye. The QR code fulfills both of these tasks. It is a visual, which catches people's eye, and it's easy to use because all the person needs to do is to point their smartphone program at it, and it will take them to the link.

The only preparation needed to use these codes is a one-time download to your smartphone of a program that scans the link. QR Reader is an example of such a program for the iPhone: (https://itunes.apple.com/app/qr-reader-for-iphone/id368494609).

Of course, this would be just one tactic of many you would use to promote sign-ups.

If you're interested in trying it, one of the sources you can use to create QR codes is QRstuff (http://www.qrstuff.com/), which is shown in Figure 13.2.

Others sources for creating QR codes include these:

• Microsoft Tag: http://tag.microsoft.com/home.aspx

• Kaywa: http://qrcode.kaywa.com/

FIGURE 13.2
QRstuff program.

FINDING IMAGES

As you might have guessed based on my comments about stock photography in several of the rules, I don't recommend that you put stale stock photos in your email. Your best image choices include pictures of your products, website images, staff pictures from events, customer testimonial photos, and so on.

However, there might be times when you do need to include photos in your email that cannot be sourced in-house. Here are a few sites that have less conventional stock images for you to consider (please be sure to check usage rights):

- Morgue File: http://www.morguefile.com, shown in Figure 13.3

- Photo Pin: http://photopin.com

- Foter: http://foter.com/

- World of photography: http://woophy.com, shown in Figure 13.4 (it has some interesting choices contributed by amateur and professional photographers)

TIP Remember that as we noted in Rule 9, "Make Ideas Tangible," if you include a visual with your text, it makes your message more persuasive than one without it.

FIGURE 13.3

Morgue File.

FIGURE 13.4

World of photography.

THANKS!

The goal of any social media marketer is to get their messages heard. Joel Rothman at Eloqua wanted to see whether he could find words to use in an email subject line that would encourage people to open the email. In his blog article "Emails That Say Thanks Get More Opens, Clicks," he detailed his findings.

He looked at 875 million email sends to determine whether any particular words were successful. He found that when "thanks" or "thank you" was put in the subject line, the open rate was higher. In addition, he found that the click-through rate (how often the links in the email are clicked) was higher too. These emails contained phrases like "thanks for signing up" or "thanks for registering."

People respond when they are thanked for taking action. It's such a simple practice, but one that your mother always encouraged you to do. Remember that the next time you're crafting your email responses.

 ## TOOLS TO CONSIDER

If you don't have a mailing list service, you might want to consider one of these services:

- MailChimp: http://mailchimp.com
- Constant Contact: http://constantcontact.com
- AWeber: http://aweber.com
- Emma: http://myemma.com/

 ## A VISUAL MARKETING METHOD

Method: How to create an email/newsletter using a quick and easy free tool called FlashIssue.

FlashIssue is a visual tool with an easy drag-and-drop interface. It also has several features that can help you get started publishing your own customer email/newsletter, including these:

- It enables you to quickly curate content from other sources so that you don't have to write everything yourself.
- It integrates with all your own blog content and channels such as Pinterest and Tumblr.
- If you already use services like MailChimp or Constant Contact and even Gmail, you can use FlashIssue with them or copy the HTML for any service not listed so that you can use almost any system.

- You can send your newsletter using FlashIssue if you don't already have a mailing list set up somewhere else.

- You can share it on your social media platforms using a link.

As you get started creating your email newsletter, there are some things you'll want to consider. Starting from the top and following the numbers, we'll look at how to fill in the template shown in Figure 13.5.

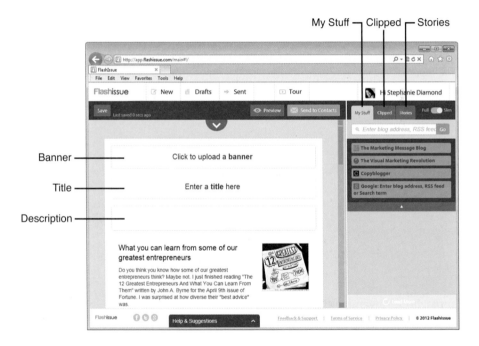

FIGURE 13.5

Template for FlashIssue post.

1. **Banner:** This is where your branding visuals go. Your logo or any heading imagery you use on your website or other channel would be appropriate.

2. **Title:** The title for your newsletter goes here. Choose a title that makes it clear what the newsletter will deliver. If readers are not interested in the title, they certainly aren't going to check it out.

3. **Description:** This is where you whet your customer's appetite for the coming benefits they will receive.

4. **Content:** To populate your newsletter with content, you get three choices for selecting content on the right side of the screen: "My Stuff," "Clipped," and "Stories." Let's look at each:

My stuff: This includes your own channel content, such as your blog and other content channels like your Tumblr and Pinterest accounts.

Clipped: If you want to clip items on the fly, you can put a plugin into your Chrome browser. When you come back to your Internet Explorer Browser, the links will be on the list of items to select.

Stories: This is for specific links you want to clip or any URL that has content you want to grab.

You also have the option of putting in original content on the fly, as shown in Figure 13.6. This can include text, images, graphics (perhaps a graphic of a coupon), or anything that adds value.

FIGURE 13.6

Original content can be added here.

TIP   There is also a Footer text block at the bottom of the template where you can put any messages or links for customers.

Here's an example of a newsletter that was created for this Rule to demonstrate the process. The content includes my blog, my curated site, my book cover graphic, and original content. Let's follow the content by numbers, as shown in Figure 13.7.

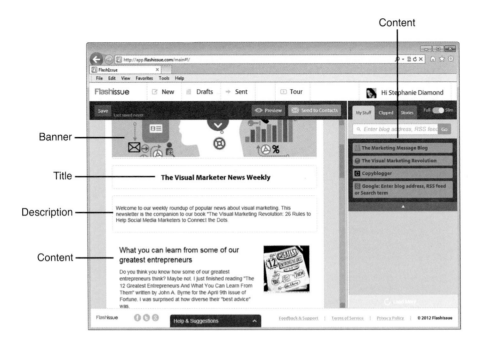

FIGURE 13.7

Example of newsletter created with FlashIssue.

1. **Banner:** This graphic was clipped from a PDF of this book cover. I uploaded it to the banner area.

2. **Title:** I used both the words *weekly* and *news* in the title to convey that I will be taking an active look at the topic each week.

3. **Description:** Here I put a welcome message that explains what the newsletter is all about.

4. **Content:** On the right side you see that I made a selection of content from my Marketing Message Blog; my Visual Marketing Revolution curator site; Copyblogger, an excellent social media blog; and a Google search box. Not visible in this shot is the content behind the Clipped tab that I did with my Chrome browser and the Stories tab that could include any URL I wanted to capture.

When you are ready to send the newsletter, as shown in Figure 13.8, you choose your From line, Subject line, and connection with an email service.

If you want to experiment with developing a newsletter, FlashIssue is a good choice.

Send

FIGURE 13.8

Programs from which you can send your newsletter.

IDEAS TO USE

Using both text and graphics together is your most powerful tool for communicating with your customer. An email newsletter is a great vehicle for doing this.

Make it a practice to consider your own in-house graphics and photos before you go to stock photography. When you do choose stock, go to a site like the ones we mentioned that are not loaded with clichéd images.

If you are going to send out your emails yourself, be sure to pick a tool that is straightforward and easy. Not all email services are created equal.

IDEA MAP

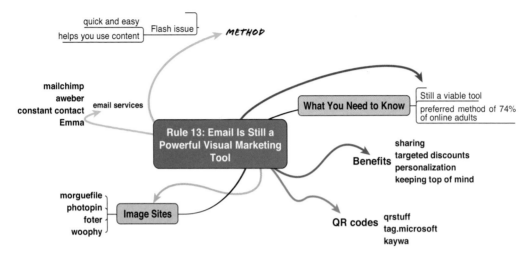

Idea Map for Rule 13

ENDNOTES

comScore. "14 Million Americans Scanned QR Codes on Their Mobile Phones in June 2011." August 2011. http://www.comscore.com/Insights/Press_Releases/2011/8/14_Million_ Americans_Scanned_QR_or_Bar_Codes_on_their_Mobile_Phones_in_June_2011.

"Email Usage." http://www.emailstatcenter.com/Usage.html.

Godin, Seth. *Permission Marketing.* Simon & Schuster, 1999.

NielsenWire. "What Americans Do Online." August 2010. http://blog.nielsen.com/nielsenwire/ online_mobile/what-americans-do-online-social-media-and-games-dominate-activity/.

Radicati Group. "Email Statistics Report, 2012-2016." http://www.radicati.com/wp/ wp-content/uploads/2012/04/Email-Statistics-Report-2012-2016-Executive-Summary.pdf.

Rothman, Joel. "Emails That Say Thanks Get More Opens, Clicks." November 2012. http://blog. eloqua.com/thankful-email-marketing/.

Webster, Tom, via Christopher Penn's blog. "How to Think Critically About Email Marketing Statistics." November 2012. http://www.whatcounts.com/2012/11/ how-to-think-critically-about-email-marketing-statistics/.

Merkle. "View from the Digital Inbox 2011." 2011.

Rule **14**

SPREAD YOUR MESSAGE WITH INFOGRAPHICS

In Rule 14, we look at what infographics are and how they are developed and promoted. We provide a structure to analyze the content you need in order to create an infographic that gets attention.

WHAT YOU NEED TO KNOW

Infographics were red-hot in 2012! Every social media marketer wanted to create or share them to get attention. What are infographics? They are a combination of visuals and text that convey information in a way that tells a larger story. They entertain and make you aware of information you can use. Some are great, some are awful, and some are just plain useless.

As you get started, you'll want to note the infographics that are popular with your audience. When something becomes popular online, you can expect to see a great variation in quality. Designers and researchers alike have complained about the lack of rigor in the design and execution of infographics. You'll need to decide what has value to your audience.

Although you might fear that infographics are a passing fad, you should be aware that infographics of one kind or another have been around for centuries. People used pictures to convey meaning back when cave walls served as a canvas. Over time, they have continued to be used to persuade and inform. This is another way that visuals help us understand the world around us. It is likely

that infographics won't continue to garner the same amount of attention as they do now, but they will have some lingering value. Make your investment accordingly.

What is new about infographics in the twenty-first century is our enhanced ability to create them. Marketers without design skills are using new tech applications to create good-looking graphics. They can then provide users with an embed code for the infographic that allows them to put it on their blog. This helps marketers increase their search visibility.

In this rule, we look at some of those tools and see how infographics are developed. Let's start with some basics.

In Rule 4, "Understand How Your Content Supports Your Business," we looked at the concept of "snackable content," which is content that can be shared quickly in small bites. Infographics, in contrast, contain several pieces of information, statistics, and other visuals that require more than a quick glance. Both are useful, but you need to know when to deploy each kind.

For example, if you are doing a short blog post, you might want to include a graphic of a quote with an interesting font to illustrate the topic. That's snackable content. As an example, Figure 14.1 shows my Pinterest board called Little inspirations.

> Although you might fear that infographics are a passing fad, you should be aware that infographics of one kind or another have been around for centuries. People used pictures to convey meaning back when cave walls served as a canvas.

WHY WE LOVE INFOGRAPHICS

- First, let's look at some of the reasons why infographics appeal to everyone:
- Infographics help us retain information more effectively.
- They entertain us and they tell a story.
- They are easier to understand than several paragraphs of text that convey the same information.
- They are shareable on social media.
- They demonstrate that we are interested in spreading information that is valuable to others.
- They increase awareness of your brand and its expertise.

Like any good visual data, an infographic simplifies the message. A look at the search term "infographics" on Google Trends shows the vast increase in popularity of the term from 2008 to 2012. On the graph, you can see the search volume recorded from 2004 to the present. In November of 2012, as shown in Figure 14.2, the search volume for the term was recorded at

100, which is the peak. "Infographics" as a search term went from being almost nonexistent to being at the top of the chart.

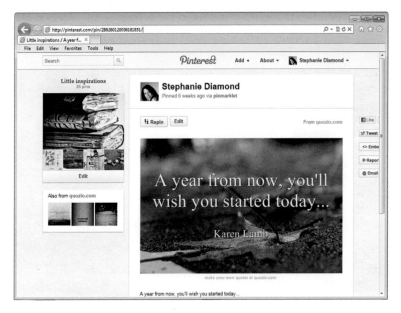

FIGURE 14.1
My "Little inspirations" board on Pinterest.

Next, let's look at the general characteristics that make up the modern infographic by looking at my Infographics board on Pinterest, as shown in Figure 14.3.

FIGURE 14.2
Search volume for infographic on Google Trends.

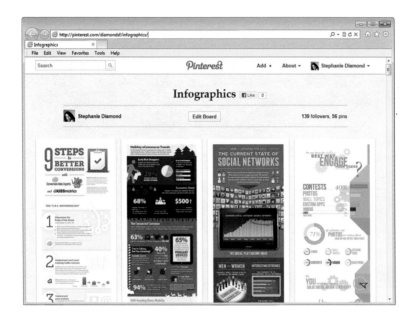

FIGURE 14.3

My Infographics board on Pinterest.

When looking at a variety of infographics, you'll find the following:

- The format most likely consists of a vertical shape with the headline at the top and the graphics cascading down.

- The headline is usually part of a well-designed header that carries through the entire graphic.

- The infographic is often divided into sections, with each providing a discrete piece of information.

- Infographics often have numbers depicted as percentages that convey a chunk of data.

- You might see illustrations that depict information. They are usually colorful and part of an overall pleasing color scheme.

- Charts, diagrams, and graphs might be included.

- Information is often displayed in steps.

- References to the research in the infographic itself should be listed at the bottom of the infographic.

- The company that creates the infographic should have its logo and branding at the bottom of the infographic.

LOOK AT EXAMPLES

A good way to learn about how infographics are put together is to study them from various fields. Like anything else that requires creativity, you want to combine great ideas from other disciplines and create something new. Spend some time looking at these examples to understand why they are appealing.

Here are a few sites that showcase infographics on different topics:

- **Daily Infographic:** http://dailyinfographic.com/. On this site you get a new infographic each day.

- **Infographic Hub:** http://www.infographichub.com. You can submit your own infographics at this site and look at the curated ones selected by the hosts.

- **Infographic Database:** http://infographicdatabase.com/. This site is made up strictly of user-submitted infographics.

- **Cool Infographics:** http://coolinfographics.com. This site contains all things infographics, as shown in Figure 14.4. It is run by Randy Krum, who is a data visualization expert whose firm creates infographics for others.

FIGURE 14.4

Cool Infographics website.

TOOLS TO CONSIDER

Various sites have tools that will help you create your own infographics. The three listed next, Piktochart, Infogr.am, and Visual.ly, have templates that you can use to create your own infographics:

- Piktochart: http://piktochart.com
- Infogr.am: http://infogr.am
- Visual.ly: http://create.visual.ly (shown later in Figure 14.6)

These next two applications, Snagit and PowerPoint, are among several that can be used to create infographics by using the application itself and working freehand. If you're familiar with either tool and you don't plan to use a template, choose the one you know best. Obviously, if you do design work, you will probably want to use Illustrator or Photoshop.

- Snagit: http://www.techsmith.com/snagit.html
- PowerPoint: http://office.microsoft.com/en-us/powerpoint/

TIP See also the "Tools to Consider" section of Rule 10, "Use Diagrams and Other Data Visualization Tools to Explain Marketing Ideas," for additional suggestions about creating diagrams and charts.

I've included a link to an infographic as shown in Figure 14.5 by Nathan Yau, a specialist in data visualization. It's a spoof of an infographic showing you what not to do.

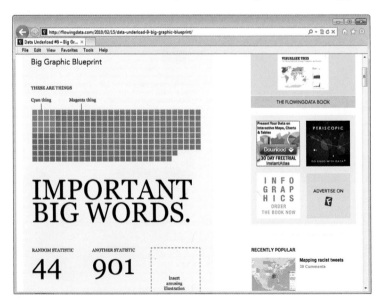

FIGURE 14.5

Spoof of an infographic.

A VISUAL MARKETING METHOD

Method: How to get started with infographics.

When you create an infographic, you essentially have three choices:

- **Hire someone to do the design for you:** Obviously, this is the easiest of the three alternatives (although the most expensive). You pay a third party and hopefully get a finished product that you are proud to share. The cost varies greatly. If you hire a professional whose work you admire, there should be no problem.

- **Use a tool like the ones mentioned previously that give you a design that you can then modify:** The design is premade by a professional and you follow the placement and choice of typography. You still need an eye for design, but if you don't stray far from the design you should be okay.

- **Use a grid and stock graphics and create one from scratch:** This choice carries some risk unless you have an in-house designer. You need an idea about how to use graphics and select content. You know whether you are capable. Do a dry run and see whether you are satisfied, and then make your decision. If you are creating the infographic to increase brand awareness and demonstrate expertise, don't distribute something that is less than professional.

PROCESS YOU CAN TRY

Regardless of the choice you make, you need to do some groundwork first. Whenever you want to communicate a message with visuals, you need to figure out how to make the message clear and simple. Here are some steps you can take:

1. **Set a goal.**

   The first thing you need to do is decide your main purpose for creating an infographic. There are several possibilities:

   - Are you creating your infographic because you want to report interesting data that you have uncovered?

   - Do you want to convey a specific message that will require you to research and find supporting data?

   - Do you want to show your company's expertise and leadership by creating an interesting infographic with your branding?

   Obviously, you might have several of these motives, but one will be the driving factor. After you have determined which it is, you can move on to creating your story.

For this example, let's assume that you found some interesting data in your analytics that you think your audience would value.

You are a company that sells software to social media marketers. You have found that using your software increases conversions by 25%. That means that 25% more people buy their services when your customers use the software tools in your product. Obviously, this is a message you want to communicate so that you sell more software. So how do you proceed to develop a basic infographic?

2. **Determine success measures.**

After you know your purpose, you'll want to determine your success measures. You need to determine this upfront so that you don't miss the valuable feedback. If you are going to the trouble of creating an infographic that could potentially go viral, you need to know whether it actually delivered on your goals. (For more see below in the section on "Share/Promote in step 5.")

3. **Determine the story you want to tell.**

You want to create a story that conveys your message, entertains your customers, and persuades people to buy. What story elements do you want to put together? You can do the following:

- Talk about who the ordinary customers are so that other customers can identify with them.

- Find the data needed. You need to find data about social media users. Your customers value information you can share about who they are as a group. You can find this in current studies and reports about who is using social media. This includes such data as percentage of males to females, age, and income. Lots of interesting factoids are available.

- Focus on data about your specific types of tools. For example, say that the conversion is highest when your customers send offers in your email tool. You would include data about the use of email as a conversion tool in the marketplace. Lots of interesting data can be found on this topic as well.

- Include your data about conversions using your software. You would also include the references for the stats you used and your branding at the bottom of the graphic. After you have collected this, you want to develop an interesting headline that would catch the eye of your customer. This takes some thought because it needs to tell the story for you.

4. **Determine the design of the infographic.**

Let's assume that you are using a service like Piktochart or Visual.ly. You need to go through various examples to see what fits your story. In this case, choose one that incorporates both percentages and illustrations that could be used to explain who the customers are. For example, peruse the examples on Piktochart (found at http://piktochart.com/themes/#all), as shown in Figure 14.6.

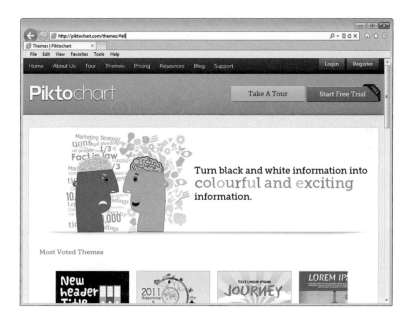

FIGURE 14.6

Piktochart.

TIP If you are designing your own infographic without a service, remember to look at the sites mentioned earlier. Look at examples that showcase different types of infographics. This is an important step that will educate you about what your customers are seeing.

5. **Share and promote.**

   After your infographic is complete, you'll want to share it with your customers and make it easy for others to share. Here are some things you can do:

   - Pin it to your board on Pinterest.

   - Send it in an email to customers.

   - Put it in a blog post that has share-it links (a tool like AddThis, at http://addthis.com, or ShareThis, at http://sharethis.com).

- Upload it to all the sites mentioned previously in the "Look at examples" section and any other sites you find.

- Put it on all the social platforms: Facebook, Twitter, and so on.

- Upload it to social bookmarking sites like Reddit, Digg, and StumbleUpon.

- Ask to write a guest post for influential blogs and include the infographic.

6. **Analyze your feedback.**

Once your infographic is online you will start to get comments from readers and information from your analytics programs. Here are some things to consider:

- If you're not using comprehensive analytics tools like Google Analytics, you'll need to be ready to monitor each platform on which the infographic is shared. This means that if you email it, you'll want to check your email analytics program.

- If you share the infographic on Facebook, you'll want to look at Insights, Twitter's analytic program, what's being said on each social platform, and so on. It's not elegant, but you want the feedback so make the effort. Then figure out how to apply that feedback to your next infographic.

 # IDEAS TO USE

Infographics can require an investment if you use a professional designer. Decide how important they are for your audience and determine the level of investment you're willing to make with that in mind.

If you are a nondesigner, consider using one of the template-based services mentioned previously.

Make sure you do all the work upfront that is mentioned in the Visual Marketing Method section. If you don't have a good story to tell and well-illustrated data, your infographic will fall short of your expectations.

IDEA MAP

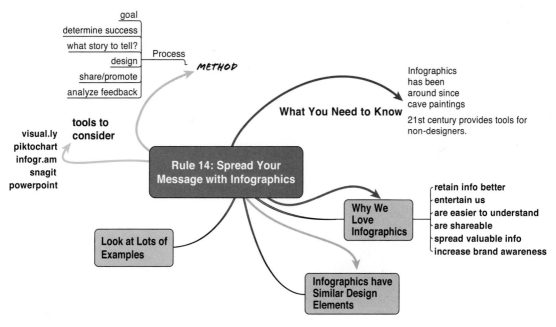

Idea Map for Rule 14

ENDNOTES

Google Trends. http://www.google.com/trends/.

Yau, Nathan. "Data Underload #9 Big Graphic Blueprint." Flowing Data Website. http://flowingdata.com/2010/02/15/data-underload-9-big-graphic-blueprint/.

DEVELOP CASE STUDIES AND REPORTS WITH VISUALS

In Rule 15, we look at why case studies and reports (CSRs) are important social media tools and how they can be made even more effective with visuals. As a social media marketer, you need to add these to your content library.

WHAT YOU NEED TO KNOW

Case studies and reports are tried-and-true methods used by marketers for decades to make the case for their products. So why am I talking about them in a book on social media marketing and the visual revolution? Aren't there more exciting ways to capture a customer's attention?

If you look at the preponderance of eBooks on every topic, you will see why it's necessary to include this category. (For more on eBooks, see Rule 16, "Digital Publishing and eBooks Are Here Now—Use Them.") CSRs are frequently used in blog posts, on websites, and in other social media channels to demonstrate how a solution is used. For this reason, it's important to include them. However, they have evolved from their earlier incarnation.

TIP I use the term CSR to include case studies, reports, and white papers. After looking at many companies that create reports and white papers, it seems that the term *report* is used as often if not more than the term *white paper*. With the prevalence of business eBooks, the term *white paper* might seem too old-fashioned so several marketers have substituted the term *report* or *guide*. The term CSR seems to incorporate all of these terms. In this rule, CSR is the term used for the new hybrid format that many social media marketers use today.

CSRs continue to be popular because they incorporate the way adults learn. Information about why case studies are still popular points to the work of the educator Malcolm Knowles, who is considered the father of adult learning.

Knowles believed that adult learning is influenced by four factors:

- **Experience:** Adult learners apply their life lessons to what they learn.

- **Maturity:** Adult learners are more focused on their needs and can understand the value of the information they are given.

- **Relevancy:** Adult learners can decide quickly whether the information relates to them.

- **Immediacy:** Adult learners know whether they can immediately apply what they learn to a problem they need to solve.

CSRs fulfill these needs by proving clear examples that specifically tell readers how a problem was solved and how they can apply it to their own situation. That's why they are unlikely to fade from use. They will simply be adapted to meet customer needs. They are used by business schools, trainers, and online businesses alike.

> CSRs continue to be popular because they incorporate the way adults learn. Information about why case studies are still popular points to the work of the educator Malcolm Knowles, who is considered the father of adult learning.

RESOURCES FOR EXAMPLES OF CSR

When business customers are looking for data, they don't have to encounter a salesperson unless they choose to. They can go to a variety of places to get information. When it comes to CSR, they have a plethora of options. It's helpful to look at examples to see what others are doing and what is popular. This section describes CSRs that focus on social media marketing topics.

One example is the Word of Mouth Marketing Association (Womma) Case Study Library (http://womma.org/casestudy/), shown in Figure 15.1.

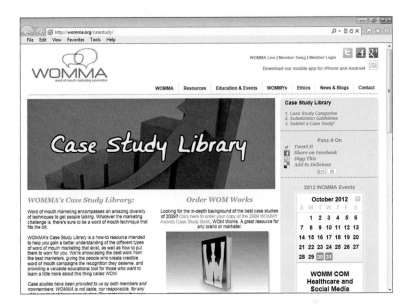

FIGURE 15.1

Womma Case Study Library.

Other good examples include these:

- Content Marketing Institute: http://www.contentmarketinginstitute.com/case-studies

- Duct Tape Marketing: http://www.ducttapemarketing.com/ebooks

- Eloqua: http://www.eloqua.com/resources (click on White Papers or Grande Guides).

- HubSpot: http://www.hubspot.com/customer-case-studies

- Marketo: http://www.marketo.com/b2b-marketing-resources

- Salesforce Marketing Cloud: http://www.salesforcemarketingcloud.com/resources/case-studies

FINDING YOUR CSR ONLINE

One of the main goals for creating CSRs is to show your target audience that you have the solution they are looking for and the knowledge to accomplish it. For this reason you want to make sure you take into account how your CSR will be found.

The title is the most important thing to choose. Just as with any book you would browse for on a bookstore shelf, the title catches the eyes first. When choosing a title, you should be aware of the keywords you want to rank for. Look at the set of keywords you normally use and decide which ones to include. In addition, you might want to add some new ones if this is a topic you want to rank for in the search engines. Also, make your title short and sweet. You have a few seconds to interest your reader. The easier it is to understand, the better chance you have to snag a reader's interest.

TIP   It is important to put your keywords at the beginning of your title so that the search engine picks them up. You will also want to make sure that these keywords are in the document itself.

You also want to be ready with a plan for distribution of this CSR before you write it. That might sound obvious, but you need to take a broad look at all the channels open to you and use as many as you can. If you plan it in advance, you can include important links in the document itself.

Consider using the following venues as part of your plan for distributing your CSR:

- Your website: Customers will likely check here to see what resources are available to them. A CSR will be considered valuable content.

- Tweets with a link to your CSR: Make sure that your Twitter followers are aware of your information.

- Your Facebook page status update: You are likely to get some traction when you put a link to a CSR here. If the content is good, others will comment.

- Your LinkedIn account: Professional content like CSRs are always well received on LinkedIn.

- Your blog or as a guest blogger: People are always looking for new content on blogs.

- Articles you place on an article directory site: A link to a CSR here will get your link clicked on more often because you are talking to people keen to find more about this topic.

- Your newsletter or email blasts: Any links your supply in an email or newsletter will get some attention. If it's a quality CSR it will be looked at.

- Pins on Pinterest: A board to display all your CSRs. Figure 15.2 shows a great example of a board created by Salesforce Marketing Cloud. It displays links to eBooks, infographics, and other content. Notice how it communicates the breadth of its content.

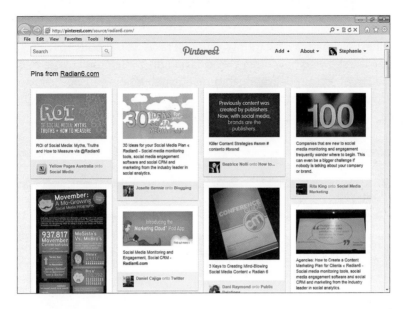

FIGURE 15.2

Pins from Salesforce MarketingCloud (formerly Radian6).

- Instagram: Take a photo of the cover and place it on all the connected social media platforms.

- A document on Slideshare.com: Slideshare has a growing audience of people looking for high-level content. A link to CSR will be well received.

- As a salesperson's collateral: It is traditional for sales people to provide CSRs to customers so they may read it.

Think of as many places to link to it as you can. Use the links multiple times, not just once. Add new places as you think of them. The idea is to get it and keep it circulating. You want to help your readers send links to their network.

TIP   Don't forget to caption all your images. See Rule 21, "Instagram Is Great for Quick Visuals from Your Mobile," for more on this.

A VISUAL MARKETING METHOD

Method: What goes into creating a good CSR?

To create a valuable CSR, you need to pay attention to three categories: the social media aspects, the visual aspects, and the content itself. Let's look at each of these.

The first category covers the elements that make CSRs perfect for social media:

- **Storytelling:** No matter what format your CSR takes, you should be telling a story. Either you are showing how other clients facing the same problem can be helped by your solution or you are delivering information about how you view a broader topic and its solution. For example, in Figure 15.3 you can see a report that clearly promises a story-based CSR.

FIGURE 15.3

Social media content in story form.

- **Multimedia formats (in the CSR or on a single page):** Your CSR is digital so that you can link from the text to various supportive materials in multimedia formats. These can include video, audio, infographics, cartoons, memes, and so on. You should take advantage of this opportunity to send your readers to other content that you have created online. Figure 15.4 shows an effective way that HubSpot has chosen to collect its content in various topics on one landing page.

  By sending readers to several places where your content resides, you help them understand the breadth of your company's offerings.

- **Social proof:** You want to do everything you can to make it easy for readers to share the CSR even if they don't choose to download it themselves. On the landing page for the Marketo eBook *How to Optimize Your Social Channels for Lead Generation*, as shown in Figure 15.5, is a set of shared links under the headline to Twitter, LinkedIn, Google+, Pinterest, and StumbleUpon.

FIGURE 15.4

HubSpot resources.

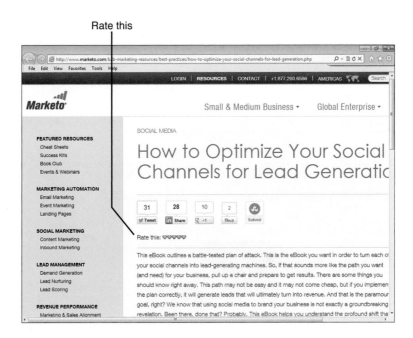

FIGURE 15.5

Marketo resources.

Notice they also have a Rate This link. If you choose to rate the eBook you are asked to which social platform you would like to send a notification of this rating so that others can see it.

- **Customer risk reducers:** One of the cardinal rules of marketing is to do things to reduce the risk the customer feels. This includes things like guarantees and liberal return policies. Show how the people in your CSR were made to feel comfortable working with you.

- **Self-identifiers:** Help the audience target themselves. If you completed your persona template in Rule 2, "Create Personas to Understand Your Customers," you know who you are targeting. Make sure you let customers know about the attributes of those in the CSR and how they relate to them. Make it easy for them to spot themselves in an example.

- **Spinoffs:** You want to be able to take the CSR and spin it off into other formats to use on social media channels. This means that you look at each of the content components and think about how you can use the same information in a different way. A good example of content that was repurposed in several ways is Sally Hogshead's Fascination line of products (see Figure 15.6). She started with a book/eBook called *Fascinate: Your 7 Triggers to Persuasion and Captivation*. Then she developed several online components, such as a test, reports, training, and video. Now she has a robust product offering for both individuals and corporations.

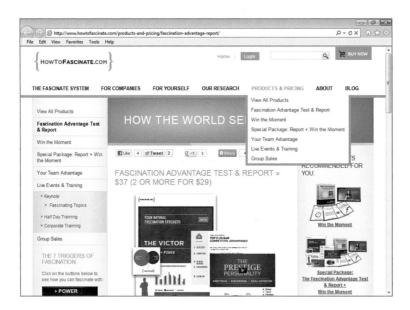

FIGURE 15.6

How to Fascinate website.

- **Promotion of thought leaders:** CSRs offer quotes that can be used to catch the eye of the media and that ultimately promote thought leaders. This tactic, employed by PR people for decades, works well in a CSR. When press releases were sent out, they always included a quote from an executive that could be used in a news article. Now journalists can locate people to interview in the same way from the CSR.

- **Links to other sources:** Be sure to include links to any other content you have that can supplement the information in the CSR. This gives you an opportunity to showcase other channels that have your information.

The second category to pay attention to covers the elements that pertain to the use of visuals, including these:

- **An inviting cover:** Don't forget that your audience is used to seeing well-designed covers on all sorts of eBooks. Make sure you deliver one for your CSR, as shown in Figure 15.7. Here we see a great cover of a CSR called "Who Really Won the brand Super Bowl? Let's Ask Social Media," by the Dachis Group.

FIGURE 15.7

Dachis Group eBook cover.

- **Up-to-date visual style:** If you have clip art or old-looking examples, you will give your audience the idea that it is not a current example. Use great design features, as shown in Figure 15.8 in a digital chapter from the book *Social Business by Design*.

FIGURE 15.8

Dachis Group eBook cover.

- **Easy-to-read text:** Remember that you want to make your CSR as easy to read as possible. Don't make it look like a heavy business document with no bullets or line breaks. Figure 15.9 shows one from ChangeThis that does a good job of laying out the text and using a pleasing design. All the manifestos published on this site follow the same format.

- **Diagrams and maps that are easy to follow:** With all the infographics and other examples of visual data, you must think about how you will depict the quantitative information. Look at Rule 10, "Use Diagrams and Other Visualization Tools to Explain Marketing Ideas," Rule 11, "Use Visual Guides That Build on Knowledge," and Rule 14, "Spread Your Message with Infographics," for specifics.

- **Images of the results:** Screenshots of the campaign itself as described in the CSR are necessary to lend credibility to your success claims. With the customer's permission, show the data that isn't confidential. Some success metrics in percentages are usually a good choice.

FIGURE 15.9

Page design used by ChangeThis.

The third category covers the content considerations that pertain to content of the CSR that haven't been covered previously:

- **Problem/solution defined:** Be sure to provide a clearly defined problem and solution.

- **Product information that shows how the product or service is used effectively:** Include as much of the product information as you need to show how results can be achieved.

- **SEO work done:** As mentioned, make sure that you have given full consideration to keywords and searches.

 ## IDEAS TO USE

CSRs are useful because they utilize the way adult learners use content. Don't assume they are passé.

At several stages of the buyer's journey (see Rule 5, "Take Buyers on a Journey"), you want to supply your potential customers with the information they need to choose you. Make it easy for them to get the information they seek by widely distributing all your CSRs.

Make sure your CSR has a great title, up-to date-visuals, and an interesting cover or customers might never get to the solid information you provide inside.

IDEA MAP

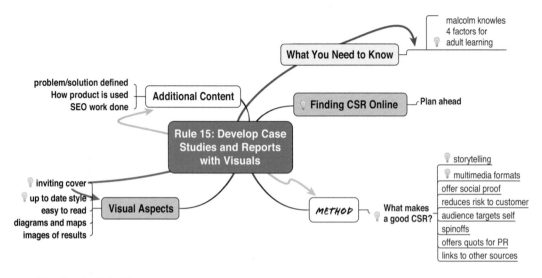

Idea Map for Rule 15

ENDNOTES

"Case Study-Based Learning." Mind Tools. http://www.mindtools.com/pages/article/newISS_94.htm.

ChangeThis. http://changethis.com/manifesto/show/48.04.DesignFunnel.

Hinchcliffe, Dion, and Peter Kim. *Social Business by Design.* 2012. Hosted on Slideshare by the Dachis Group. http://www.slideshare.net/dachisgroup/social-business-bydesignchapter5.

"Who Really Won the Brand Super Bowl? Let's Ask Social Media." http://www.slideshare.net/dachisgroup/dachis-group-super-social-2012.

DIGITAL PUBLISHING AND EBOOKS ARE HERE NOW—USE THEM

In Rule 16, we look at how social media marketers can use eBooks. We explore many of the decisions you need to make and provide worksheets to help you move forward.

WHAT YOU NEED TO KNOW

Coupled with the visual marketing revolution is the explosion of digital publishing and eBooks. As a social media marketer, I'm sure you've seen how eBooks have been used as incentives, premiums, and lead generators.

TIP   Also check out Rule 15, "Develop Case Studies and Reports with Visuals," which includes information about eBooks in the form of case studies and reports.

With all the interest in eBooks, you are probably convinced that publishing an eBook would be a great tool—whether or not you charge for it. The purpose of this chapter is to help you figure out the attributes your eBook will have before you write a single word. The key is to determine what your customer values.

Note that this chapter doesn't cover how to write an eBook, which is a separate topic for another book.

The Deloitte "State of the Media Democracy Survey," Sixth Edition, 2012, found that 36% of respondents preferred to download books, magazines, and newspapers to a digital device. That number will continue to grow as more people become accustomed to using digital readers. Research by Gary Small at the UCLA Center for Longevity was reported by Nick Bilton in his 2012 *New York Times* article "Disruptions: Your Brain on E-Books and Smartphone Apps." Small found that regardless of age, a person adapts to new technology in seven days. With the increase in the number of first-rate devices, people will be increasingly adopting new habits.

So how do you determine what kind of eBook is right for your business? I've created two worksheets you can use to evaluate how to achieve your eBook goals for each project you undertake.

> The Deloitte "State of the Media Democracy Survey," Sixth Edition, 2012, found that 36% of respondents preferred to download books, magazines, and newspapers to a digital device.

 ## A VISUAL MARKETING METHOD

Method: How to decide what kind of eBook to create.

These are the five categories that require decisions:

- **Purpose/revenue considerations:** Why are you creating your eBook and will you charge for it?

- **Content:** What shape will the content take?

- **Document conversion and distribution:** How will you convert and distribute the eBook?

- **Added-value options:** What should you include with your eBook to add value for the user?

- **Promotion:** How will you make sure that you get wide distribution?

The first worksheet, shown in Figure 16.1, is a map of the categories and the factors you need to consider. We go through each item so you can make decisions. We also show a benefits category that will help you call them out on your map.

The second worksheet, shown in Figure 16.2, holds your decisions so that you have a project record of your eBook and can return to it when you want to create another one like it.

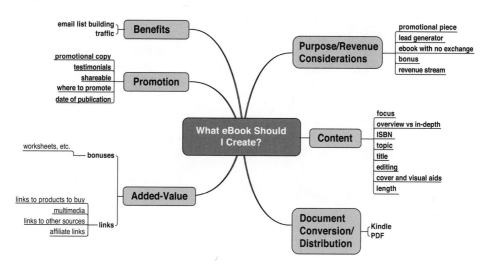

FIGURE 16.1

"What eBook should I create?"

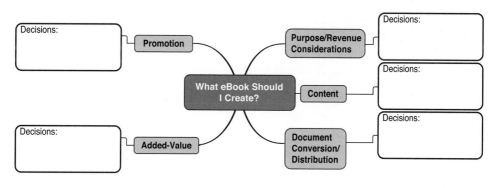

FIGURE 16.2

"eBook decisions."

Let's get started with the first worksheet.

PURPOSE/REVENUE

Do you want to charge for this eBook? One way to answer that question is to look at your purpose for creating it. When you know how it will be used, you will know whether it should have a price attached to it. Here are some of the ways you can use an eBook:

- **A promotional piece:** This eBook features the benefits of your product category. For example, you can create an eBook about how single-cup coffee makers save money as a promotion for your own single-cup coffee maker.

- **A leader generator:** You get an email address or other information in exchange for the eBook. In the example shown in Figure 16.3, Eloqua, a marketing systems company, has a line of eBooks on various topics called "Grande Guides." These guides are well written and help Eloqua establish its authority as experts in marketing.

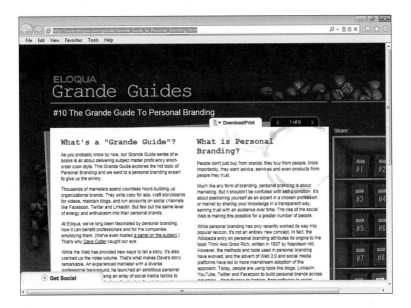

FIGURE 16.3

Eloqua Grande Guides.

- **An eBook with no exchange:** The user can download the eBook without exchanging anything. This tactic is used to get name recognition for thought leaders. The upside is that this type of eBook will be more widely downloaded than an eBook with reciprocity attached. The downside is that you can't build an email list with it.

  In the example shown in Figure 16.4, marketing guru David Meerman Scott offers several eBooks that customers can download without having to put in their email address. These eBooks have been widely praised for their content and availability.

- **A bonus with another offer:** This option is used to increase the value of a product/service you are offering. In the example shown in Figure 16.5, writer Jeff Goins sells his eBook *You Are a Writer (So Start Acting Like One)*. He offers various packages with different price points that include bonuses.

FIGURE 16.4

David Meerman Scott eBook Library.

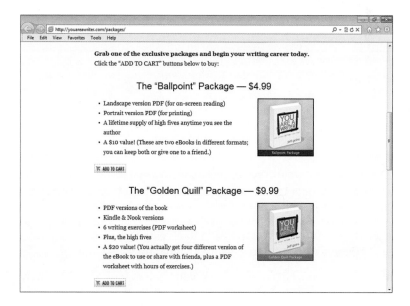

FIGURE 16.5

Packages for the Jeff Goins eBook.

- **An eBook with a price:** This is an eBook that you feel has enough value and demand to charge for. The example shown in Figure 16.6 is Angie Dixon's Kindle Single *Write As Fast As You Think*.

FIGURE 16.6

Angie Dixon's eBook with a price on Amazon.

CONTENT

After you have determined the purpose of your eBook and whether it will generate revenue, you can focus on the content. Following are the factors you should consider:

- **Focus:** Do your readers want several solutions or one specific solution? eBooks can be centered around a bigger topic and supply a collection of tips and hints or they can solve one particular problem.

- **High-level or in-depth:** Are you speaking to an audience of executives who want the overview, or people who need to execute on what they are reading?

- **Topic:** When deciding which topic to pick, you need to look at your content on your blog, website, and other channels. What are the topics that get a great response? You can test topics on your blog and see what your readers have to say. It is likely that because these are marketing vehicles, you don't want to stray too far from your most important content. You don't want to risk picking a topic that hasn't been thoroughly tested. A safer bet is to choose to take a deeper dive into the same topic.

- **Title:** The title of your eBook can make or break it. When choosing the title, make sure that there is a benefit right in the headline. A good example of this would be the book title, *Decisive: How to Make Better Choices in Life and in Work*, by Chip Heath and Dan Heath. It tells you right in the title what it will help you achieve if you read it.

- **ISBN:** If you plan to sell your eBook or offer it on a platform like Amazon, you need to get an ISBN (International Standard Book Number). It is the number used by commercial sellers to identify books. To learn more about it or to obtain a number, check out this source: http://www.isbn.org/standards/home/index.asp

- **Editing:** You need to decide whether you will use an outside editor. If you want to have an eBook you will be proud of, consider having a professional or someone who is well versed in your topic read it and supply edits. If you have an eBook that is riddled with errors in grammar and spelling, or has misinformation, you will defeat the purpose of publishing your eBook.

TIP When I have purchased an eBook that is poorly edited, I make it a point to never buy from that source again. I'm sure most readers feel the same way. It doesn't matter whether you sell the book or give it away, you want to be thought of as an expert. If the quality of your eBook is poor, you will turn customers away. You are better off not publishing it.

- **Book cover and content visuals throughout the book:** These elements are crucial. I cover them in depth later in this chapter.

- **Length:** Are your readers people who are short on time? Make your eBook under 30 pages. If this is a specific problem, send an executive summary–style document instead.

DOCUMENT CONVERSION AND DISTRIBUTION

To know how to convert your document after it is complete, you need to decide how you will distribute it. To make things easy, you might want to narrow your choices to the formats that have the largest distribution. Here are two to consider:

- **Amazon Kindle:** Amazon has the largest audience, so if you are creating an eBook with a price tag, you might want to choose the Amazon Kindle format. It can be showcased to all of Amazon's members, and your audience can download a free application that enables them to read it on their Windows or Mac computer, iPad, iPhone, Blackberry, or Android. Amazon offers a royalty for each book sold and has various lending and promotion options.

  To learn more about the Kindle Publishing Program, check out this link: http://www.amazon.com/gp/feature.html?ie=UTF8&docId=1000234621, as shown in Figure 16.7.

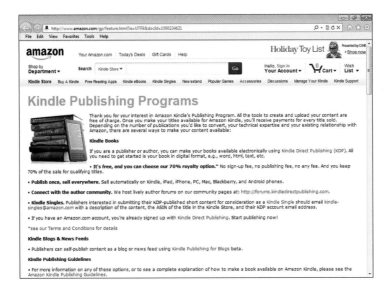

FIGURE 16.7

Amazon Kindle Publishing Programs.

- **Adobe PDF:** If you are not charging for your eBook and you don't want to have to deal with conversion issues, you might want to publish your eBook as an Adobe PDF. It can be widely distributed to all computer users. For more information, check out the link shown in Figure 16.8 or visit http://www.adobe.com/products/acrobat.html.

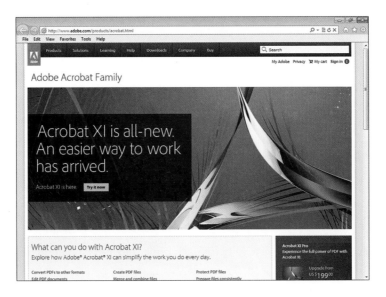

FIGURE 16.8

Adobe Acrobat format.

An example of an eBook published as a PDF is ChangeThis (http://changethis.com), as shown in Figure 16.9. ChangeThis publishes manifestos by top writers with a point of view. They use the PDF format so that anyone who is interested can read it without an eReader device.

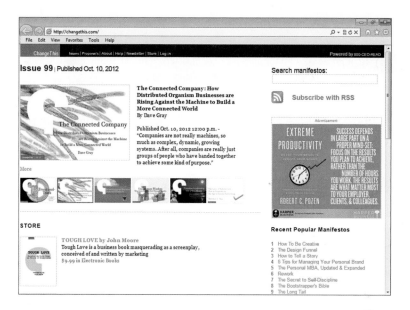

FIGURE 16.9

ChangeThis.

At the time of this writing the Amazon Kindle format is the most popular because it can be read on so many devices.

ADDED-VALUE

You also want to add content to your offer to sweeten the deal. People always like the idea that they are getting free stuff. Some items that add value are:

- **Bonuses:** Decide whether your eBook should have a bonus attached to it (particularly if you are selling it). If you are not selling it, you might conclude that it can stand on its own. But remember, if you have a specific goal in mind that can be enhanced with a bonus such as a free consultation, consider using the bonus.

- **Links:** Because you can include links in your eBook content, consider adding links to other online content that will enhance the understanding (and value) of the eBook. The types of content you might link to can include these:

    Multimedia: Audio or video content that you have created specifically for the book or have on hand that is pertinent.

Other web sources: Additional sources of content on other sites or your own.

Other products/discounts: A current product you are selling to gain another promotion channel, and possibly a discount to purchase that product.

> **TIP**
>
> If you are selling your eBook, you might want to create affiliate links that enable others to promote your eBook and get a commission. Remember that if you do this, you need to set up a program to support commission payments.

Don't go overboard on these items. If you load up on too many they begin to lose value.

PROMOTION

You'll want to think about specific copy that will sell your content and add social proof. Here are some things to consider:

- **Copy:** Will you be writing your own promotional copy or will you have a professional do it? Obviously, if the stakes are high, you should use a professional.
- **Testimonials:** To cut the risk the reader feels about downloading your content, it helps to have testimonials of people who have read the eBook or are happy with the work you have done for them. Even if you are not charging for the eBook, testimonials help shore up your credibility.

> **TIP**
>
> When you add testimonials, try to include a picture of the person who provided it to add credibility. If you can get him or her on video, that is even better.

- **Shareable:** eBooks are often shared so remember that you will want to make it as easy as possible for your reader to share it with his network. Depending on the venue, you can use tools such as ShareThis (http://sharethis.com), as shown in Figure 16.10, or AddThis (http://addthis.com) to the promotion page.
- **Where to promote:** Unless there is some reason not to, you will want to promote your eBook on as many channels as you can. This means that you will promote from your website, social media platforms, LinkedIn, your newsletter, and email lists. (See the example in the "Purpose/Revenue" section.)

> **TIP**
>
> Aside from promotion on social networks, blogs, and so on, another way to promote your eBook is on sites such as Goodreads (http://www.goodreads.com). You list your book on the site and encourage site members you know to read and review your book.

FIGURE 16.10

Share this.

- **Date of publication:** Think about when you will launch the eBook. Is there a reason to hold it for a special date or should you release it as soon as you're ready? If it is seasonal or ties to a holiday, obviously, you'll choose that date.

IMPORTANCE OF BOOK COVER AND VISUALS

In a book that champions the use of visuals as an adjunct to copy, it's important to reinforce the use of visuals for your eBook. Let's start with the cover. The choice of a cover is critical to the success of your eBook. Here are examples of some successful covers and visuals:

- ***47 Handy Facebook Stats and Charts,* by HubSpot:** This cover (see Figure 16.11) demonstrates the clear promise that you will get 47 items with a big number 47 in the corner. When you look inside, you get exactly that.

- **Seth Godin eBooks:** It's hard to pick one eBook from well-respected marketer Seth Godin's collection because all of his covers are spectacular. Figure 16.12 shows a roundup of his covers for you to peruse. Notice the use of color and clear, simple graphics.

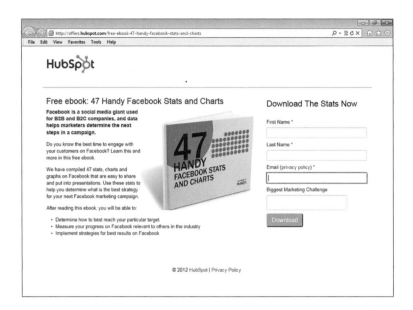

FIGURE 16.11
HubSpot cover.

FIGURE 16.12
Seth Godin's book covers.

- ***The Right Brain Business Plan*, by Jennifer Lee:** This book cover (see Figure 16.13) shows you exactly what you'll get inside. It sets the mood for a process that will have you using your own DIY skills to create a visual business plan. When you look inside, you see great illustrations of plans people have created.

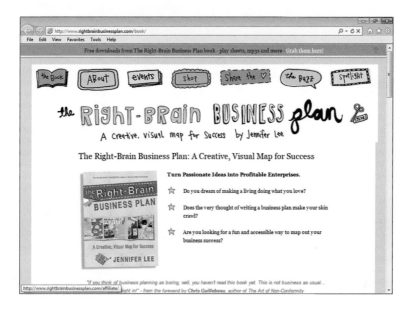

FIGURE 16.13

Jennifer Lee's book cover.

IDEAS TO USE

Make sure you know what purpose your eBook will serve before you write one word. The purpose will dictate all your other decisions.

Include links to your other online content (multimedia) from the eBook so that readers can find new places to read your materials and learn about your capabilities.

Ensure that your eBook will entice readers by adding a well-designed cover and visuals inside that support the ideas.

 IDEA MAP

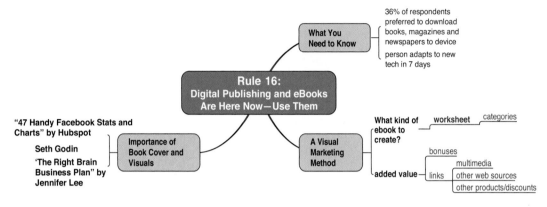

Idea Map for Rule 16

ENDNOTES

If you're interested in reading about book cover design theory, here's an interesting article in the *Guardian* newspaper about the theories of Jon Gray and Jamie Keenan, two very successful book designers: http://www.guardian.co.uk/books/booksblog/2012/aug/16/book-cover-theories-edinburgh-festival.

ROCK YOUR VISUAL BRAND ON SOCIAL MEDIA

In Rule 17, we look at what you should consider including when you are working on your branding. We include a template that helps you evaluate your branding efforts on social media.

WHAT YOU NEED TO KNOW

Do you sometimes feel a bit jealous of the companies that have successfully created a popular brand using social media? It doesn't matter what size your company is, you want to be part of a brand that people respect and admire. But don't assume that achieved status is a result of deep pockets.

There are large companies that have thrown big money at the problem and never solved it, and there are small companies that have nailed it. J.C. Penney is still struggling but Z Squared Media, founded in 2007 by Joe Pulizzi, is on the 2012 Inc. 5000 list of America's Fastest Growing Companies at number 9 in the Media Category. It takes more skill than money.

DUNKING IN THE DARK

A great example of a company using more skill than money on social media happened during the 2013 Super Bowl. During the game between the San Francisco Forty-niners and the Baltimore Ravens, there was a 34 minute blackout. Oreo, the cookie company, sent out a tweet with a picture that said, "You can still dunk in the dark." This message was retweeted more than 10,000 times in one hour, and Oreo got a sweet bit of attention.

The key was that Oreo seized the moment. Of course, Oreo has an advertising agency that jumped in, but arguably, any company could have done something similar because every advertiser had the same opportunity to send out a tweet during that time. Oreo's picture was an image with a caption—a very simple image to create. All they needed was a good idea—something all the money in world can't always produce.

Branding is not a topic that is easily understood. But don't think you need to sit on the sidelines wishing you had the answer.

There are things you can do to get your social media branding house in order. We cover some of them in this Rule on visual branding.

Branding involves understanding what is in your customers' mind when it comes to your company. As branding guru Marty Neumeier says in his book *The Brand Gap*, a brand is "a person's gut feeling, because brands are defined by individuals, not companies, markets, or the public."

This makes branding a natural ally of social media because it establishes a dialogue with the customer. By integrating your social media with your branding efforts, you create a powerful channel to reach customers.

Outside of social media, brands need to capture the imagination of their customer by participating in the community in which they live. They need to show customers that some of their profits go back into the local economy, as well as the country as a whole. They need to be perceived as insiders.

Branding is also about what customers think about themselves. As with most things that involve psychology, it is hard to predict the outcome. Branding involves complex factors such as these:

Some brands inspire love; some are showered with indifference. If you are a social media marketer, you know that branding is an important key to your overall success.

- How your customer wants to feel when she uses your product

- What the customer was raised to believe is of value and how that value translates itself to pricing

- What part of the world the customer comes from

- Whether the customer thinks your voice is authentic and trustworthy

- What the customer believes about your interest level in your customers

- Whether the customer thinks she fits into the community that surrounds your brand

- Whether the customer believes that talking about your brand to others will increase their reputation

The list goes on and on. Needless to say, your brand should invoke positive feelings and it should be emotionally satisfying. Some brands inspire love; some are showered with indifference. If you are a social media marketer, you know that branding is an important key to your overall success.

TIP If you capture your brand's essence, you can create loyal customers. But it's not always easy to know what customers will think about your brand no matter how much you research and plan. You need to talk to them on a regular basis and understand what makes your brand attractive to them.

According to Forrester Research, in their 2012 report "How Social Media Is Changing Brand Building," a survey of marketing leaders found the following:

- One-third of their online users have become fans on social platforms like Facebook and Twitter.

- Ninety-two percent believe that "social media has fundamentally changed how consumers engage with brands."

- Ninety-three percent say they will reinvent their branding efforts to integrate mobile and social media.

Clearly, social media is having a major impact on branding. If you build your brand using social media, you will find that branding offers some important benefits, such as the following:

- **Provides a micro message:** It provides a shorthand way to grab your customers' attention.

- **Inspires loyalty:** It helps your customers band together as a community under one banner.

- **Holds your historical record:** You don't need to reiterate everything about your company each time you promote it. The brand is the repository for its history and goodwill.

- **Stabilizes your message:** After you establish yourself in a category, you'll stay in that category. (Most brands want to remain in a particular category—rebranding is hard.)

- **Nurtures employee satisfaction:** It helps employees understand your message, rally around it, and reinforce it with your customers.

ANALYZING YOUR BRAND

To get organized to evaluate how well your brand is doing and what you need to do to revise it, let's look at a template of items to consider (see Figure 17.1). This is by no means a complete list, but it will get you started.

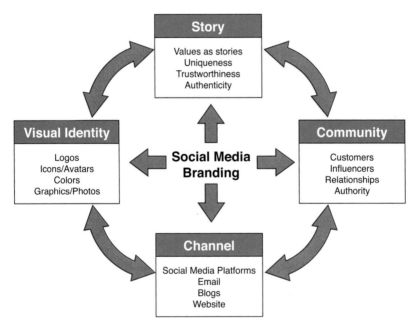

FIGURE 17.1

Social Media Branding.

Branding as it relates to social media is a subset of traditional branding. If you combine this template with the others in the book, you should have a complete picture of your social media branding.

Let's look at the template by following a clockwise pattern.

1. **Story:** As we have discussed throughout the book, your story is your brand on social media.

    *   **Values as stories:** Have you explained to your customer what you believe in and why you are running the business? Whether you are large or small, this story either resonates or fails with your customer.

        If customers don't know what values you hold, they will guess at them. This is not something you want your customers to have to construct by themselves. They will want to see your commitment to the community in which you live, the environment, or any other philanthropic causes you support. Be sure to convey this in as many formats and channels as you can.

    *   **Uniqueness:** I'm sure you've heard about your unique selling proposition (USP). That's old school for determining why your customer should choose you. With all the competition for your attention, you need to make this as easy to understand as possible. You won't get a lot of time to make this case. On social media you have to constantly reinforce this message.

    *   **Trustworthiness:** This involves demonstrating your credibility with social proof, that is, testimonials, press mentions, and so on. Without trust in your company, a customer can't really think about pulling out his credit card.

    *   **Authenticity:** You need to be who you say you are. If your reputation is damaged or not up to par, you won't be able to sustain an audience. There are too many other choices for your customers to waste time on you if they have any question in their mind about your credibility.

    Following are questions to answer about your story:

    *   Have you made your stories easy for your customers to tell? If not, work on making sure they can tell their friends why you are worth buying from.

    *   Do you know what makes you unique? If it's not clear in your mind, you'll discover that your customers will prefer competitors who make that choice clear.

    *   Do you monitor your reputation online? If you aren't constantly watching what's being said about you, you won't be ready to step in when a crisis hits.

2. **Community:** Your community reflects the value of your brand. You need to look at each of the following constituencies:

    *   **Customers:** If you have clearly delineated your target customers and developed personas, you know who will respond to your brand and why. A community of interested people will have formed around your brand that provides you with feedback, ratings, focus, and ideas.

- **Influencers:** You need to know what the major influencers in your market are saying about you. If they are unaware of you, your brand is not as strong as it could be. If you can connect with them, you can partner with them to strengthen both your brand and theirs.

- **Relationships:** Strong relationships among your ecosystem of vendors, colleagues, and customers will support your brand. Creating such groups as brand ambassadors that carry your message will do a great deal to keep your brand growing. They can bring your brand to places you can't go, like a closed networking group.

- **Authority:** You know how much authority you have in your marketplace by seeing who repeats your stories and who values your leadership. If you are in a large company, are you the one asked to speak at events?

Following are questions to answer about your community:

- Do you nurture your community and provide customer service on various platforms? Your brand will gain recognition by providing customer service in all its forms.

- Have you considered creating a brand ambassador program to leverage the value your customers bring?

- Does your company have a consistent presence at conferences and forums? Does the press pick up on your stories or seek a quote from you?

3. **Channel:** Your participation on social media channels will make or break your brand value. Here are some venues to consider:

- **Social media platforms:** You need to have a presence on the major social media channels unless you are absolutely sure your customers are not there. It is hard to believe that with the major audiences on platforms like Facebook and YouTube, you won't want to be there. The question you need to tackle is how you can leverage those audiences.

- **Email:** Despite what you read, email is not dead. In fact, it is still going strong. It should be part of any branding effort you make whether in the form of a newsletter or regular email communication.

- **Blogs:** This is another format that can sell your brand. Some smaller companies do all their branding through their blogs. It's a great way to spread your brand stories and provide a consistent message.

There are so many tools that allow you to monitor your blog's traffic, and it's valuable information about your audience that you can't afford to overlook.

- **Website:** This is your hub. You know that your branding is on view here every day. If you don't have your visual brand nailed down, you can tell that when you visit your website.

Following are questions to answer about your channel:

- Have you figured out your social media strategy?

- Are you consistently providing valuable content on these channels? Do you keep in regular contact with your customers via email and newsletters? When they hear from you, are they expecting to get a pitch rather than something of substance?

- Does your website reflect your brand or does it provide mixed messages that confuse the viewer?

4. **Visual Identity:** Your visual identity will be what the customer sees in his mind when thinking about your brand. If you pair that with the right messages, you will have a powerful tool that supports your branding efforts. Here are some visuals to consider:

- **Logos:** These can be a visual depiction of your company's letters such as IBM's (see Figure 17.2), Nike's (see Figure 17.3), and the Disney Channel's (see Figure 17.4).

FIGURE 17.2

IBM on Facebook.

FIGURE 17.3

Nike on Facebook.

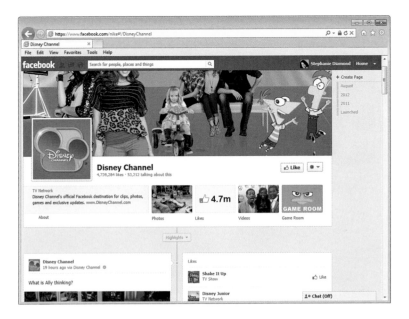

FIGURE 17.4

Disney Channel on Facebook.

- **Icons/Avatars:** These support your brand because although they are small, they make a strong visual impact.

- **Colors/Fonts:** Obviously, this is at the heart of your brand. Two things that people will remember are the color scheme and the message the fonts send. They will probably not be aware of them unless they are familiar with your brand. But the visual effect is strong.

- **Graphics/Photos:** As we discuss in this book, the visuals and photos communicate your brand in a way that text alone never can.

  Following are questions to answer about your visual identity:

- Is your logo professionally designed and used the same way each time? Design rules dictate that the logo must be portrayed exactly as it is designed and cannot be changed based on the venue or promotion.

- Do you pay attention to the icons and avatars used on social media? This is not insignificant.

- Is your story told with memorable graphics? Do you make sure that your graphics do not signal that your company is too amateurish to use design effectively? You will be judged.

VISUAL EXPECTATIONS

In today's marketplace, we know that customers are in control of the messages they receive. They can do the following:

- Use the Back button on their browser

- Click the Mute button on their TV remote

- Fast-forward through the commercials on their DVR

- Ignore you on their mobile phones

On the flip side, customers can talk back to a brand and let their opinions be heard. This makes one-way control obsolete. You are in a dialogue with your customer whether you want to be or not.

But what about their visual expectations; have they changed, too? Advertisers have always known that visuals are important. The Web has multiplied that need with its facility for making visuals easy to share on social platforms.

If you wonder whether social platforms have changed our visual expectations, all you have to do is look at the list of social media platforms covered in Part IV of this book, "Tactics for Social Media Platforms." Many of them weren't even around five years ago, including these:

- Pinterest, launched 2010

- Instagram, launched 2010

- Google+, launched 2011

- iPad, released 2010

Note that these are visual tools for the most part and have contributed to a change in our visual expectations. Most notably, Pinterest and Instagram are solely visual in nature.

Tools like these have changed our branding needs. For example, you need such visuals as these:

- A timeline image for Facebook

- A photo header for Twitter

- Photos using Instagram

- Boards for Pinterest

It's hard to keep everything consistent and fresh. Even the major brands have been slow to adopt these changes. That's because it's not easy to get right. If you look around Facebook, you can see that some major brands haven't developed a great visual display.

Laura Ries, in her book *Visual Hammer*, says that in today's marketplace it is critical for brands to use what she calls a visual hammer to nail an idea into the customer's mind.

Previously, it was easy to capture the attention of the customer with a tag line. But with advertisers fighting for customer attention, she says that using a visual is the only way to take that verbal message and make it memorable.

For example, she cites how the contoured Coke bottle has endured in people's minds as the symbol for Coca-Cola. On Coke's Facebook page they use the bottle as their defining picture (see Figure 17.5).

This ties into the neuroscience research cited throughout this book that tells us that using visuals and text together is the most effective way to reach the customer.

Design companies today have to be creative about the visual messages they create. A great example of this creativity is shown in Figure 17.6 and can be seen on the blog of design and branding company Stitch Design Company, by founders Amy Pastre and Courtney Rowson, at http://www.stitchdesignco.com/blog/.

FIGURE 17.5

Coca-Cola on Facebook.

FIGURE 17.6

Stitch Design Company's Made to Measure blog.

This interactive design was created as the invitation to the AIGA South Carolina Chapter InShow. It's not what you'd expect and it demonstrates how an unusual metaphor grabs attention.

 # A VISUAL MARKETING METHOD

Method: Use the branding template to ask yourself the questions covered in this section. After you have gone through it once, you will have a better understanding of how to influence your branding.

 # IDEAS TO USE

Establishing a great brand using social media doesn't take deep pockets. It takes an understanding of all the elements that go into making your brand: story, community, channel, and visual identity.

Your brand is a micro message that holds all your history and goodwill.

If you haven't developed brand stories that demonstrate your values, do so immediately. You don't want your customers to supply their own versions, which might be inaccurate.

IDEA MAP

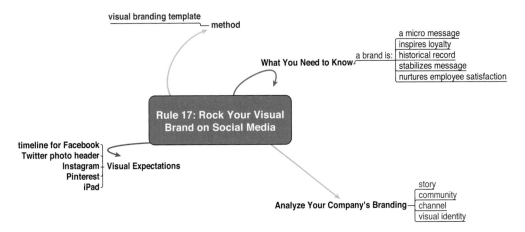

Idea Map for Rule 17

ENDNOTES

Neumeier, Marty. *The Brand Gap: How to Bridge the Distance Between Business Strategy and Design.*" Indianapolis, IN: New Riders, 2006.

Ries, Laura. *Visual Hammer: Nail Your Brand into the Mind with the Emotional Power of a Visual.* Laura Ries Publisher, 2012.

Stitch Design Company. http://www.stitchdesignco.com.

Stokes, Tracy. "How Social Media Is Changing Brand Building." Forrester. May 7, 2012.

Rule 18

LANDING PAGES WON'T PERFORM WELL WITHOUT VISUALS

In Rule 18, we look at how using visuals can be a "make or break" for your landing pages. We give you a working template to evaluate them so that they deliver the conversions you expect.

WHAT YOU NEED TO KNOW

Throughout this book, we discuss the impact visual content has on social media marketing. I hope by now that you're convinced about how important it is. But in case you need more proof, a study by ROI Research in 2012 called "Life on Demand" found the following:

- Thirty-five percent said pictures that they took are the content people enjoyed most from their friends.

- Forty-four percent said pictures are the content they most engage with from a brand.

- Fifty-six percent said digital pictures are what they prefer when both digital and offline formats are available.

I'm sure you're noticing a trend. Pictures are a hot commodity, and you can't expect your online sites to perform unless you include them. The key is to choose the right images for the vehicle you are creating.

ABOUT LANDING PAGES

What are landing pages? They are the pages you rely on to capture a lead. They are the place where you want your customers to "land" when they are making a decision about engaging with you. Marketers found that it was very inefficient to send someone to their home page from a link and hope they could locate the information from the advertisement or offer.

They realized it would be much more effective to have a dedicated page to sell something or acquire a lead from an interested customer. Enter landing pages. Typically the page will have specific information and either a sign up box where the customer inputs their contact information or a button that takes them to a place to buy something.

Visitors to these landing pages come from various places. Most likely they are coming from a link you created to get them here. These links are from both the ads and media you pay for and ones that are free. For example, it could be a link from a paid ad on Google, a link in a press release you paid for, or a free social media or blog post link.

Landing pages ask your customers to take a specific action. For example, you can ask them to do the following:

- Put in their email address in exchange for content such as an eBook or a newsletter subscription

- Call a phone number to get information they want

- Make an appointment to speak with you

> What are landing pages? They are the pages you rely on to capture a lead. They are the place where you want your customers to "land" when they are making a decision about engaging with you.

TIP

In this context, I am not referring to a sales page from which you can purchase a product. Sales pages are much more detailed than a landing page. Your landing page needs to have just enough information to get your customers to take the action you want them to.

Because you want customers to take some action, you first need to determine the answers to two revenue-related questions:

- **What is the ROI if the customers take the action?**

    Many marketers ignore this question when creating landing pages. They are so focused on the outcome that they forget about the value it has to them. Obviously, you want to get that email address or get them to call you, but what does that mean as far as revenue goes? Are you getting a return from your phone calls? If you get someone to call you, does the call convert customers? Do you know the cost of acquiring a new customer?

One reason this question is so important is that you have to set priorities. No matter how hard you or your team works, you won't get to do everything you'd like to. No matter how well funded you are, you still need to make choices.

If you know that a call converts better than another method, the landing page promoting a call is the one you will choose to test and improve first. When that page has been optimized, you can focus on optimizing others. If you have lots of resources, you can work on them simultaneously.

- **"What's in it for me" (WIIFM), the customer, if I take the action?**

As you know, everything is competing for your customers' attention both online and offline. For this reason, you want to make sure that you are providing something that the customer perceives as valuable.

You should be very clear about what your customers value and in what quantity. You might think that sending them a 50-page eBook will be greeted with delight when, in fact, it makes them feel burdened. A 5-page summary might be appreciated much more. You need to gauge that by knowing your customers' preferences.

RULES OF PERSUASION

In Rule 1, "Recognize the Power of Visual Persuasion," we looked at the "Six + Five Rules of Persuasion" and demonstrated the use of a template to analyze a website. To analyze a landing page, we need to focus on a subset of that template because the goals are more focused. Let's revisit the template used in Rule 1 and make some revisions to it so that it works for a landing page. We are going to use this template without the following six items:

- **Commitment and consistency, liking, and relationship building:** A landing page requires a commitment, so your content on a landing page would make these items a requirement.

- **Scarcity:** You can choose to put this in your top banner with your story, but it's something you need to think through carefully. If it looks as though you are manufacturing it, it won't work. Also, putting short deadlines on the landing page requires you to update it frequently.

- **Green attitude:** Your brand needs to reflect this on your website. It would be difficult to call attention to this in a landing page.

- **Word of mouth:** There is nothing wrong with sharing links on your landing page, but most companies focus on the traffic from the specific links they have chosen to tie to these.

We are going to add this to the original template:

- **A call to action (CTA):** This is the goal of the template and should be front and center.

With these changes, the landing page template will have six items listed under Persuasion:

- Story and visuals (banner)
- Social proof
- Authority
- Reciprocity
- WIIFM
- CTA (listed separately on the map)

This template is used later in this chapter, but for now, let's look at what components are required to build your landing page.

MECHANISMS OF A LANDING PAGE

There are several mechanisms you need in order to create your landing pages:

- **Form:** You need an input form so that the user can give you the critical lead information you want. This form sends the data to a database so that it can be utilized.

  It's important to note here that you should think carefully about what you need to capture in your form. You can depress the response simply by asking for too much information. Do you need to know the customer's phone number on the first pass? Get by with the least information you can. If the person is interested, you have several chances to get information from him. This matters.

- **Database:** This is where your captured information from the form is stored.

- **Autoresponder:** When the user inputs the information you requested, the autoresponder sends information or gives him a link to the item he requested.

- **Analytics:** This provides a way for you to track the behavior of the people who interact with the landing page. If it isn't built into your autoresponder you would want to use a program like Google Analytics to tell you such things as who clicked on the link and whether they went on to take some action.

TIP In the "Tools to Consider" section later in this chapter, I list several tools that incorporate the mechanisms together in one tool. You might or might not be able to use them based on how your company handles internal databases and so on.

COMPONENTS

Next, let's look at the actual components that make up a landing page:

- **Text:** This refers to the copy that is used on the page. It includes everything you think should be included to generate your lead. Most important of these is the headline to grab attention.

- **Visuals:** These are the images and video components that help your user better understand what you are trying to convey.

- **Search Engine Optimization (SEO):** This is placed here because it is a part of the process you include when creating the text and visuals. You need to pick out which keywords and tags should be included in the code of these components. If you leave this out, you risk not being found.

- **A/B testing:** This refers to the ongoing tests you conduct to see what works best. Visuals play an important part here. For example, to improve the click rate, you would test the headline, the visuals—like the picture of the product or a line drawing, and the Call To Action (CTA) button. You want to make sure that no one item is making the conversion rate go down.

WHERE ARE BUYERS IN THE JOURNEY?

Next, you need to look at where you believe the buyer is in her journey (see Rule 5, "Take Buyers on a Journey") and make sure you can support her interests. The key here is to provide enough information so that a person ready to click has sufficient content and a person who is not ready to click will be interested enough to bookmark the landing page to return to it later.

The time you spent analyzing and developing your personas comes into play here. When you are creating the landing page, you should be talking to your personas. If you forget to target them, you are missing out on an opportunity to home in on the people who care about you the most.

The next two items tie back to our template:

- **Story:** You want to make sure that you are telling a story. As you'll see on the landing page that we analyze in the "Method" section, the landing page has a story. It can be subtle, but you need a narrative that helps the user understand features, benefits, and values. Only a story can easily bring those elements together.

- **Persuasion elements:** The persuasion elements are on the template and are discussed in Rule 1. They are social proof, authority, reciprocity, WIIFM, and word of mouth.

EFFECTIVE HANDSHAKE

The handshake refers to the journey from the link you've set up to the landing page. For example, one link can be from an ad, another from Twitter. For each of the links you set up, you need to make sure there is consistency. Take the visual trip yourself. You want to make sure that the wording with the link smoothly fits with the landing page. If you create confusion, you destroy the handoff.

EMAIL MARKETING

Although this section is devoted to landing pages, because email marketing uses some of the same mechanisms that landing pages use, it's appropriate to discuss email marketing here.

If you look at the mechanisms we discussed, emails (and newsletters) also need the following:

- **Form:** Subscribers need to be able to sign up using a form to put in their contact information.

- **Database:** As a marketer, you need a place to house your email list.

- **Autoresponder:** When subscribers sign up, you want to send them something that acknowledges them.

- **Shareability:** If subscribers are excited about the content and want to send it to a friend, you want to make that as easy as possible by providing links to social platforms and other links.

What's different about emails is that you want to use them to establish an ongoing communication with the subscriber. Where landing pages perform a specific function, emails help you keep your name in front of the customer. If you send an email newsletter on a biweekly basis, your customer will expect to hear from you. The key is to make the email fulfill the promise every newsletter or regular email makes: to provide the customer with something valuable. It's new information, a discount, an upcoming webinar, and so on.

In case you're wondering, you can use the same template items for emails that we use for landing pages: CTA, story/graphics, social proof, authority, reciprocity, and WIIFM.

Just note that there is a difference for the CTA. The CTA in an email is different from that of a landing page. The landing page is used most often to generate a lead. When you send a newsletter or another email, you already have subscribers' contact information. What you are trying to do with a newsletter is encourage them to continue to engage with your company in some way.

For example, customers can do the following:

> Purchase from a discount code in the newsletter
>
> Forward the newsletter to a friend
>
> Tweet information contained in the newsletter
>
> Send in a question
>
> Make a comment on your blog

All of these would be valuable engagement with your company.

If you want to establish an ongoing communication with your customer, there are many services that provide newsletter style services, including these:

- Constant Contact: http://constantcontact.com

- MailChimp: http://mailchimp.com

- 1ShoppingCart: http://1shoppingcart.com

- AWeber: http://aweber.com

 # A VISUAL MARKETING METHOD

Method: Evaluating landing pages. We picked three landing pages to discuss: Basecamp Software, WorkFlowy, and SEOmoz. Note that the numbers on each of the figures corresponds to the numbered list in the discussion that follows it.

BASECAMP SOFTWARE

We begin with Basecamp Software. Figure 18.1 is an example of a great landing page. We can analyze it with our template to recognize the most important components.

Basecamp (http://basecamp.com/signup) is popular cross-platform project management software. The company that created the software is 37signals, which launched it in 2004.

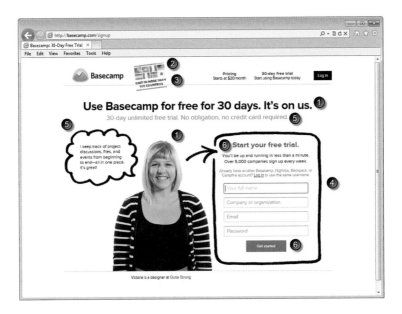

FIGURE 18.1

Basecamp.

I chose this landing page because it is cleanly designed and it sits above the fold. More important, it does a lot with a simple design. When you look at it you don't feel overwhelmed. It tells a story and is supported by its visuals. Let's look at the page more closely:

1. **Banner Headline and Graphic**

   Content components: Story and graphic. The story on this landing page is about Victoria, a designer at Quite Strong who uses Basecamp. You see her picture and assume that she likes the product enough to allow her image to be used. Basecamp also provides a link to her site to prove she is real.

2. **Social Proof**

   Content components: Graphic saying that the product is used by people in 180 countries, and a photo of Victoria, someone you can relate to.

3. **Authority (Credibility)**

   Content components: Again, the graphic saying that the product is used by people in 180 countries. This does double-duty as proof of its credibility. I call this out separately because if a brand is large with great authority, it will want to call that out separately.

4. **Reciprocity**

   Content components: An input form attached to a sign-up mechanism. In exchange for typing in my contact information, I can get a free 30-day trial.

5. **WIIFM**

   Content components: The opportunity for me to try the application for 30 days without having to give my credit card number. In addition, I see the benefit that Victoria gets when she uses the product.

6. **CTA**

   Content components: Headline that says "Start your free trial," which you initiate by putting in your contact information. After you do that, you have to click on the Get Started button. Both are clear calls to action.

WORKFLOWY

WorkFlowy (https://workflowy.com/) is an online application that is essentially a dimensional outline that can create lists within lists of any structure you desire.

I chose this landing page because of its unique construction, as shown in Figure 18.2 and Figure 18.3. It puts the sign-up graphic right in your face. There is no mistaking what you are here to do. Cleverly, though, WorkFlowy supplies a lot of information below the sign-up box that covers all the questions and concerns you might have. As you go through the analysis, notice all the content that is neatly packed onto the page.

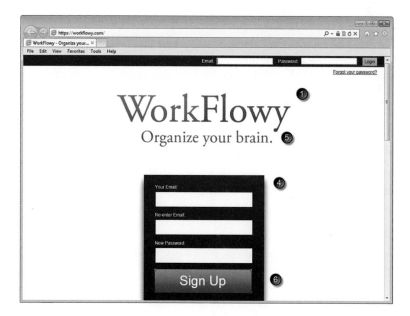

FIGURE 18.2

WorkFlowy part 1.

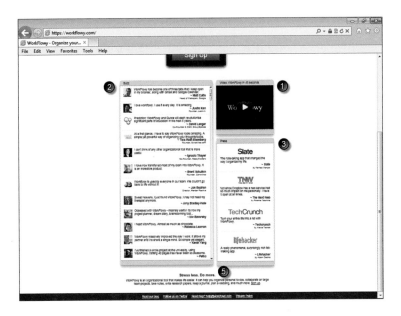

FIGURE 18.3

WorkFlowy part 2.

Let's look at the page more closely:

1. **Banner Headline and Graphic**

   Content components: Sign-up graphic, marketing video, and headline with benefit statement. The entire area above the fold is taken up by the sign-up box and the headline, which is the product name and the benefit, "Organize your brain." If you need a quick intro, Workflowy provides one that is approximately 45 seconds. The image they are trying to portray is simple, easy, and quick, just like the product.

2. **Social Proof**

   Content components: A "Twitter-style" stream on the left side that shows you a collection of comments made on social platforms. Note the company mentions each person's name and picture and goes on to show you the positive comments made.

3. **Authority (Credibility)**

   Content components: Press mentions with logos. On the right you see major tech press outlets saying that the application is "life changing." These reviews are impressive and assign credibility.

4. **Reciprocity**

   Content components: Text you don't see is the key here. Note that you see nothing about pricing. You are asked to sign up, but not asked for a credit card. The implication is that there is a free version, which is always a great quid pro quo.

5. **WIIFM**

   Content components: A headline that gives a benefit, "Stress less. Do more." Under that you see suggestions for the application's use and get a total of six suggestions, including keeping a journal and planning a wedding.

6. **CTA**

   Content components: A big Sign Up button, located at the bottom of the sign-up box—you can't miss it.

SEOMOZ

SEOmoz (http://www.seomoz.org/freetrial) is a set of applications related to SEO management and deployment. I chose this landing page (see Figure 18.4) because it does a good job of handling the amount of information you need in order to persuade a buyer to sign up for a free trial with a credit card in a two-step process.

FIGURE 18.4

SEOmoz page 1.

Let's look at the page more closely:

1. **Banner Headline and Graphic**

   Content components: A blue background to highlight the main area. The headline starts with the authority factor by mentioning that it is "the #1 SEO software" and using the word "free." SEOMOZ uses a graphic robot character for appeal. The headline under SEOmoz Pro also says "free," as does the CTA banner.

2.   Social Proof

Content components: A long rectangular box on the right side of the page that says that you should join over 10,000 other companies (no risk here). Also at the bottom you see a headline that says, "Voted Best SEO Tool 2010."

3.   Authority (Credibility)

Content components: A list of actual names of the major, well-respected companies that have used the product. Note the effective use of their logos as a visual column.

4.   Reciprocity

Content components: A callout box in the center of the page with the 2x2 configuration. They tell you what you are getting—a platform, experts, tools, and a big community, with a picture for each. They repeat these in the center for the WIIFM (see the next item).

5.   WIIFM

Content components: Three major subheads that call out the benefits (shown below the headline). The benefits are listed as "dozens of SEO tools & valuable SEO resources," a mention of the big community, and an easily managed web application.

6.   CTA

Content components: A big banner that says, "Try It Free Today." To reduce risk, again they mention canceling anytime with no contract.

Figure 18.5 shows the second page of the sign-up.

The second page is devoted to the sign-up. They begin the sign-up process with the headline "3 Easy Steps" to prepare the user to follow an orderly process.

Note the following:

Graphic: Note that the graphic robot is now standing in an "at your service" pose.

Authority: Because of the credit card requirement, the company shows the VeriSign logo to reduce concern about security.

Reciprocity: A big graphic button signals that you can do a live chat if you have any questions.

CTA: The big CTA button is at the bottom. In the billing section is a repeat of the conditions under which you will be charged.

FIGURE 18.5

SEOmoz page 2.

TOOLS TO CONSIDER

Unbounce: http://unbounce.com/. Creates landing pages.

KickoffLabs: http://www.kickofflabs.com. Creates landing pages and emails.

Google Content experiments: Works with your Google analytics account and has built-in A/B testing. http://support.google.com/analytics/bin/answer.py?hl=en&answer=1745147

Optimizely: https://www.optimizely.com/. Has built-in A/B testing.

Pippity: http://pippity.com/. Pop-ups that capture leads from your website.

ClickTale: http://www.clicktale.com/. Heat maps that tell you how your customer interacts with your landing page.

InstaPage: http://www.instapage.com. It says it self-optimizes landing pages.

IDEAS TO USE

Use visuals along with your text to engage customers on all your landing pages.

Make sure you know the value to you and your customer if someone clicks on your CTA on your landing page.

Check your landing pages against the Idea Map below to make sure you've covered all your bases.

IDEA MAP

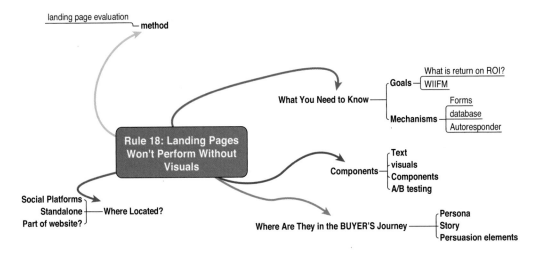

Idea Map for Rule 18

ENDNOTE

"Life on Demand: Participant Behavior and Social Engagement." Performics Study. ROI Research, 2012.

Part IV

TACTICS FOR SOCIAL MEDIA PLATFORMS

VISUALS ARE A MUST ON FACEBOOK

In this rule, we look at how visuals affect your impact on Facebook and determine how to increase their use. Paying attention to how visuals supplement your content will bring results.

WHAT YOU NEED TO KNOW

In October of 2012, Facebook reportedly reached one billion users. If you are asking yourself why you need a presence on this social media platform, that's probably the answer: one billion users. But don't get me wrong. Just because Facebook has one in seven of the people on earth using the platform doesn't mean you will easily build a big audience.

Facebook users are there for a multitude of reasons. Your ability to draw an audience on Facebook will tie back to your ability to connect with your customers on any online channel. If you aren't forming relationships with them on other channels, you aren't even on their radar screen.

It is most likely that the people who seek you out on Facebook are already familiar with your company or have done business with you. For this reason, they might take a look at what you're doing on Facebook. So you have to give them a reason to engage with you on Facebook. You won't succeed if you don't have the right complement of visuals and entertainment and information to engage your specific audience.

TIP Habit plays an important role in capturing audience attention from social media platforms. You don't want to try to create a new habit for your audience. What you want to do is capitalize on a habit they already have. Because such a large audience already has the habit of interacting on Facebook, you want to add interacting with you to that habit.

Here are some of the questions you need to ask yourself about Facebook:

- **What are my goals for this platform?**

  You need to know why you are on Facebook. It can't just be because everyone else is. I've heard clients say they need to be there because of a competitor. Then they squander their time and money as a copycat brand.

  If you get into the mind of your customer (see Rule 2, "Personas Are the Key to Understanding Your Customers"), you'll know what they want from you on this platform.

- **Who is on Facebook?**

  According to a report by Royal Pingdom,

  - 60% of Facebook users are female; 40% are male.

  - The average age of a Facebook user is 40.5.

- **What kind of value can I be sure to deliver?**

  Value and engagement should always be uppermost in your mind. Your management might feel comfortable being able to tell their stockholders they are on Facebook, but if they get little or no return, that sentiment will fade quickly. Be able to give answers about what value your customers are getting and how that translates into revenue for your company.

- **What resources will I employ?**

  To do a thorough job on Facebook, you will need resources. These include all the same resources that you need for any social media platform—creation of content, people to monitor the site, people to respond to customers, and so on. You have to make a commitment to Facebook to give it the time and attention it requires. The good news is that you might be able to repurpose content you already have. (See Rules 7 and 26.)

> Your ability to draw an audience on Facebook will tie back to your ability to connect with your customers on any online channel. If you aren't forming relationships with them on other channels, you aren't even on their radar screen.

- **How will I know I've engaged my audience?**

    This is an important question. See what metrics you can use to quantify your results. ROI is a continuing problem for everyone dealing with social media, but try to at least tie metrics to a specific campaign or test. Use short-term examples with specifics rather than sweeping global answers.

- **Do I know the real value of a "like"?**

    The impact of a like is not easy to assess. That's because there are several different places where likes show up and it's hard to determine what kind of action they spur. All likes aren't created equal.

    For example, you can like a business page, as shown in Figure 19.1.

— Like page

FIGURE 19.1

Lifehacker on Facebook.

You can like the content shared in a status update.

You can like content you find on a blog or website and share that on Facebook.

WHAT'S A LIKE WORTH, ANYWAY?

As with any tactic, marketers are eager to be able to determine the real value of a Facebook like to the brand's earned media value. Several studies have been done to see if a monetary value could be placed on it. Syncapse (www.syncapse.com), a social media company that specializes in community building and digital measurement, undertook such a study with Hotspex in June of 2010 called "The Value of a Facebook Fan: An empirical review." They examined six measures they believe contribute to the value of a Facebook fan: product spending; loyalty; propensity to recommend; brand affinity; media value; and acquisition cost. One of the studies concluded that if an influencer designated as a "social media producer" made a recommendation it generated $22.93 in earned media value.

Businesses on Facebook need to tolerate a bit of uncertainty about the direct value their likes produce. Obviously, you want the value of being where the action is and gaining recognition among your target audience. Just don't convince yourself that you are getting direct revenue unless you can track it with a promotion or an ad. That doesn't mean it doesn't have value. It just means you can't track all of it with an analytics program.

TIP   Don't overlook the value of social proof as we have discussed throughout this book. If users on Facebook see that you have lots of likes for your page and content, it can strengthen their initial interest in you.

Just because you can't trace back each like doesn't mean that you can't get valuable feedback. For example, Macy's, the venerable old retailer, gives a lot of weight to the likes they get from their customers.

According to an article filed by the Associated Press, Macy's polled their Facebook users during the 2011 holiday season about the colors they wanted for their holiday jeans. The majority of likes went to neon colors over pastels. They therefore went with bright colors and were able to satisfy their customers. This translated into holiday revenue and helped them avoid a mistake.

A MORE VISUAL FACEBOOK

The year 2012 saw the blossoming of a new, more visual version of Facebook. This was evidenced by the following:

- The restructuring of pages to display a visual timeline rather than a text stream

- The purchase of Instagram in April

When the timeline was introduced, it received mixed reviews. Some users were fearful about the amount of content it exposed. But almost no one criticized the look of the timeline itself.

So what is the timeline all about? According to Facebook, the timeline is a "collection of the photos, stories, and experiences that tell your story."

Facebook's goal for the timeline was to bring to the top the content users engaged with most. Clearly, this means that visual content of any kind will frequently be seen. Facebook users love to post photos. Gizmodo reports that 300 million photos are uploaded on Facebook every day. But do these photos have an impact?

According to HubSpot, Facebook photos received 53% more likes than posts without photos. So should you consider adding more visuals to your social media content? Yes, that's a winning strategy. (See the section "A Visual Marketing Method" later in this chapter for tactics on adding visuals to the timeline.)

TIP It's important to be aware that as of January of 2013, Facebook has adopted a new policy for Facebook covers and sponsored stories. It says that no picture can have more than 20% text. Photos that are not sponsored are not affected. This means that all the photos you take to share with friends and family are not subject to this policy.

To understand where visuals fit in, first let's briefly look at the two types of pages you can create on Facebook:

- **Personal profile:** The personal profile is where your timeline is displayed and where you connect with friends and family. Only they can see your activity, which means that you must approve each viewer. This is different from a business page that must be created separately. If you are a solopreneur or want to be known as one person rather than a business entity, you might use a personal page to connect with a select group.

- **Business page:** If you are a business and you want a Facebook presence, you can create a business page. The key thing about a business page versus a personal page is that you don't have to approve each person. Anyone can like your page to view the content. Obviously, this is an advantage when you want to get the widest distribution of your content. This is why businesses are always coming up with new ways to get you to like their content.

To create a page, the first thing you need to do is choose what type of page you want to create, as shown in Figure 19.2. Then simply follow the instructions.

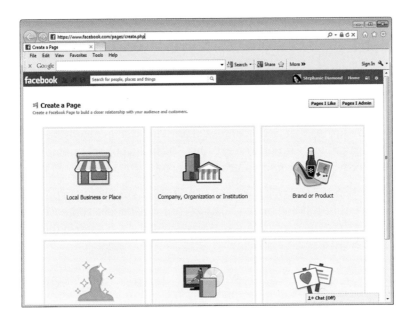

FIGURE 19.2

Page to "create a page" on Facebook.

 # A VISUAL MARKETING METHOD

Method: Looking at the visuals you can add on Facebook to capture more of your audience's attention. As with the other social platforms we discuss in this book, my focus is primarily on the visual content. Let's look at the places on Facebook where you can have an impact with visuals.

The profile of a personal or business page has several image components: the cover photo, the profile photo, and the album photo. This section looks at each of these.

The cover photo is the large photo at the top of the timeline, as shown in Figure 19.3. Facebook recommends that the image size be 851 pixels by 315 pixels.

Cover photo

FIGURE 19.3

Facebook's own Facebook page.

The cover photo is the largest real estate you get for an image, and it's the first thing a user sees when he comes to your page. It's like the banner you have on your website. For this reason you want to give some real thought to what your cover photo says about you or your business.

You don't want a blatant promotion or image that says, "I'm selling you something!" (Facebook restricts this kind of photo.) You should select something that shows that you are interested in communicating with your customers.

It's a good idea to look at what other brands have done and see what response they got. For example, consider a small business like BarkBox.com, shown in Figure 19.4, that shows their Pup of the Week on the cover photo. BarkBox offers a service that sends you a monthly goodie box for your dog. By showing the dogs of the owners they send boxes to, they enable you to get to know who is in their community.

Or take the example of a big brand like Volvo that positions its car in front of a river, as shown in Figure 19.5. The image implies that you can have an adventure in their car. Notice it doesn't show the car sticker on the window or a salesman eager to sell you one.

FIGURE 19.4

BarkBox on Facebook.

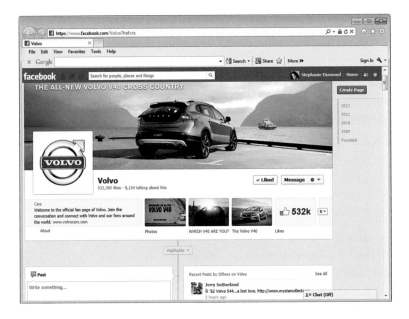

FIGURE 19.5

Volvo Cross V40.

Think about how you can inspire your customers and use that as the jumping-off point for your image. If you need some help with your cover images, here are some tools you can consider:

- Pagemodo: http://pagemodo.com. Easy-to-use free tool to help you create a photo cover (see Figure 19.6).

FIGURE 19.6

Pagemodo.

- InstaCover (see Figure 19.7): http://insta-cover.com/. Create a Facebook cover with Instagram.

In addition to cover photos, you can also use a profile photo. Facebook recommends that this image be 125 pixels by 125 pixels. The profile photo can be your logo, if a business, or your portrait. Some people have gotten creative and tied the profile photo into the larger cover photo. Figure 19.8 shows one from Martha Stewart Living that uses Martha's photo and a colorful image.

FIGURE 19.7

Insta-cover.

Profile photo

FIGURE 19.8.

Martha Stewart on Facebook.

Finally, the photo album is where you have the opportunity to start building relationships with images. The idea is to start to build stories about your company supported by images. You want to have a narrative that people can pick up on. Remember that storytelling is about action (see Rule 3, "Social Media Is Storytelling, So Tell Stories"). If nothing happens, it's not a story. You need to make your pictures follow a larger storyline. Then you need to repeat that storyline with different types of multimedia content. This is key! You need to repeat ideas so that people remember them. Think about how you want your customer to fill in this sentence:

"This is the company that _____." Here are some ways this sentence is answered in the marketplace:

- **Amazon:** This is the company that has one-click ordering.

- **Zappos:** This is the company that has free shipping and returns.

- **Apple:** This is the company that has products with amazing design.

Notice that I picked big companies. It's no accident that you have their idea firmly in your mind. One reason for this is that they have been around long enough for you to see their branding many times.

It has been shown that people need to see something at least seven times before they remember it. Smaller companies can achieve brand recognition by remembering to show their brand as often as they can on as many channels as they can.

Think about how you want to build the ongoing narrative about your company and what will support it. Here are some ideas to consider:

- **Dedication to customer service:** Photos of your staff in your offices serving customers with stories about how they saved the day. Post video testimonials of happy customers with some larger point you are making about your company.

- **Interest in training customers:** Photos of a training event where your staff is working with a customer. Post about training you provide and have plenty of free training they can download.

- **Focus on design:** Photos of your influencers wearing, eating, or working with something you produce. Let them say what they like about the design. Think about the photos you already have and add text to give them context.

To enhance your photos, here are some tools from the Facebook App Center that you might want to consider:

- **Muzy:** This tool helps you create collages and interesting displays that can instantly be posted.

- **PhotoMania:** This is a photo editor with lots of interesting features. You can use this to apply filters to your photos if you are not using Instagram.

You can find both tools at the link shown in Figure 19.9.

FIGURE 19.9

Photo apps on Facebook.

IDEAS TO USE

You know intuitively that images enhance content on any social media platform, but take note of the fact that Facebook redesigned their pages to be more visual and purchased Instagram. Obviously, they are betting on the power of the image. You should, too.

Just because you can't track your ROI in the same way you track other marketing tactics doesn't mean that it doesn't exist. There are lots of benefits that being on social media confers to brands that can't be tracked with an analytics program. Just be sure to have a strategy and tactics planned, and then monitor what's happening so that you learn what works for your company.

Tell your company story using the image placement that Facebook has designed—use the cover photo, the profile photo, and the photo album.

IDEA MAP

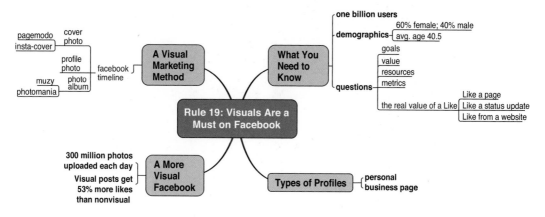

Idea Map for Rule 19

ENDNOTES

Syncapse and Hotspex, "The Value of a Facebook Fan: An empirical review," June, 2010 http://www.syncapse.com/category/white-papers/

Chan, Casey. "What Facebook Deals with Everyday." Gizmodo, August 2012. http://gizmodo.com/5937143/what-facebook-deals-with-everyday-27-billion-likes-300-million-photos-uploaded-and-500-terabytes-of-data.

Choi, Candice, and Christina Rexrode. "Facebook Users Hit 'Like,' Stores Jump into Action." Associated Press, December 18, 2012. http://news.yahoo.com/facebook-users-hit-stores-jump-action-162256521--finance.html

Corliss, Rebecca. "Photos on Facebook Generate 53% More Likes Than the Average Post" Nov 15, 2012 HubSpot. http://blog.hubspot.com/blog/tabid/6307/bid/33800/photos-on-facebook-generate-53-more-likes-than-the-average-post-new-data?source=Blog_Email_%5bPhotos%20on%20Facebook%20G%5d.

"Social Network Demographics in 2012." Royal Pingdom. http://royal.pingdom.com/2012/08/21/report-social-network-demographics-in-2012.

USE TWITTER TO LINK TO VISUALS

In Rule 20, we look at how Twitter has evolved from a platform that allowed only 140-character messages to a more visual site that allows you to view photos from within the site without using a third-party service.

WHAT YOU NEED TO KNOW

Twitter has enabled a global public conversation in real time. Everyone who wants to voice an opinion can do so using a smartphone or another digital device. Major world events are played out right on Twitter. It is storytelling at its most potent. With Twitter you can do the following:

- Get breaking news

- Find out what people around the world are thinking and doing

- Share links to interesting information

- Display photos related to your business

- Hold conversations with like-minded people

- Conduct a conference using a predesignated hashtag

- Provide a link to sign up for a newsletter

- Offer a promotion or discount via a special link

- Display a photo of a customer using your product
- Find influencers and those already talking about the brand

Twitter has grown in 2012 more than any of the other social networks, according to Ignite Social Media's infographic "The Current State of Social Networks." Reports put users at around 500 million but there is some question as to how many of those are active. Needless to say, it's a powerful platform that you as a social media marketer can't afford to ignore. It's been said that if Twitter were a country, it would be the 12th largest in the world.

Who are Twitter users? According to the September 13, 2012, Pew Internet Study, "Photos and Video as Social Currency Online," Twitter users in the online adult population are

> Almost equally divided between men and women
>
> More likely to have higher incomes
>
> Likely to have at least some college education

So what are people tweeting? According to the infographic "A Day in the Life of Twitter," created by Diffbot.com, the top five things shared on Twitter are

> Images: 36%
>
> Articles: 16%
>
> Videos: 9%
>
> Products: 8%
>
> Front page 7%

Previously, links to images were just that—links. But interestingly, in keeping with the current trends, Twitter has gotten more visual in 2012. The company introduced several features that demonstrate its acknowledgment that visuals are an integral part of social media.

Several media pundits suggest that they are trying to keep up with Instagram. Clearly, whatever the motive, they are moving in a visually oriented direction.

To understand how Twitter has enhanced the handling of photos and images, let's look at Twitter's basic structure, as shown in Figure 20.1.

- **Profile:** In your Twitter Profile you have a brief description, a profile picture, and link to a dedicated landing page or your website.
- **Followers:** This is the number of people who have chosen to follow you.

> Reports put users at around 500 million but there is some question as to how many of those are active. Needless to say, it's a powerful platform that you as a social media marketer can't afford to ignore.

- **Tweet:** This is the single container where your 140-character message resides.
- **Hashtag:** This tag with a "#" sign lets people search and find tweets on that topic.

FIGURE 20.1

The Today Show Australia on Facebook.

These are the basics units. The following sections show how Twitter has modified the use of images to make a more visual display. You'll want to take advantage of these additions so that you are using the full power of visual messages.

A MORE VISUAL TWITTER

Previously, when you composed a tweet, you could add *links* to photos, videos, or other sites. To insert pictures, you had to use a third-party service such as Twitpic, Yfrog, or Flickr.

Starting in the spring of 2012, Twitter has made several visual changes, including these:

- **The capability to upload pictures directly to Twitter:** The service added the capability to upload pictures directly to Twitter so that they can be viewed from within the tweet. In Figure 20.2 you can see the View Photo link. The format of the image can be .jpg, .gif, or .png and it can be no larger than 3MB.

View photo

FIGURE 20.2

National Geographic on Facebook.

When you click on the link, you see the photo below the Tweet, along with the number of retweets and favorites (see Figure 20.3).

Photo link
click

FIGURE 20.3

Photo below the tweet.

- **A new header design:** Twitter instituted a new header design that gives your profile more of a Facebook style (see Figure 20.1). You see a profile picture used as the background to the text content of the profile.

  To upload a new header, follow the link https://twitter.com/settings/profile and choose Change Header, as shown in Figure 20.4. Twitter recommends that an image have the dimensions 1252×626.

Change header

FIGURE 20.4

Change header on Twitter.

 TIP   For more information from Twitter on creating your header design, check out https://support.twitter.com/articles/127871#. You might have to experiment to get your header's design just the way you want it.

- **A display of top images and videos:** The visuals displayed when you search are also enhanced. You see the matching images and video displayed above the search results. In Figure 20.5 you see a search for "#dog" that yields some great photos above the tweets. Previously, these images were displayed to the left of the tweets and were less prominent. Also displayed are videos that match the hashtag.

Search hashtag dog

FIGURE 20.5

Search for #dog.

- **A background image that is controllable:** Twitter revised the way the background image is placed so that you can position it using your cursor to look the way you want it. This helps make the display more cohesive.

- **Twitter mobile apps:** In an effort to help the iPad version catch up to the iPhone and Android versions, Twitter updated its iPad app in September of 2012. It too is more visual. When tweets are displayed that have photos in them, the photos pop open immediately without your having to click for them. Your profile picture is backed with a new solid-color background and images are bigger when you click on them. All in all, a better visual experience.

So what does all this mean for your social media account on Twitter? In a nutshell it gives you more branding space. You can more easily incorporate product visuals, team photos, and anything else that will alert your readers to your branding and the qualities you want them to remember.

You need to make sure that you have carefully thought through how you want to represent yourself. You can see that the trend is to have more visual space. If you haven't nailed down your visual content strategy, you are not going to gain the kind of attention you want. Now that it's easier for people to access photos, they are more likely to look at them. If yours are subpar, they will send the message that your company doesn't care.

In the section "A Visual Marketing Method," we look at how Southwest Air handles its Twitter account.

"TWITTERIZE YOURSELF"

Various companies have created lots of clever tools with visual applications just for fun. You might be interested in checking out one created by Visual.ly (http://visual.ly/), a firm that creates data visualizations and infographics for online companies. I mention it here because you can create a visual avatar from your Twitter profile. It's called "Twitterize Yourself" and it can be created with just a few clicks. First, you can choose to either "Twitterize" your own profile or compare yourself to another Twitter profile. Then you choose from custom options like gender and hair color, as shown in Figure 20.6, and then click the Generate Infographic button. This app is another example of how images can be used to get attention for your company.

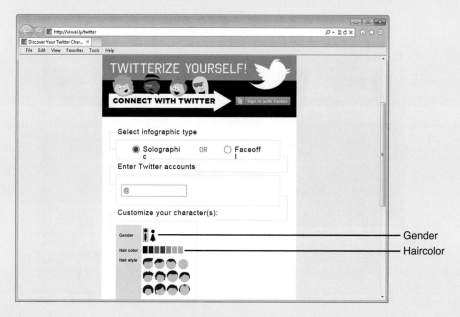

FIGURE 20.6

Create an avatar for yourself.

TOOLS TO CONSIDER

There are lots of tools created for Twitter. If you'd like some free tools that focus on visuals, following are some to consider:

- **ThingLink** (http://www.thinglink.com/): If you love images, you'll want to try this application. It enables you to make any image an interactive one. What that means is that, using the ThingLink application, you can embed all kinds of multimedia links right into the image. You can get creative and link to music, video, your online store, social media sites, maps, and so on.

  For example, you can take an image you have modified and upload it to Twitter. In Figure 20.7 you can see what Fiat has done with a photo of one of its car models. If you roll over the car image as shown in this figure, you see several embedded links, including one to Fiat's online store.

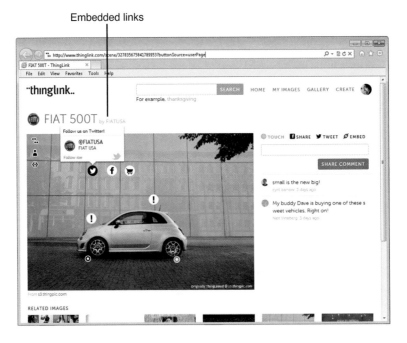

FIGURE 20.7

Fiat on Thinglink.

  You can also link to their page on Facebook or anything else that is applicable. This is a great way to pack a lot of information into one image. And because it's novel, you are more likely to get people to explore all the links.

- **Mentionmapp** (http://mentionmapp.com): Type in search terms, brand names, or other terms, and a mind map–style result is returned. You see a great visual display of people who have mentioned you and their most important followers (see Figure 20.8). It's a great way to see what's being said about you and who those people influence.

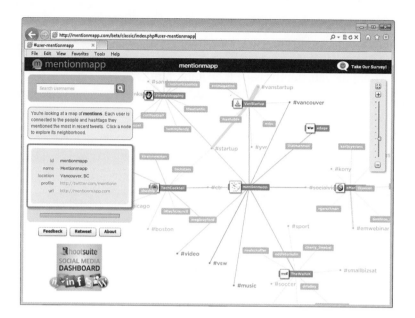

FIGURE 20.8
Mentionmapp's visual map.

- **Twitonomy** (http://twitonomy.com/): This app shows analytics in visual form. Two features that are helpful are a pie chart and thumbnails of people you interact with.

- **TweetStats** (http://tweetstats.com): This app gives you a quick graph of tweets per month and hour. It shows you a timeline and also gives you reply stats.

- **Followerwonk** (https://followerwonk.com/): This app does a good job of helping you drill down and get to know your followers and influencers.

 A VISUAL MARKETING METHOD

Method: Let's look at a brand on Twitter that has over one million followers—Southwest Air—and see what "Takeaways" we find.

Follow the numbers on Figure 20.9 to see our analysis.

1. **Strategy:** Notice that SA has chosen to keep its customer service separate from this account. A notice above the account says, "We will not address specific Customer Service issues on this site." In addition, they put a direct link in their business account header that takes you to a help page with contact information. This decision makes perfect sense because the magnitude of questions would obliterate the conversation. On the other hand, you know that they are interested in serving you because they put the link right in the header.

Takeaway: You have to decide how you will handle your customer service with regard to Twitter. Some companies have a separate account, some abstain and hope for the best, and others handle it right in their main account. Obviously, you need to decide what is right for you, but the issue is an important one. If you ignore it, the customers will decide. If you choose the wrong method, they'll let you know that, too.

FIGURE 20.9

Southwest Airlines on Twitter.

2. **Branding:** In the header text, Southwest Air uses the tagline "The LUV Airline" in keeping with its overall branding. (The company launched from Love Field in Dallas in 1971.) The company has converted to a Twitter business account and has chosen to show one of its planes as the header design. The header is colorful and clean and easy to understand at a glance. SA also has "verified" its account (see the check mark next to the name) to show that it is the official account of the airlines and not an imposter.

Takeaway: It's obvious that branding is a key component of anything you do on social media platforms. There should be one consistent message that you modify to suit the platform. You wouldn't communicate the message the same way on LinkedIn as you would on Twitter. But there needs to be consistency in the overall tone and content.

3. **Community building with quality images:** Southwest Air includes images that show a wide range of activities: celebrities at airport sites, interns training for service, people enjoying a concert they sponsored, and so on. The goal is to let you know that the airline is out in the community interacting with customers.

   Takeaway: There are two components to this. One is the connection your company has with your community. The other is documenting that activity. If you don't show what you are doing, very few people will know about it. If you start the ball rolling and show pictures of people, they will join in and document their experiences. That is the goal of photo sharing.

4. **Choice of content:** Southwest Air tweets a variety of content, all designed to show that the company has value to its customers. It includes such things as recipes during holidays, pictures of children enjoying flights, and notices about current delays.

   Takeaway: Do you have your messaging for each of your social media platforms nailed down? If you don't, you can't decide which content to choose. Make that a priority.

5. **Connecting with other channels:** On the blog (see Figure 20.10) SA puts its Twitter feed right up front to show that it connects with its customers. It is called the "'Southwest Social Stream."

FIGURE 20.10

Southwest blog.

Takeaway: It can be a good idea to put your Twitter feed on your blog or website. The idea is to show action and community. If you want to encourage others to follow you on Twitter, you need to make it easy and entertaining. It also helps with social proof for other customers to see the number of Twitter followers you have.

IDEAS TO USE

Twitter has become more visual in 2012 so you need to step up your game. Over 36% of content shared on the network is photos and 9% is videos. Think through your visual strategy and test what works for each social media platform.

Be sure to switch over your Twitter account to a business account, verify it, and carefully choose your header image. It's also important to decide which link you will choose to put in the header. It's likely that people will click it first.

There is an abundance of third-party tools that have been developed for Twitter. Decide what you want to accomplish and then pick the tools that work. Don't get overwhelmed. You don't need to try everything right away. As the account grows, you can determine which analytics you need. Pick one to start.

IDEA MAP

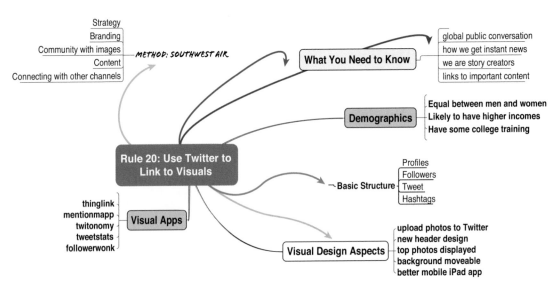

Idea Map for Rule 20

ENDNOTES

"A Day in the Life." Diffbot.com, Infographic. http://mashable.com/2012/08/16/twitter-day-in-the-life-infographic/

Rainie, Lee, Joanna Brenner, and Kristen Purcell. "Photos and Videos as Social Currency Online." Pew Internet and American Life Project, September 12, 2012. http://pewinternet.org/Reports/2012/Online-Pictures.aspx.

Tobin, Jim. "Social Networks Winners and Losers 2012." August 2, 2012. http://www.ignitesocialmedia.com/social-networks/2012-social-networks-winners-and-losers/.vvvvvv

INSTAGRAM IS GREAT FOR QUICK VISUALS FROM YOUR MOBILE

In Rule 21, we look at how Instagram can be used to enhance your social media communications. We give you examples and tell you why the examples work so that you can apply them to your site.

WHAT YOU NEED TO KNOW

Instagram launched in 2010 and it exploded onto the social media scene. It is popular with celebrities and politicians, and as of July 2012 it had 80 million users and was bought by Facebook. In September of 2012, Mark Zuckerberg reported that Instagram was up to 100 million users. As with Pinterest, its amazing growth is attributed to the capability to easily share photos on social platforms.

Want to know the demographics of Instagram users? According to a global study done by InSites Consulting called "Social Media Around the World, 2012" Instagram users are

- 43% male and 57% female

- 49% between the ages of 25 and 34

In addition, according to Mike Isaac in his September 2012 *Wall Street Journal* article, "Instagram Beat Twitter in Daily Mobile Users for the First Time, Data

Says," smartphone owners spent more time on Instagram in August 2012 than they did on Twitter. They also returned more frequently and stayed longer.

Instagram can be accessed from the Web or your mobile device.

Here are some quick facts to get you started:

- You can easily share your photos to Facebook, Twitter, Flickr, Tumblr, Posterous, Foursquare, or an email address right from the application.

- The main feature that makes Instagram so popular is the built-in filter tool: It enables users to add visual filters so that they can put their own stamp on their pictures. The reason filters are so popular is that most people don't have photography skills. Add to this the fact that smartphone cameras don't have professional settings. By adding filters that users can easily apply, Instagram differentiated itself from other photo apps. By applying the filters, users get a better photo than the one they would have taken without them.

The filters as of this writing include the following:

Normal	Toaster
Amaro	Brannan
Rise	Inkwell
Hudson	Walden
X-Pro II	Hefe
Sierra	Valencia
Lo-Fi	Nashville
Earlybird	1977
Sutro	Kelvin

There's no magic way to know which filter to select. Until you get familiar with the filters, the best way to select one is to try several and pick the one that fits the mood. Experiment and you'll develop favorites.

TIP   Another popular feature built into Instagram is the "tilt-shift" feature. When you apply it, you change the viewer's perception of the depth of the scene. To try it, go to the Choose button and click on the droplet icon.

- To view photos on Instagram, you can go to several sites that let you search and view the photos. These sites include Pinstagram, Statigram.com, and Webstagram.com.

  For example, on Pinstagram the photos are available for searching, as shown in Figure 21.1. Remember to put the URL from the site on your website or blog so that others can view your collection of photos.

FIGURE 21.1

Food photos on Instagram.

- To preserve your photos, you can download them from the site. One easy way to do that is to use Instaport.me, as shown in Figure 21.2.

 TIP If for some reason you want to make your photos private, you need to go to the setting under Privacy in the Profile tab; otherwise, your photos will be public. Of course, you can't be followed if you do this.

- Instagram photos are square. Don't forget to consider how the borders will look.

FIGURE 21.2

Instaport.

A WORD ABOUT CAPTIONS

Before we move on to looking at why you want to use Instagram for social media marketing, I want to again highlight the importance of using captions with photos. (For more on this topic, see the section "The Power of Visuals and Text" in Rule 1, "Recognize the Power of Visual Persuasion.")

People are hard-wired to read captions. If they read nothing else, they'll look at your picture and caption before leaving your page. If you write an interesting caption, you might entice readers to stay longer and read the rest of the text. Instagram has a built-in caption feature. It's incredibly easy to add one. Don't ever send out a photo without a caption.

Of course, the key is to figure out which caption has the most impact. Start by looking at why you chose to send that specific photo. The caption should support that purpose. In addition, if you can, add humor, which will make an impression. Just be careful that you don't say something offensive. Humor is tricky.

WHY INSTAGRAM IS GREAT FOR SOCIAL MEDIA

Now let's look at what makes this an important social media tool. If you look at the list, you'll notice that Instagram has most of the same features that popular social networks have. The added value is that you can share photos on most of the other major social networks. Here are some of the features you'll find on Instagram that are popular on most other social media platforms:

- **Profile:** You can create your own profile with a picture. Make the most of your profile to attract new viewers. Think carefully about what name you'll give the account.

- **Followers:** People can follow your brand and you can follow other people's brands. Find businesses you admire and follow them to see how they use Instagram. Go to Find Friends in Settings.

- **Hashtags:** Create a hashtag for your business; also check out what others are using so that you can interest new followers with similar interests. Creating your own hashtags is best because your community can find you more easily.

- **Push notifications:** These notifications let you know who is looking at or commenting on your photos. Obviously, you want to be aware of the engagement followers have with your pictures. To set it up, you have to go to the Settings page on either your iPhone or your Android phone.

- **Connect to social networks:** As mentioned previously, you can easily share pictures by setting up a connection between Instagram and your social networks.

- **Location tags:** Marketers can include the location of the photo when they upload it so that it can be identified with a particular area and searched using that location. This is important for local businesses.

  In relation to location, Instagram has a feature that is called an Instameet, which can be found at http://instagram.meetup.com/ and is shown in Figure 21.3. If you want to create a meetup with your followers, this is an easy way to get started.

- **Photo Contests:** An obvious outgrowth of sharing pictures is the idea of a photo contest. Use a tool like Statigr.am, as shown in Figure 21.4, to set up and run the contest.

A company that uses Statigr.am repeatedly to launch contests on Instagram is the Swatch watch company. One example is the contest in 2012 to mark the introduction of their Gents Lacquered Collection of watches. Users were asked to take pictures of the world's most inspirational streets and post them using the hashtag #FromTheStreets. Three winners had their pictures displayed on Swatch's Facebook, Tumblr, and Twitter accounts and received a Gents Lacquered watch. The contest brought in many entries and the watches received the publicity they were seeking.

TIP Would you like to use filters on all your photos, not just the ones on Instagram? You might want to consider using Perfect Effects: http://www.ononesoftware.com/products/perfect-effects-free/.

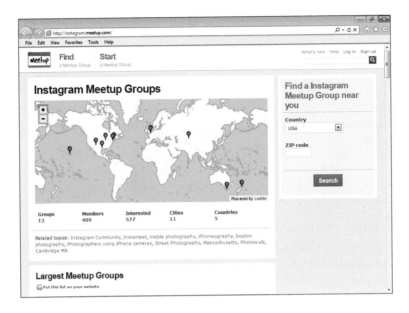

FIGURE 21.3

Instagram Meetup Groups.

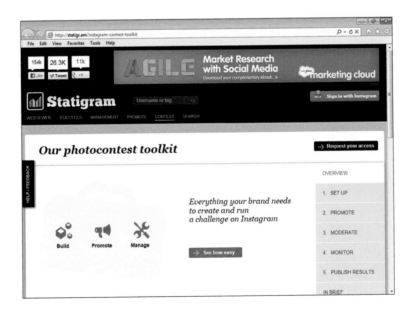

FIGURE 21.4

Toolkit to set up contest on Statigr.am.

WHAT SHOULD YOU PROMOTE?

It's probably not that hard for you to come up with a few pictures to promote your business. The hard part is continuing to come up with interesting photos on a regular basis. If you attract followers and then post infrequently, you will lose them quickly. Users look for novelty.

To help you think about what you can do to keep the photos coming, here are some options:

- **Product photos:** Not only should you show your products, but you can also to try get users to send in photos using the products. This has the added benefit of encouraging users to identify with your product. People who like to be tagged will also send photos.

- **Customer testimonials:** Customer testimonials are similar to the previous idea but have the added benefit of providing captions with pictures that you can use on your website and other channels.

- **Events:** Be sure to capture pictures of your staff and customers at conferences and major events. Whenever possible, you want to add social proof that people are interested in your products. Ask your customers who attended to share their photos.

- **Training pictures:** Whenever you hold training sessions or product tests, ask for permission to take photos of users and encourage them to take their own.

- **Team photos:** Take photos of your staff in action. It helps humanize your company and lets customers know that real people are hard at work serving them.

 ## A VISUAL MARKETING METHOD

Method: How to determine what can be done with Instagram by looking at some good examples.

As you can imagine, making it easy to tell photo stories on social platforms opens up a big opportunity for businesses to promote and share. Because the content can be shared so many different ways, some companies have gotten creative about how they use Instagram.

We're going to look at how a retailer uses it, how designers are using it, and how a medical facility uses it to educate people around the world. Let's start with the retailer.

Luxury retailer Bergdorf Goodman (BG) is a New York store located on Fifth Avenue. It has been in business for

As you can imagine, making it easy to tell photo stories on social platforms opens up a big opportunity for businesses to promote and share. Because the content can be shared so many different ways, companies have gotten creative about how they use it.

111 years and attracts shoppers to visit from around the world. BG created an Instagram application to show off its shoe collection on a map called "Bergdorf Shoes About Town."

To make it easy to show you the moving parts, I marked up the map as shown in Figure 21.5 using the "landing page template" we used in Rule 18, "Landing Pages Won't Perform Well Without Visuals."

FIGURE 21.5

Bergdorf Goodman on Instagram.

What's great about this Instagram shoe display map is that the methods BG employs are subtle and appropriate for this type of application. They created it to let shoppers share their favorite shoe pictures, but it does much more in an unobtrusive way. Let's look at what they did to be successful. Note the Figure numbers correspond to the numbered list below:

1. **Banner Headline and Graphic**

   Content components: This is a great example of storytelling. The graphics are modern and fun. The map is done in a playful way instead of being realistic. It shows pictures of shoes taken by BG shoppers around the country. It's not limited to New York shoppers. So if you click on a picture on the map, you can find pictures of shoes taken almost anywhere.

   In addition, the store adds its own pictures of shoes to make sure that the site has lots of pictures they want to promote. They also provide a scale tool so that you can focus in and find your location if you are local.

2. **Social Proof**

   Content components: The shoe picture links around the map show that lots of shoppers have participated and are interested in showing off their stylish shoes. In addition, the scrolling shoe bar demonstrates the volume of pictures.

3. **Authority (Credibility)**

   Content components: Notice that they have included sharing links for Facebook, Google+, and Twitter showing you that they are present on these sites and that people are interested in them.

   There is also an Info link in the upper-right corner that tells you what hashtag to use (#BGShoes) and says that the "shoes are the stars here, so pose them well." It also says, "Don't forget to visit the newly expanded shoe salon at Bergdorf Goodman." This lets you know that they are thriving and expanding, as well as encouraging you to buy shoes.

4. **Reciprocity** and

5. **WIIFM**

   Content components: If you look up at the left corner, you'll notice a check box that enables you to see only shoes the store has posted, ensuring that you are looking at "approved" photos. They also let you know that you are able to upload and show off pictures of your own shoes. If you want to link to this site from your own, you demonstrate that you are part of the action.

6. **Call to action (CTA)**

   Content components: In the left corner there is text that says, "Like what you see?" It displays a phone number and a link to the online store, making it easy for you to browse and shop at the online store or contact it.

USING INSTAGRAM PHOTOS AS PART OF A BUSINESS PLAN

Printstagram is an example of a company that has folded Instagram into its business model. Users submit photos from Instagram to be made into a variety of items, as shown in Figure 21.6. You can create calendars, memory boxes of photos, photo squares, stickers, minibooks, tiny books, and posters.

I selected this company to showcase because it takes the byproduct of another company and uses it as the centerpiece of their own business. Of course, the downside is that if the platform folded, they would be out of business.

In this case, that's not a big risk because Facebook bought the application in 2012. It is unlikely that they will dismantle it any time soon.

FIGURE 21.6

Printstagram.

Think about how your company might use the byproduct of another to develop a product or service that can generate revenue. It doesn't have to be at the heart of the business. It can be an adjunct that fits well with your other products.

A HEALTHCARE COMPANY EDUCATING PEOPLE AROUND THE WORLD

Swedish Health Care is a nonprofit medical association based in Seattle, Washington. Patient Eleanor Day, age 79, consented to allow her cochlear implant operation to be documented step by step, as shown in Figure 21.7.

The medical group did a masterful job of using all the social media available to live stream and Instagram the procedure and the activation of her implant. When you look at how all the information was broadcast online, you see how widely the information was disseminated:

- On social platforms such as Instagram, Twitter, YouTube, Storify, Twitpic, and Facebook.

  Check out this link on Storify that shows all content from the different social platforms: http://storify.com/swedish/live-tweeted-and-instagrammed-cochlear-implant-hea.

- In magazines, such as *Forbes* and *The Atlantic*.

- On news sites, such as Mashable and the local news channel.

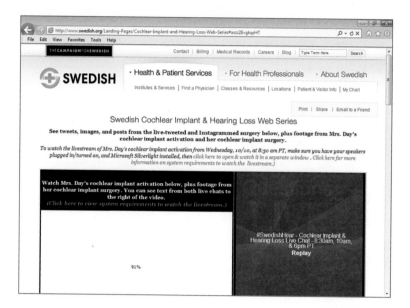

FIGURE 21.7

Swedish Health Care.

Swedish Health Care was able to educate millions of people around the world about what steps are taken when a patient opts for a cochlear implant. They used video, audio, photos, and text to tell a story with great impact. In fact, they developed a web training series as a companion to the online broadcast

Think about the vast reach of this one story. You don't need to have something serious to catch the eye of the media, however. In addition to the gravitas of this situation is the notion that you can watch any story unfold, meet the people involved, and learn how everything is done.

Your social community can be taken behind the scenes just like this one was. For example, you can show the play-by-play of your team getting ready for a conference, showing the sales collateral as it's created, and conclude with the conference participants reacting to your products.

IDEAS TO USE

Instagram makes it easy to tell stories and engage readers with visuals. Take advantage of this easy opportunity.

See whether you can find a way to incorporate Instagram photos into an application that lets your community share photos with each other to make an impact.

Your readers are anxious to share their professional-looking photos taken with Instagram. Figure out all the ways you can get them to photograph themselves with your product.

 IDEA MAP

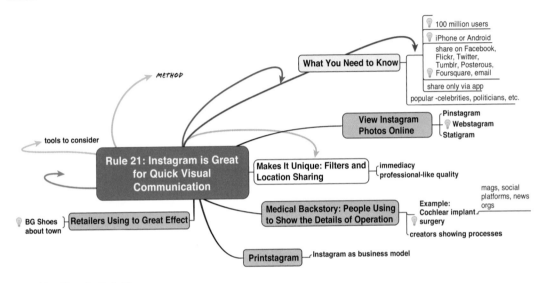

Idea Map for Rule 21

ENDNOTES

To get more Instagram business tips, check out the blog devoted to this topic at http://business.instagram.com/blog/.

InSites Consulting. "Social Media Around the World 2012." http://www.slideshare.net/InSitesConsulting/social-media-around-the-world-2012-by-insites-consulting

USE PINTEREST AS A MARKETING HUB

In Rule 22, we look at the current use of Pinterest and its potential for social media 'marketers. We also help you evaluate its potential for creating your own marketing hub by looking at a successful retailer with millions of Pinterest followers.

WHAT YOU NEED TO KNOW

If you are a woman in the U.S. who is personally active on social media, chances are you are already on Pinterest. If you are a social media marketer, you should definitely learn more about its potential. It has all the components needed to make it a powerful marketing hub.

It is imperative to cover Pinterest in this book because the focus is on the use of visuals. If our sole focus was on the aesthetics of the images, there would be plenty to talk about; but the more important discussion here is about how this platform can impact your revenue numbers. For you as a social media marketer, that's your main concern.

Think about Pinterest as your interactive social media billboard. No matter what online content you have residing elsewhere, you can aggregate it in a meaningful way and display it on Pinterest. Marketers are starting to experiment, so don't be left out. The sooner you start using it, the sooner you will see how to make it valuable for your brand.

TIP   An important concept to note right upfront about Pinterest is that you have a potential built-in "sales force" of people who might choose to repin your content, thus amplifying it and making it easier for others to find it. Pinterest is gaining new users every day. It's a great distribution vehicle for content.

So let's focus on the basics and then move on to looking at the impact it can have on your bottom line. Pinterest is one of the fastest-growing social media channels in history.

A Compete.com's "Online Shopper Intelligence Survey" found the following:

- Pinterest had 20 million unique visitors daily as of May 2012.

- Twenty-five percent of social media users report spending more time on Pinterest, thus taking time away from other social networks, most of all Facebook.

- Twenty-five percent of users bought a product after seeing it on Pinterest.

- The most popular category on Pinterest is food (57% of users).

When we look at the demographics of Pinterest, they are equally interesting. According to the infographic "Pinterestingly Enough" by BuzzReferrals.com in their blog post "Pinning Down the Interest in Pinterest," Pinterest users are predominantly female (80%), 50% have children, and 55% are between the ages of 35 and 54. That's a potent demographic!

But don't be put off if Pinterest's current demographic is not your exact target market. Pinterest, by virtue of its capability to manage content, advertise, and show off your brand in its best light, is a potential marketing powerhouse.

One of the most interesting facts about the aforementioned infographic is that Pinterest pins have strong referral value. Customers who come from Pinterest referrals are 10% more likely to make a purchase than customers from other social networks. Have I got your attention now?

So what quick facts should you know about using Pinterest? Here are a few:

- Pinterest is free to join, and you can set up pins and boards free. You can join by connecting from your Facebook or Twitter account or by using your email address.

- Creating a pin is easy. You can put a "bookmarklet" into your browser after you sign up and click it when you find

> But don't be put off if Pinterest's current demographic is not your exact target market. Pinterest, by virtue of its capability to manage content, advertise, and show off your brand in its best light, is a potential marketing powerhouse.

an image you want to pin. To get the bookmarklet button, click on the About link, as shown in Figure 22.1, and select Pin It Button.

FIGURE 22.1

About link for bookmarklet.

- The image you choose to pin from a web page needs to be at least 80×80 pixels; otherwise, you won't be able to pin it. If you are struggling to pin a thumbnail, now you know why it doesn't work.

PINTEREST FOR BUSINESS

In November of 2012, Pinterest launched its business accounts. Previously, they requested that no commercial activity take place on personal sites. This change was inevitable because businesses were already using the platform and requesting more business-related tools.

To convert the account from personal to business involves a quick set of clicks. The new account doesn't look any different, but allows brands to use their brand name instead of a first and last name. You can also put your URL link right in your profile by verifying your site. That can encourage traffic to your site.

TIP   If you have a personal account, it's a good idea to switch over to a business account now so that you can use the widgets that are immediately available. Most important, you will want to be ready to use the tools that will be added shortly to support business accounts.

To learn more about the specifics of the business account, go to http://business.pinterest. com/. There, you will see case studies, tools, brand guidelines, and information about buttons and widgets.

Two new widgets are available:

- **Profile widget:** Displays 30 of your latest pins on your sites.

- **Board widget:** Displays 30 of your favorite board's latest pins. This is helpful for marketers because it enables you to concentrate on a specific topic that you want to promote. For example, if you have a board specifically for infographics, it will make a nice display for your website.

In addition, when you convert your account (or sign up for the first time) as a business account, you are given three of what Pinterest calls "secret boards." Secret boards are ones that are invisible to other pinners. Only you and the people you authorize can see the board and add pins to it. This is a useful collaboration and planning tool. You can add project document visuals and stage designs internally. You can either prepare a board and make it visible when it's ready or keep it private and use it for teamwork.

THE "EYES" HAVE IT

Two articles published on Mashable by Sara Kessler, called "Eyes on Pinterest: How People Look at your Boards" and "How Pinterest Changed Website Design Forever," talk about the effect that Pinterest is having on the way we look at images on the Web. A study done by the EyeTrackShop.com found that Pinterest boards are looked at differently from websites. Instead of moving our eyes from left to right as we do on websites, we look at pinboards from the top down, as shown in Figure 22.2. This can have a lasting impact on the use of visuals on the Web as more people become accustomed to viewing images in this configuration. You'll also see more websites begin to use this visual layout.

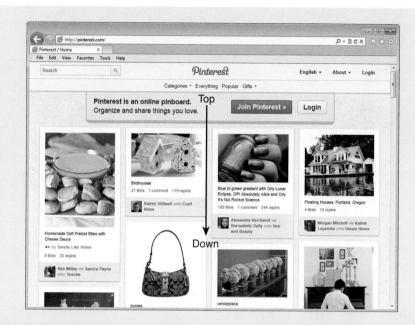

FIGURE 22.2
Eyes move top down.

VALUE TO YOUR CUSTOMERS WHEN YOU USE PINTEREST

Pinterest is structured so that as you develop your boards, you are providing your customers with some inherent benefits. These include the ability to do the following:

- **Show aspects of your products and services:** The key to marketing with Pinterest is to grab your customer's attention from within Pinterest itself. As with any page on the Web, the fewer clicks someone needs to take to find something interesting, the more likely it is that he will stay and explore.

    That's one reason why Pinterest designers allow each board to feature one pin image that is larger and serves as a billboard for the others. An interesting graphic whets your appetite for others on the board and encourages you to explore.

    One way to show more information about your site before customers link to your site is to use a tool like Snapito. Snapito, as shown in Figure 22.3, takes a shot of your website and turns it into a pin. In this way, you preview what your viewer will see on your website. You can use a board to pin product pages and other important content that the viewer can see right in Pinterest.

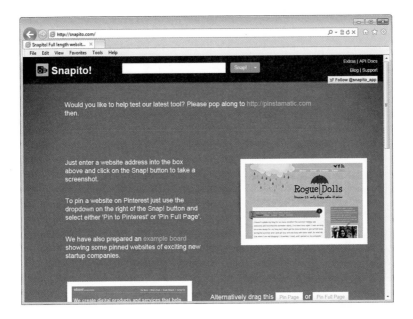

FIGURE 22.3

Snapito.

- **Help your target audience find you:** Getting found is the key to being successful on the Web. By pinning interesting graphics about your brand right in Pinterest where they can easily be found, you are going to reach people who might not find you any other way.

- **Get people to endorse your products:** Pinterest by its very nature demonstrates the interest others have in your product. When people repin your content, they are implicitly endorsing it. You didn't force them. They make that decision by virtue of their interest. If several people repin your content, it can become viral on Pinterest. You can also repin those again to encourage visibility.

TIP   Just remember that although people are electing to repin an image, this doesn't mean they will automatically do anything beyond that. You need to determine whether a repin translates into a purchase, a visit to your website, a sign-up for a newsletter, or some other show of interest. That's where the real value is.

WHAT MAKES PINTEREST GREAT FOR SOCIAL MEDIA?

Next, let's look at why Pinterest is an important social media channel. Pinterest is a distribution channel for content of all kinds that are attached to an image. It has several key elements for social media marketers that give it a great deal of potential beyond its current usage.

Here are several reasons why:

- **Huge built-in audience available to find your content:** You can create boards (think billboards) of content to display to anyone who follows you. In turn, those following can repin the content to their followers. As a marketer, you are being given digital space to display content of all kinds. (Think about it like an aggregated visual Facebook feed or enhanced Twitter stream.) Add this to the fact that you have a huge audience of Pinterest users. This gives you the potential to be seen by millions.

- **Content management:** You can also think of Pinterest as a content management tool. Because you can link all kinds of content, you can create boards with podcasts, videos, and any other media that you have. This becomes an easy way to put like content together (on a specific topic) and display it.

  If warranted, you can create a board that displays a podcast series or a video series hosted on YouTube along with tutorials and case studies. Create boards that your salespeople can send to potential customers to educate them. Pretend that you are making a physical corkboard to bring to your customer's location. Include everything you would want a potential customer to know. Make it as visual as you can, assuming that people would be walking by. (Obviously, you won't disclose any proprietary information.)

- **Multimedia formats:** You can have links to articles, product photos and information, webinars, "kits," case studies, white papers, blog posts, videos, audios, tools, infographics, and maps. Try to use as many as you can to keep it interesting.

- **Selling:** A potent way to use Pinterest is to take advantage of the fact that it is not perceived as a hard sell if you link to a product for sale. However, if you are selling retail products such as food, jewelry, or clothing, you might elect to use the gift-pricing scenario that puts a price right in the pin. Here are your choices:

  Gifts: You can put items on your board and list them for sale in the gifts section by putting either a dollar sign ($) or an English pound sign (£) and a price in the pin info. The pin will then be added directly to the Gift Section, as shown in Figure 22.4, and the price will be on a banner on the left side of the pin.

Prices ranges

FIGURE 22.4

Gift Section in Pinterest.

Links: You can link back from a pin directly to a product or service for sale. This has the added benefit of enabling you to track a customer's visit on your site with your analytics program.

You need to assess the value of putting prices right in the pin. Look at what other users are doing. If you see that other sellers in your category are not putting prices right on the pin, you might want to avoid doing it yourself. Try it and see.

- **Connections to/from other social media platforms:** Pinterest can link both to and from social media. Click on your account link and choose Setting. You can set up a link to Facebook, the Facebook timeline, and Twitter.

- **Apps for iPhone and Android:** Pinterest has apps for the iPhone, Android, and the Kindle Fire. Customers can view your boards while on the go and follow your link to purchase a product. What makes it so appealing is that a pin or a board doesn't look like a standard advertisement. The iPad is especially conducive to pinning while people are away from their computer because the display is very close to a desktop experience. The apps are available for download here: http://Apps.Pinterest.com.

- **Capability to collaborate on boards:** Pinterest allows you to authorize multiple pinners to work on the same board, as shown in Figure 22.5. This board is a collaboration among several inbound marketing companies that joined forces to provide the best information they could find online. The information pinned to the board is considered more valuable because of the diversity of knowledge and the quality. Do you have someone you want to partner with to create a board?

FIGURE 22.5

Inbound Marketing Gold Dust.

- **Sharing buttons:** Pinterest has easy sharing buttons that you can put on your website or other third-party site:

  Pin items from your website: You can place a Pin It button next to any content that is right for pinning.

  Follow Me on Pinterest button: As shown in Figure 22.6, Williams Sonoma.com, a high-end kitchen goods store, has a Follow Me on Pinterest button positioned at the bottom of their home page to encourage new followers.

Follow me button

FIGURE 22.6

Follow Me on Pinterest button.

TOOLS TO CONSIDER

There are a multitude of great tools available for Pinterest, and new ones are being developed daily. Two that seem particularly useful are Pinstamatic and Pinsearch.

Pinstamatic (http://pinstamatic.com/) is a good, free, all-purpose tool for making boards unique. As shown in Figure 22.7, the icons at the top let you do the following on a board (from left to right):

- **Pin a picture of your website:** This can send traffic to your site by showing a preview.

- **Make a quote pin:** Do you have a quote or saying that you want to use to inspire your viewers? Ask customers to send in quotes of their own and repin the best ones.

- **Put on a sticky note:** Sticky notes always get people's attention. If you have something you want to alert people to, use one on your board.

- **Add a song and an album cover from Spotify:** This is an interesting one. If you can think of a song tie-in to something, pin it to your board using this tool.

- **Pin your Twitter profile:** Want to get more Twitter followers? Create a Twitter profile pin so that pinners can see what your Twitter profile looks like.

- **Make a calendar date pin:** Create a board for an upcoming conference or event and prominently feature the calendar date pin.

- **Pin a map:** Help local customers find you by putting a map pin right on a board.

- **Add captions to photos:** Remember that captions are key to helping photographs be understood.

FIGURE 22.7

Pinstamatic.

These tools are all great additions that will help your boards stand out and also provide helpful content. Can you think of ways to add these to your boards?

Pinsearch (https://chrome.google.com/webstore/detail/pin-search-image-search-o/ okiaciimfpgbpdhnfdllhdkicpmdoakm?hl=en-US#detail/pin-search-image-search-o/ okiaciimfpgbpdhnfdllhdkicpmdoakm?hl=en-US) is a tool for the Chrome browser, as shown in Figure 22.8. When installed, it adds a Search button to your pin when you mouse over it. When you click the Search button, you are shown all similar images on Google. This is a great way to see where your pins are being placed and how the images are being used.

Additional useful Pinterest tools include these:

- **Reachli:** http://www.reachli.com/overview. This tool enables you to track visual content.

- **PinAlert:** http://pinalert.com. This alerts you when someone pins your web content on Pinterest.

- **PinGraphy:** http://pingraphy.com/. This application lets you schedule pins so that you add a steady stream.

- **Pinvolve:** http://www.pinvolve.co. This enables you to put your pins on Facebook.

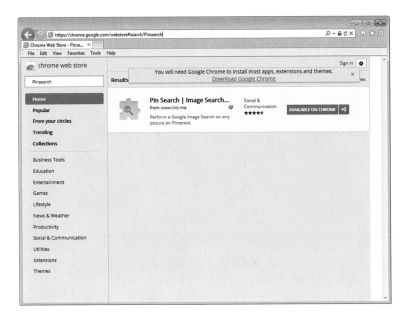

FIGURE 22.8

Pinsearch.

A VISUAL MARKETING METHOD

Method: How to use Pinterest as a marketing hub.

Let's look at what Nordstrom is doing on Pinterest to see how you can use their best marketing ideas to create a hub of your own. We can start by using the company's profile, as shown in Figure 22.9, to examine the anatomy of a Pinterest account.

1. **Profile:** Notice that in the Nordstrom profile description they put their customer service phone number and the names of the staff on the social team. This demonstrates that they want to make it easy for you to contact them with your questions. They also want to convey that they have real people working behind the scenes.

Profile

Search

Followers

FIGURE 22.9

Nordstrom on Pinterest.

2. **Followers:** They currently have more than 3.4 million followers who loyally repin their content.

3. **Search:** If you type "nordstrom" in the Search box and click on Boards, as shown in Figure 22.10, you'll see the huge number of people who have dedicated entire boards to Nordstrom.

Next let's look at the key concepts for Pinterest that retailers like Nordstrom take advantage of:

- **Branding:** Notice that the company's logo is the picture chosen for its profile. This is a logical choice and you would probably use yours or something that denotes the brand.

- **Quality images:** As a retailer, Nordstrom makes it a rule to have high-quality pictures of everything they recommend and sell. This gives them a vast supply of images to use on Pinterest. But the key to making the boards popular is giving them themes that are educational, entertaining, and persuasive. As shown in Figure 22.9, you see such themes as Gift Ideas and Stocking Stuffers.

- **Community Building:** Pinners can also add comments and reuse hashtags on individual pins, as shown in Figure 22.11. Here is a pin with a #boo hashtag to document Boo the dog's visit to Nordstrom, along with comments by pinners.

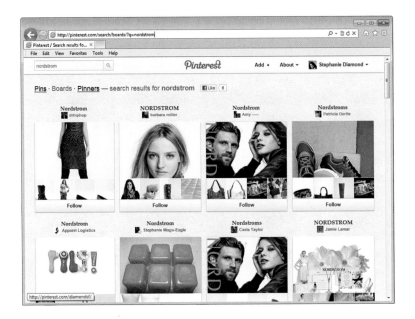

FIGURE 22.10

Search Nordstrom on Pinterest.

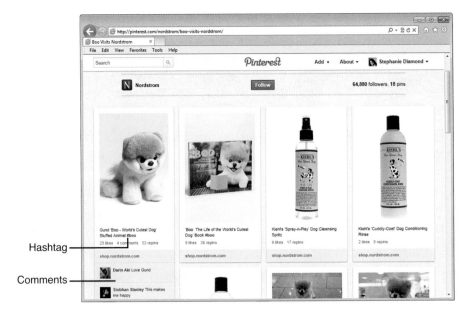

Hashtag

Comments

FIGURE 22.11

Boo visits Nordstrom.

Remember to add hashtags to all your pins and read all your pinners' comments to stay abreast of their interests. By doing this, you see what your community responds to and who the influencers are.

Nordstrom uses the hashtag #NSales on all their sales items. Customers who want to see what's on sale can put the hashtag directly into the search box and see what comes up. See how you can do that with your promotions.

- **Well-thought-out board themes:** It's important to provide a variety of board themes. If you don't entertain your customers, you won't grab their attention. For example, Nordstrom has boards about the following:

  Gift guides

  Trends

  Quotes

  Fashion shows

  Catalog pages

  If you are a company that sells technology, services, or less glamorous commodities, you can still mix up your boards and demonstrate that you have a grasp of the problems your customers face. You'll probably want to take advantage of multimedia like video and podcasts. Nordstrom will probably do more of this in the coming year.

- **Selling:** Nordstrom provides a link back to its online store for every product shown. In this way, it controls the path and ensures that the customer can make an impulse buy for whatever they like. To buy, customers need to register, so this also drives Nordstrom's email list.

- **Apps for iPhone and Android:** Nordstrom has mobile apps so that customers can shop from their smartphones and tablets.

The key to Nordstrom's popularity on Pinterest is that they are dedicated to making it easy for you to view, share, and buy everything they sell. They also provide context so that you can see how the items are used. Don't forget that you want to show your customers using and finding value in your products.

 ## IDEAS TO USE

Be sure to use linking to and from Pinterest as your most valuable asset. By adding your pins to platforms such as Facebook and your website, you amplify the content.

Use multiple formats to engage pinners. The key is to use well-designed graphics to represent the pin. For example, if you have a great podcast, be sure to represent it with a design that adds excitement. Think visual for every link. Take the time to create a graphic if you don't have one and plan to do that for all content that doesn't have any branding. Make the graphics simple but eye-catching.

Be ready to do more with your Pinterest account as the Pinterest for Business offering expands. You'll see great strides made in this next year.

 IDEA MAP

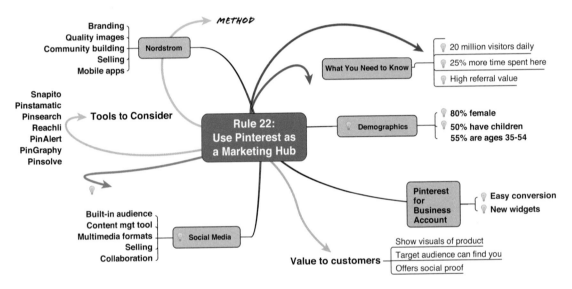

Idea Map for Rule 22

ENDNOTES

Caine, Jason. "Pinning Down the Impact of Pinterest." June 2012. Compete blog. http://blog.compete.com/2012/06/28/pinning-down-the-impact-of-pinterest/.

Kessler, Sarah. "Eyes On Pinterest: How People Look at Your Boards." May, 2012, http://mashable.com/2012/05/29/pinterest-eye-tracking-study/#66227Better-Homes-and-Gardens-Brand-Page.

Kessler, Sarah. "How Pinterest Is Changing Website Design Forever." February, 2012, http://mashable.com/2012/02/07/pinterest-web-design.

Buzz Referrals, "Why the Interest in Pinterest." June. 2012. http://blog.buzzreferrals.com/2012/06/whats-interest-with-pinterest.html.

TUMBLR MAKES IT EASY TO SHARE VISUALS

In Rule 23, we look at Tumblr, a microblogging platform that was created to simplify the sharing of visual content. We also show you some of the creative ways you can approach a Tumblr blog (aka tumblog).

WHAT YOU NEED TO KNOW

When you started blogging, did you wish for a tool that was incredibly easy, was free to set up, and could accept any kind of multimedia content you could throw at it? Welcome to Tumblr!

Tumblr is a free microblogging platform that was launched in 2007. David Karp, the founder of the service, said he created it to help bloggers quickly and easily share visual information.

Unlike a platform like WordPress that encourages long text posts, tumblogs usually focus on visual content. Most of its users post a short comment along with an image or another form of multimedia. The fact that it's free and hosted by Tumblr is another great feature. You can set it up and be ready to post in short order.

In my experience, social media marketers are often afraid to start blogs because of the need to create unending content. They rarely focus on the structural aspects of running a blog. If you have a webmaster, that problem is solved. If you don't, maintaining your blog can be an issue as well. If you haven't

considered Tumblr, maybe you should. It might just be the solution you are looking for.

According to Tumblr's own blog (http://www.tumblr.com/about), 85.7 million blogs and 38.4 billion posts have been created as of December 2012. It continues on an upward trend as users become familiar with its features.

So what are the demographics of Tumblr users? Quantcast reports that as of December 14, 2012, this is the demographic of the Tumblr user:

- Female

- Age 18 to 24 (with a large cohort of users age 25 to 34)

- No children in the household

- Income average $50K

> In my experience, social media marketers are often afraid to start blogs because of the need to create unending content. They rarely focus on the structural aspects of running a blog.

TIP   If this is not your demographic, you should still consider trying Tumblr because you can also use it to showcase your visual content and link to it from your other channels. Magazines such as *National Geographic* (http://nationalgeographicmagazine.tumblr.com/) and *The New Yorker* (http://newyorker.tumblr.com) use their tumblogs that way.

GETTING STARTED WITH A TUMBLOG

When you set up a new blog, you can choose a URL with Tumblr.com in the address, such as http://yourname.tumblr.com/, or you can use a URL of your choosing. To make the blog your own, you'll want to go to your dashboard and click on the Customize tab, as shown in Figure 23.1.

On the dashboard, you can select a theme to personalize your blog. There are free and fee-based themes. It's easy to experiment because you can preview the themes before you select one. Also look at designs posted on the Web that offer you various options. They are inexpensive and easy to set up.

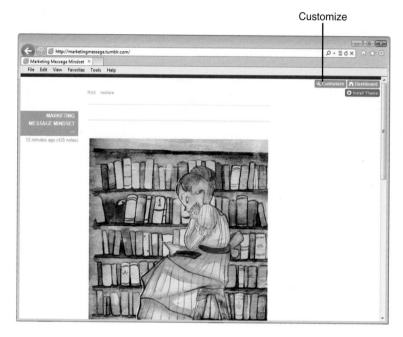

FIGURE 23.1

Customize link on Tumblr. Illustration credit: copyright Rachel Smythe.

BLOG TYPES

Tumblr has two kinds of blogs you can set up. They are called a primary blog and a secondary blog.

- **Primary blog:** The first blog you set up is always designated as your primary blog. It has all the social features, such as follow, like, reply, ask, and submit. You can't make this blog private.

- **Secondary blog:** Subsequent blogs you set up are called secondary blogs and can be made private via password protection. You can also add more users and a group blog. The limitation on a secondary blog is that you can't initiate social functions, such as like, follow, ask, or submit. The secondary blog is used for private groups and multiple users. It is totally separate from a primary blog.

POSTING

The blog post is set up so that you can easily select the content type you want to post. Types of content are text, photo, quote, link, chat, audio, and video (see Figure 23.2).

FIGURE 23.2

Content types. Credit: Pencilfury.

When you click on the content type, you are taken to a post that is configured to accept that content. An example is shown in Figure 23.3. Here, the video icon has been selected.

TIP

Do you want to email something to your tumblog even if you are not in your account? You can do that by using the email address given to you when you signed up. You can find it by going to Settings, clicking on the name of your blog from the list on the left, and scrolling down to "Post by email."

CURATION

Curation is the act of selecting other people's content to highlight and share. As you do so you need to credit the original author. To select content as you surf, you can install the Tumblr bookmarklet by dragging it, as shown in Figure 23.4. Then, whenever you see something you want to share, you can click on the bookmarklet.

FIGURE 23.3

Send fan mail.

FIGURE 23.4

Tumblr bookmarklet.

WHY TUMBLR IS GREAT FOR SOCIAL MEDIA

Tumblr might look deceptively simple. Because it's so easy to use, you might think it doesn't have all the robust tools that other social platforms have. But that's not true. Here are some of the features that make it valuable to you:

- **Built-in audience:** According to comScore, Tumblr reached 26.9 million unique visitors in July of 2012. Those numbers continue to increase.

- **Content management of multimedia:** As we noted previously, you can share most content types online using the built-in sharing mechanism.

- **Links:** There are built-in settings that enable you to automatically post the same content to Facebook and Twitter. Of course, you can also grab those links and place them in emails, and so on.

- **Follow:** If you find other bloggers whose content interests you, you can follow them. You can also be followed, which helps you identify your community.

- **Like:** The ubiquitous Like feature is present on this platform so that you can show your approval.

- **Fan Mail:** This feature has a nice name for a feature that enables you to send messages to other bloggers. You can access the Send Fan Mail button by clicking on the envelope at the top of the dashboard, as shown in Figure 23.5.

FIGURE 23.5

Send Fan Mail button.

- **Ask:** You can enable an ask feature that allows you to answer questions others ask you. You can choose whether to make them public.

- **Reply:** Users can comment if you allow, but you can't comment back.

- **Submit:** If you want to allow other users to submit posts to your blog, you enable this feature. You don't have to publish the submissions if you choose not to.

- **Apps:** Apps are available for your iPhone, iPad, and Android device. They have been beefed up in 2012 to provide a better visual experience.

- **Sharing buttons:** Just like the other social platforms, Tumblr has sharing buttons, as shown in Figure 23.6. You can put them on your other marketing channels to encourage users to spread your content with their community.

FIGURE 23.6

Sharing buttons.

- **Reblogging:** This is the equivalent of retweeting on Twitter. It can help content go viral. Obviously, if you reblog someone's content, that person will be more likely to reblog yours.

ASK DAVID

According to an article in *The New York Times*, David Karp, the founder of Tumblr, gave his top three tips for making your tumblog stand out: (1) Be inventive: He suggests that you look at the tools available on the platform and try to use them in unexpected ways. (2) Give your fans a peek behind the curtain: Most people love to learn about the process behind your finished product. Let them be a fly on the wall. (3) Start a community effort: You can open your blog up to submissions so that others can be a part of your community.

TOOLS TO CONSIDER

Here are two tools that let you extend the functionality of your Tumblr:

- Create polls for your users: http://polldaddy.com/.

- Provide the capability to receive and moderate comments: http://disqus.com/.

A VISUAL MARKETING METHOD

Method: How to evaluate the visual aspects of a tumblog.

Obviously, as with any good blog, you are going to have a strategy. You'll know why you are creating the blog and what value you plan to deliver to your customers. In this section, we are going to focus on some of the visual aspects of the blog to help you consider your options. Let's start by looking at some tumblog examples:

- **Minimal Design:** The Daily Lit uses a minimal design that suits its content perfectly. You'll notice that it displays a poem of Emily Dickinson with no embellishment, as shown in Figure 23.7. Think about your content and decide whether it stands on its own.

- **Simple design:** The Social Business blog by IBM uses a simple yet effective design, as shown in Figure 23.8. The goal of this blog is to impart interesting information.

    Note that below the fold you see additional links to other tumblogs and QR codes for their mobile apps, as shown in Figure 23.9. If you have several discrete types of content that you want to separate into secondary blogs, consider this type of design.

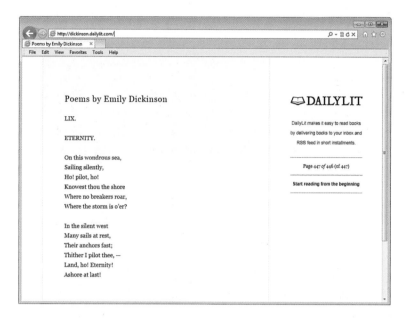

FIGURE 23.7

Daily Lit.

FIGURE 23.8

The Social Business Blog.

Other links to blogs and apps

FIGURE 23.9

Links to mobile apps.

- **Highly designed content:** Beautiful Type is a blog that makes good use of its left navigation, as shown in Figure 23.10. Here the content is the star and the interface supports that. If you have content that is highly designed, think about positioning it this way.

- **Crowdsourced:** Eat, Sleep, Draw is a tumblog that accepts beautiful art submissions from its users, as shown in Figure 23.11. If you have an active user community and the content has visual potential, consider this type of blog.

TIP   Remember to tag your images so that they are searchable. You want them to be found by as many people as possible.

FIGURE 23.10

Beautiful Type.

FIGURE 23.11

Eat, Sleep, Draw.

THEMES/BRANDING

Now that you've looked at some examples, you need to evaluate your own content. Let's do that by looking at social media superstar Gary Vaynerchuk's tumblog, as shown in Figure 23.12.

FIGURE 23.12

Gary Vaynerchuk's Tumblr blog.

- **Interface versus content:** It's helpful to decide beforehand whether you have visual content that needs to be the star. If you intend to have minimal text and mostly multimedia as your content, be sure to select a design that supports visuals like social media.

- **Where you want to display your links:** You'll note that the left column displays all the social media links in one place, as shown in Figure 23.12. This is a great way to direct people's attention to community. In addition, one of Vaynerchuk's goals is to share his information with his community, so he has a Have Me Speak button in the same place.

- **Content variety:** Vaynerchuk has content from all his different social media channels (in a Pinterest-style display), which keeps the blog updated and interesting. It's a good use of a tumblog (see Figure 23.13).

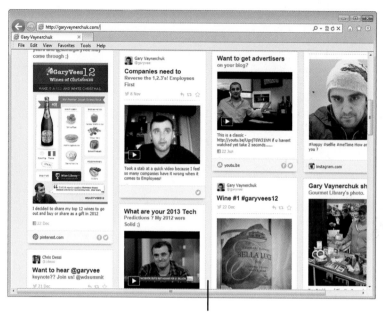

Pinterest Style display

FIGURE 23.13

Content display.

PROMOTING YOUR TUMBLOG

Most people overlook registering their tumblog on Technorati as a way to promote it. Be sure to establish a claim using this link: http://technorati.com/blog-claiming-faq/. The term claim is used to refer to registering your blog.

The Tumblr staff spotlights blogs at this link: http://www.tumblr.com/spotlight/business. You can't make your blog appear there, but if you do your best to create something interesting, you just might land there.

 ## IDEAS TO USE

Creating a blog on Tumblr could be a good fit for you if you have lots of visual content and are looking for an easy way to share it with your community.

Study other tumblogs before you create something yourself. Be sure to look through the themes available and consider a fee-based theme.

Tumblr has a built-in audience that is constantly growing. Don't overlook the opportunity to reach them via a tumblog.

IDEA MAP

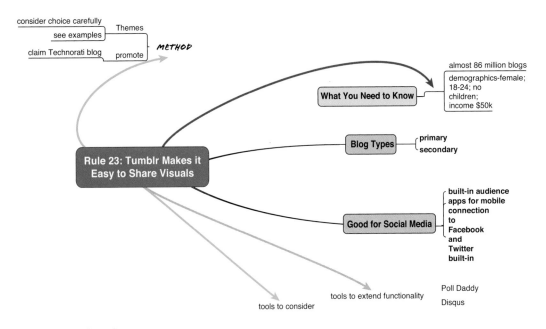

Idea Map for Rule 23

ENDNOTES

Quantcast: http://www.quantcast.com/tumblr.com.

Tumblr blog: http://www.tumblr.com/about.

"Tumblr Tips from Tumblr's Founder." *New York Times Magazine.* The Sixth Floor Blog, July 12, 2012. http://6thfloor.blogs.nytimes.com/2012/07/12/tumblr-tips-from-tumblrs-founder.

If you're looking for more tips about Tumblr, you can check out TumbTips, a blog about Tumblr: http://tumblrtips.com/. Here are some additional tumblogs with interesting designs:

- 52 Weeks of UX: http://52weeksofux.com/.

- Made with Paper: http://madewithpaper.fiftythree.com/.

GOOGLE+ IS MORE VISUAL THAN YOU THINK

In Rule 24, we look at the ways Google+ can be used to increase your visibility among potential customers. We show some examples of ways to improve your profile and add visuals.

WHAT YOU NEED TO KNOW

Your business is probably on Facebook and Twitter and has lots of social media connections. You or your staff spends a great deal of time figuring out how to maximize your efforts. You ask yourself, "Do I really want another social media platform to worry about?" If you're talking about Google+, the answer is yes.

There are several reasons why you should be on Google+ if you are a social media marketer, not the least of which is that it is owned by Google. This means that your profile is tied to Google's dominant search engine.

If you pay attention to search engine optimization (SEO), you will find that you can move your content higher up in the search results as you add content to Google+. This is significant. You know that being found is the single most important factor that affects your business online. If customers can't find you, it doesn't matter what you do.

The good news is that Google+ is easy to use and sets up quickly. Don't pay attention to all the "ghost town" rhetoric. As of September of 2012, Casey Newton, a blogger for CNET, reported that Google+ had 400 million users; 100 million are active. Does this sound like a ghost town to you? Would you consider your website a success if you had 100 million active users? Of course you would!

If you think about Google+ by comparing it to Facebook's numbers (approximately 800 million active users), then you are looking at the wrong end of the telescope. Although you might see some similarities, Goggle+ and Facebook are not competing platforms.

Google+ was created primarily to tie all the Google properties together. Therefore, your social strategy on Google+ should be to optimize all the tools Google+ offers to gain prominence by sharing great content with selected groups of like-minded people.

So who is using Google+? Alissa Skelton on the Mashable blog reports that the typical Google+ users

- Are male (71%)

- Are 24 years old or younger (50%)

- Most commonly are engineers, developers, and designers

> There are several reasons why you should be on Google+ if you are a social media marketer, not the least of which is that it is owned by Google.

Not your demographic? Don't let that worry you. According to a Bright Edge Technologies study, "Tracking Social Adoption and Trends," 75% of the 100 biggest brands are on Google+. Obviously, there are compelling reasons to be there beyond a specific demographic. One good reason: Brands with Google+ pages are showing up higher on the search engine results page(s) (SERP).

GETTING STARTED WITH GOOGLE+

Let's dive in to the features that Google+ offers so that you can see how they differ from those of other social platforms. You need to begin by setting up a Google account if you haven't already done so. You'll find the sign-up at https://accounts.google.com/NewAccount?service=writely and as shown in Figure 24.1.

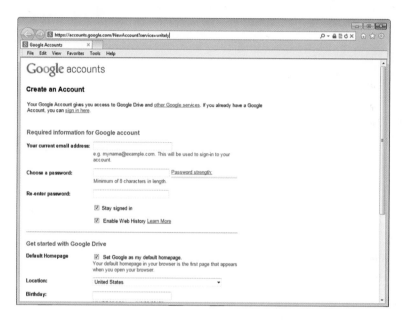

FIGURE 24.1

Google account signup.

After you've created the account, you need to set up a Google+ profile. You do that by creating a personal profile with your own name. If you want to create a business page after you create your personal page, you can leave the first one as a personal profile.

Obviously, if you are a thought leader or have a service business built around your skills, you might want to keep your personal profile. If you have a business that serves local customers or is an active online business, you'll want to create a business page.

To begin, start with the About Page. This is the place where you serve up the content you want your users to see first and the content the search engine should display, as shown in Figure 24.2. (See also Mashable's About page in the section "A Visual Marketing Method.")

FIGURE 24.2

Google+ About Page.

Here are some of the other features you need to know about. Follow the callouts shown in Figure 24.3.

1. **Circles:** This is one of the key differentiating features of Google+. You can create circles that target your personas. For example, after you have identified people who use your product, you can send them a steady stream of "tips and hints." See what feedback you get and develop more content for your other channels that supports their needs.

2. **Share what's new:** This is where you place your status updates. Note that there are links you can click to support the different types of content:

    Photos

    Video

    Events

    Links

    Use those to make updating easy. Remember to add hashtags to help people find your content topics.

3. **Stream:** Below your status update box is the stream of content from those in your circles.

4. **Comments:** You can read other people's comments and add your own.

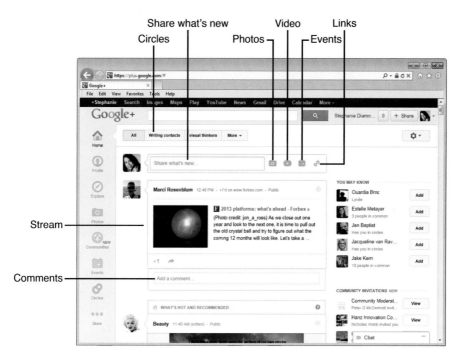

FIGURE 24.3

Anatomy of a Google+ page.

> **TIP**
>
> Remember that all the content you share should be optimized. That means that you want to include your keywords whenever possible. Also, remember to tag your multimedia so that it can be found. In addition, be sure to make all your general content "public." You want the widest possible audience. If you have specific content you are pushing to a particular circle, you can select that circle when you post that content.

WHY GOOGLE+ IS GREAT FOR SOCIAL MEDIA

As we have done with other social platforms, let's look at why Google+ is great for social media marketers:

- **Built-in audience:** The Google+ audience is steadily growing. It pays to get in early and establish yourself.

- **Hangouts:** Want to speak to your customers directly? Host a video chat called a Hangout. Hangouts enable you to see and speak to your customers in real time. You can use Hangouts to test new product ideas, give product demos, and conduct focus groups.

- **Events:** This is a powerful marketing tool that can be integrated with Google+ Hangouts if you need an online venue. You can create a private event that hosts customers and/or staff, or a public event. You can also allow invitees to post their own photos—a great feature.

- **Google Communities:** Google has a feature called Communities. You can create a public or private group and invite like-minded people. The value of creating or joining a community is that you can use all the built-in functions Google+ provides to communicate with your group. You can find more information at http://www.google.com/+/learnmore/communities/.

- **Google+ local:** If you list your business on Google Places, you can be rated by your community. It pays to take the time to create a good profile of your business with photos and useful information.

- **Ripples:** Ripples refer to the number of shares you've gotten on your public content. You can find that activity laid out on a visual chart by looking at the upper-right corner of your post and clicking on the drop-down arrow. From the choice select View Ripples. (Obviously, if the content hasn't been shared, you won't find that option in the list.)

- **Sharing buttons:** Google+ has badges and +1 buttons. The badge can be placed on your website to encourage people to circle you on Google+. The +1 buttons are what followers use to "like" your content. Not only should you encourage people to +1 your content, but you also should do the same for content you admire.

- **Social extensions:** This is a valuable tool for marketers who use Adwords. It lets you integrate your +1 content with Adwords. This way users can see who in their circles has clicked on the ad. You can find more information about this tool at http://services.google.com/fh/files/misc/socialextensions1pgr.pdf.

- **Apps:** Don't forget to download the Google+ app for your Android device, iPhone, or iPad. When you're on the go, you can still be active on Google+ as you are on Facebook and Twitter.

TOOLS TO CONSIDER

There are lots of companies that are creating tools to integrate into Google+. Several of them have fees attached. HootSuite, http://hootsuite.com, has a free version that is now integrated with Google+, so if you already use it, you'll want to add Google+.

A VISUAL MARKETING METHOD

Method: Let's look at Mashable, a very popular brand across all social media, to see how they've specifically grown their followers on Google+.

Mashable is well known for its excellent content and up-to-the-minute news on social media and technology. It was founded by Pete Cashmore in 2005. As of this writing, 1.1 million people have circled Mashable, as shown in Figure 24.4.

FIGURE 24.4

Mashable on Google+.

> **TIP**
>
> Don't feel that because Mashable is a mega-content creator you can't model some of the company's best practices. In this example, the company shows you the types of content you can share when you can choose from an almost limitless supply.

Let's look at the specifics of their brand page and see how you can apply this info to your brand.

- **Visual branding:** As shown in Figure 24.5, Mashable has a really striking image that is displayed across the page. The page uses a logo that stands out and is clear. You also see social proof based on the number of people who have +1ed their content (more than 1.2 million). Think about what graphics you could use to get people's attention and portray what your company is about. You might not have the graphics now, but you can create them specifically for this venue.

Graphic

FIGURE 24.5

Mashable's cover image.

- **About page:** On the About page (see Figure 24.6), Mashable discusses its mission and online reach. Links include the following:

  Email address

  Website

  Google+ URL

  Facebook page

  Twitter account

These show the depth of participation on social media and they point you toward the major channels.

After this page is created, you will see this listing to the right of your Google search page when you search for Mashable, as shown in Figure 24.7. These are the search results when I searched Google+ while displaying my personal results. You can see that the content is pulled from the Google+ profile. Your profile will display the same way so think carefully about what content should go here.

Links

FIGURE 24.6
Mashable's About page.

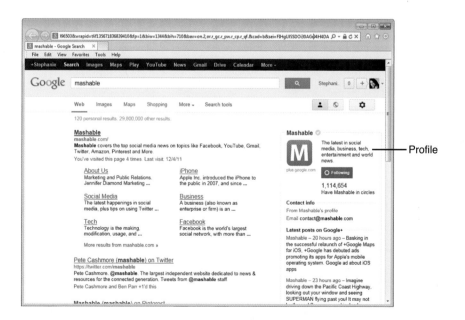

Profile

FIGURE 24.7
Mashable profile display on Google.

- **Photos:** Mashable's photos (see Figure 24.8) cover a range of topics; there are photos from posts, event photos, and Hangout photos. You can see that Mashable has engaged staffers who interact with the community.

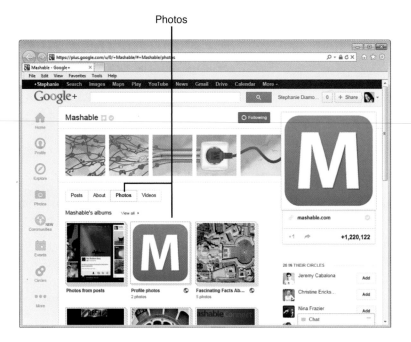

FIGURE 24.8

Mashable photos.

- **Video:** Rather than discussing the videos Mashable displays here, we will discuss Mashable's YouTube channel in Rule 26, "YouTube is *the* Place to View Videos."

As you look at the contents of Mashable's profile, you should note that nothing here is uncommon. The key is providing the kind of content that people want to +1. That should be your goal. If you please your community, no matter how small, you will be successful.

 ## IDEAS TO USE

Don't make the mistake of comparing Google+ to Twitter or Facebook. Your goal on Google+ should be to share content that will help you rise in search results so that you can be found by your community. After they find you, engage them directly by creating targeted circles.

Use the relationship features like Hangouts, Communities, and +1 buttons to build relationships with your audience.

Be aware that using visuals will increase the attention your content will receive. Make it a practice to include them with all your updates.

 ## IDEA MAP

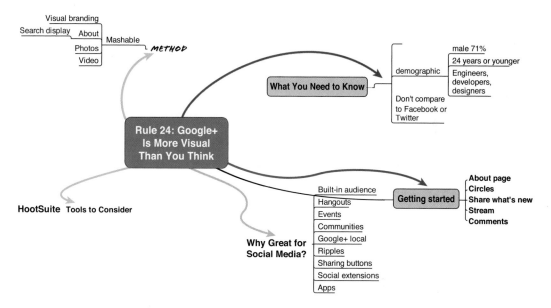

Idea Map for Rule 24

ENDNOTES

Hof, Robert. Forbes, July, 2012. http://www.forbes.com/sites/roberthof/2012/07/31/brands-flock-to-google-but-facebook-twitter-still-more-active/. Cited: BrightEdge SocialShare. "Tracking Social Adoption and Trends." http://www.brightedge.com/social-share-july-2012.

Newton, Casey. "Google+ Signs Up 400 Million Users, with 100 Million Active." CNET blog, September, 2012. http://news.cnet.com/8301-1023_3-57514241-93/google-signs-up-400-million-users-with-100-million-active/.

Skelton, Alissa. "Social Demographics: Who's Using Today's Biggest Networks [INFOGRAPHIC]." March, 2012. http://mashable.com/2012/03/09/social-media-demographics/.

MOBILE APPS PROVIDE VISUAL OPPORTUNITIES

In Rule 25, we look at how mobile apps have impacted visual marketing. We consider what visual tools you can use to be more productive and provide value to your customer.

WHAT YOU NEED TO KNOW

You already know that many of your customers are interacting with you on social media platforms and browsers via mobile. But has that influenced your mobile strategy? You're not alone if you feel you are behind in creating your mobile strategy.

If you are following the path of the majority of major online advertisers, it is likely that your mobile strategy is dictated by your desire to deal with mobile apps rather than your customer's needs. According to internal data reported by Google on its site ThinkWithGoogle.com, 79% of the major online advertisers haven't optimized their websites for mobile.

That's an astounding number. In fact, in this area, it can be easier for smaller companies to compete in the mobile arena because they have more focused content and fewer legacy issues. So how can you change that situation for your company?

Let's start by looking at what constitutes a mobile experience for your customer. From their mobile devices, your customers might use the following:

- **A browser:** A user searches with a browser on a mobile device in the same way he searches on a computer. In some cases the content might be optimized for viewing. A user will decide, based on the ease of use, whether he wants to continue this activity on a mobile device.

- **A mobile app:** A user downloads a mobile app that is customized to view specific content from a mobile device. If you have found that your customer wants to conduct a specific activity relating to your company via a mobile device, consider creating an app.

According to internal data reported by Google on its site ThinkWithGoogle.com, 79% of the major online advertisers haven't optimized their websites for mobile.

To evaluate what you want to do, you need to look back at your personas (Rule 2, "Create Personas to Understand Your Customers") and decide where and how your customers access your content. To further evaluate this question, it is helpful to understand what mobile users prefer to do on apps versus browsers. Then you can determine which of the following you need to do:

- Create a custom app so that customers can access your specific content

- Optimize your site for mobile

- Do nothing (not recommended)

A Yahoo study reported by Dave Chaffey in his article "Understanding Consumer Mobile Usage" on the Smart Insights site, found that when

- Connecting, 69% prefer an app

- Navigating, 65% prefer an app

- Informing, 61% prefer an app

- Managing, 54% prefer an app

- Entertaining, 60% prefer a browser

- Searching, 63% prefer a browser

- Shopping, 73% prefer a browser

Looking at the data, we might conclude that a mobile user prefers to interact with a dedicated app for business activities such as navigating and reading information.

Then, they switch their preference to a browser when it comes to such activities as shopping and entertainment. Remember that this is general data. You should make an investigation that relates directly to your audience before you spend time and resources creating an app.

CAN VISUAL REINVENTION WORK?

Before we look at tools and techniques, let's see how a major brand, *USA Today*, has attempted to revitalize itself by focusing on visuals and creating mobile apps to accommodate its customers.

On the occasion of its 30th anniversary in January 2012, *USA Today* unveiled its newly designed product. Although it is the second-largest newspaper in the country, its revenues have slipped 20% in the past three years.

In the face of falling revenue, management decided to visually reinvent the paper. *USA Today* has always been a visually appealing newspaper, so it's no surprise that it turned to designers to boost circulation. It has also been reported that the paper was particularly interested in enhancing the reading experience on mobile devices. This has been borne out by its attention to mobile apps.

Many have said that the redesign makes the digital version on a browser appear like an iPad app. In Figure 25.1, you see the Tech section of the paper, which has a rectangular border and resembles an iPad app.

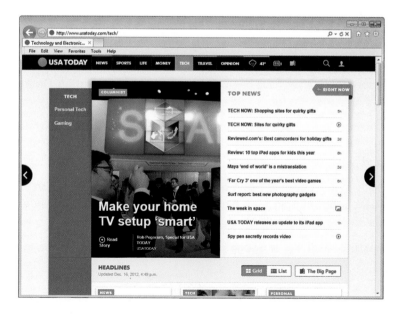

FIGURE 25.1

Tech section.

A feature of the design that is particularly interesting is that you can choose to view your stories in a grid pattern or as a list pattern (see Figure 25.2). This gives the reader a chance to personalize the visuals.

Grid or list view

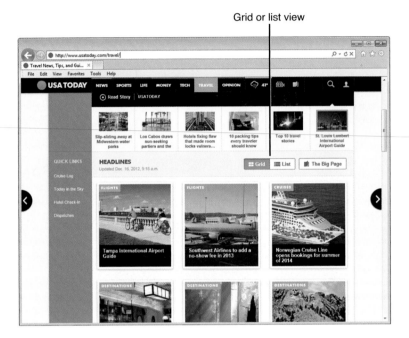

FIGURE 25.2
Display options.

The mobile apps themselves have been given a great deal of attention. Figure 25.3 shows that there are versions for phones, tablets, and Kindle (seven to date).

So why should you care what a newspaper is doing with its visual content? Aren't newspapers on their way out? I included this redesign because it shows you one example of a major brand that is betting that its visual brand is one of its most important assets.

It is likely that you don't have as heavy a burden to revise your identity. But you do need to give it some thought. Ignoring it will hamper your ability to increase revenue as more and more mobile devices go mainstream.

As Eric Schmidt, former head of Google, has said, "Put your best people on mobile."

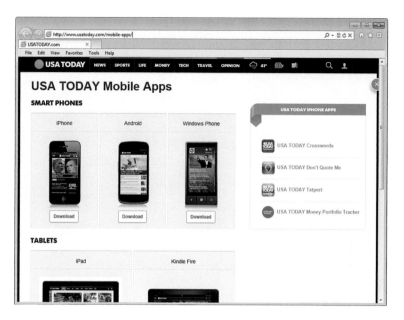

FIGURE 25.3

Mobile apps.

TOOLS TO CONSIDER

As with all the other rules, we're focusing on the visual aspects of our topic, in this case content for mobile. Mobile apps by definition enable you to send content back and forth through email and social networks. I also wanted to focus on mobile apps that assist you and your staff when drawing, brainstorming, or creating images for publication.

I've divided the mobile apps into the following: apps to make you more productive, apps that educate and entertain your audience, and apps that encourage staff collaboration.

MORE PRODUCTIVE

If you are a mobile user, you probably access your email on your mobile phone. But have you considered using visual apps to assist you in being more productive? Following are some apps you might want to consider:

- **Image/Font Tools**

  - **Cropp.me:** http://cropp.me/ (free). This isn't a mobile app; it's a cloud app. But I included it here because it can help you auto-size any image you have to make it shareable with mobile apps.

After you upload an image, all you need to do is select the size you want (see Figure 25.4). When you're happy with the image, you can download it and use it as you like. This is a great tool for nondesigners who need to crop an image to a particular size for social networks or other platforms.

Sizes to choose from

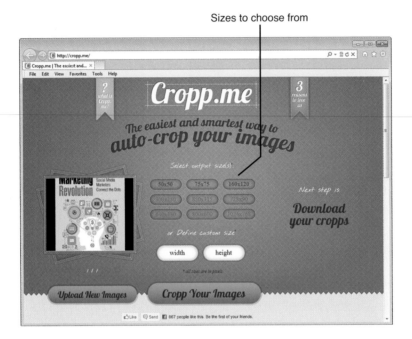

FIGURE 25.4

Cropp.me.

- **Typefaces:** https://itunes.apple.com/us/app/typefaces/id292461457?mt=8 (It's free and available on the iPad). This is a great little utility app that shows you all the fonts on your iPad (see Figure 25.5). If you are creating on the iPad, it's helpful to know which fonts are available to you. This helps spur creativity.

TIP

Some studies indicate that you can be more productive if you use two screens. Although those studies cite larger screens, it might be useful to add another screen using your iPad or Android tablet. iDisplay (http://getidisplay.com/) is an app that turns your tablet into a second screen. It's available for the iPad, Android; fee.

FIGURE 25.5

Typefaces app.

- **Visual Note Taking**

  - **Note Taker HD:** http://notetakerhd.com. (iPad; fee) This application was created by Dan Bricklin, who is often called the "father of the spreadsheet." He created VisiCalc, the first spreadsheet software program, in 1979. Note Taker HD is a robust app that has a host of interesting features. You can draw with your finger or a stylus, as shown in Figure 25.6. It's easy to use and you can create sketchnotes.

  - **Notes Plus:** http://notesplusapp.com. (iPad; fee) This app is a bit more complex to use than Note Taker HD, but it has lots of interesting ways you can make creative handwritten notes (see Figure 25.7).

- **Board Displays**

  - **Springpad:** http://springpad.com (iPad, iPhone and Android; free). Springpad is an application that can be used in various ways to capture notes and photos of items you want to remember. (See the section "A Visual Marketing Method" for a discussion on how to use it.)

  - **Corkulous:** http://www.appigo.com/corkulous (iPhone and iPad; free and fee versions). Corkulous is an app that uses a corkboard as a metaphor, as shown in Figure 25.8. You can put all kinds of content on the board and sort it any way you like. You can create an unlimited number of boards.

FIGURE 25.6

Note Taker HD.

FIGURE 25.7

Notes Plus.

FIGURE 25.8

Corkulous.

- **Drawing**

  - **Paper from FiftyThree:** http://www.fiftythree.com/ (iPad; free). Not surprisingly, this app was named one of the "25 most disruptive apps of 2012" by Business Insider. Most outstanding about it is the beautiful interface and collection of tools you can use to draw and share content (see Figure 25.9). The content is collected in notebooks that make it easy to organize.

  - **Tapose:** http://tapose.com/ (iPad; fee). This app allows for easy mixed content creation in notebooks. You can easily clip multimedia content and position it on notebook pages.

EDUCATE AND ENTERTAIN YOUR CUSTOMERS

We've already discussed creating visual content such as blog posts (Rule 9) and infographics (Rule 14) and using services such as Instagram (Rule 21). In this section, you learn ways of presenting content in a unique way using mobile apps.

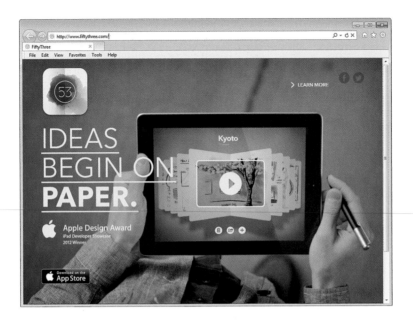

FIGURE 25.9

Paper from FiftyThree.

Here are some apps you can use to present visuals:

- **Flayvr:** http://www.flayvr.com/ (iPad, coming soon to Android; free). Flayvr is a fun tool that lets you group your images and display them on your mobile, as shown in Figure 25.10. This app was also named by Business Insider as "one of the 25 most disruptive apps of 2012." Here are some of its main benefits:

  Organization: What's so unique about this app is that it automatically organizes photos on your mobile that have the same location and timestamp. You can then name the group and remove any photos that don't belong in that group. You can also showcase one photo as you do in Pinterest.

  Elegant display: You can show your photos on your mobile in the tiled display, as shown in Figure 25.10. This can work for product photos and professional events so don't only think about personal photos. This can be especially useful to salespeople and presenters who need to show images at a customer location.

Sharing: To share this photo group, you can send friends to a link created by Flayvr from your favorite social platform. When the user clicks on the link, he is sent to view the photos in a tile view on the Flayvr site. Only the photos you designate are shared. All others remain private.

FIGURE 25.10

Flayvr.

- **Mixel:** http://mixel.cc/ (iPad; free). Want to create unique collages of your photos? Mixel makes it easy to compose interesting arrays of photos to share.

ENCOURAGE STAFF COLLABORATION

Here are some apps that encourage collaboration:

- **Jot Whiteboard:** http://tabularasalabs.com/ (iPad; free and fee versions). We all know the value of a whiteboard to help spur collaboration. This application lets you share the whiteboard in real time. It's easy to use and has a simple interface (see Figure 25.11).

- **GoToMeeting mobile app:** http://m.gotomeeting.com/fec/web_meeting?type=mobile (iPad, iPhone, Android; free). You don't need to pay a subscription to attend a meeting, only to call one—so this app is free to mobile users.

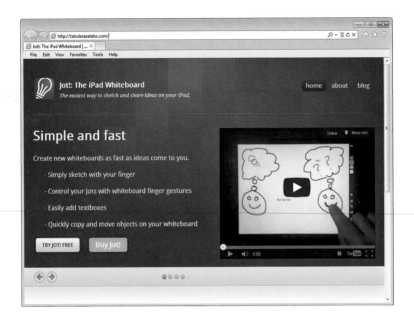

FIGURE 25.11

Jot Whiteboard.

 A VISUAL MARKETING METHOD

Method: Using your camera with Springpad and a Whitelines notebook to capture handwritten notes, bar codes, and other content with your mobile device.

The reason I included this system is that it is an easy-to-use visual system that can make you more productive. In addition, there are things you can do with it to assist your social media marketing efforts.

There are a couple of online services that have created a notebook capture to online system. In Rule 9, "Make Ideas Tangible," I mentioned the system created by Evernote to capture notes from a Moleskine—a very elegant solution. (This notebook can also be used to send items to your Evernote account.)

In this exercise, I want to discuss another system you might want to try. This one was created by using Springpad.com to capture notes from a Whitelines notebook.

Springpad is an application that enables you to create collections of multimedia content from the Web and your camera and load it into notebooks you create, which can be displayed as visual boards similar to what you find on Pinterest.

A whitelines notebook has paper with white lines on a gray background. When you photograph it, the lines disappear—hence the name Whitelines. The notebook that you use for the Springpad system is called Whitelines Link. Here is their website: http://whitelines.se/link/

Now that you know about the application Springpad and the notebook Whitelines, you are ready to get started. First, you need to download the free Springpad app from one of the following locations:

- From the iTunes store: https://itunes.apple.com/se/app/whitelines-link/id552914549?mt=8

- From Google Play: https://play.google.com/store/apps/details?id=com.springpad

Next, you create an account. Your account online is your home base where you will keep your notebooks and boards. You can create as many notebooks as you like and all your mobile devices are synced.

To clip items from the Web, you need to add the Spring It button to your browser. You can find this at http://springpad.com/resources/#clipper.

To give you an idea of what you can capture, Figure 25.12 shows the item types. Click the New Spring button on the left side to see this screen. (In the figure the Spring It button is in the darkened background showing you what it looks like once it's clicked.)

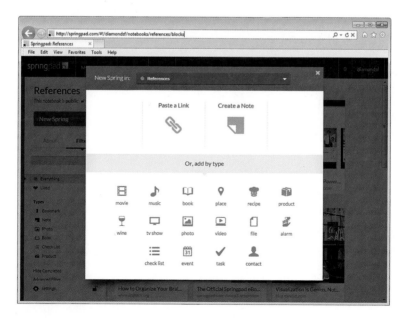

FIGURE 25.12

New Spring.

Now you're ready to collect more content. You can click on the Explore tab at the top of the page to search for suggestions from other users or use the Spring It button as you surf the Web.

Figure 25.13 is an example of my online notebook. You see clippings from the Web, content from people I'm following, and other material including my notes. You can follow other people's notebooks and keep yours private or share them.

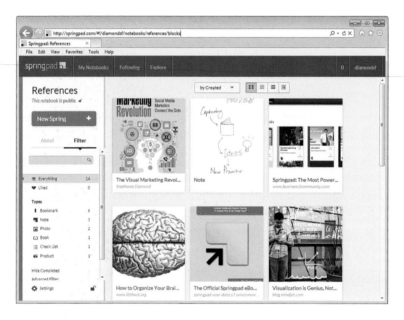

FIGURE 25.13

My online notebook 'References' in Springpad.

CAPTURING YOUR HANDWRITTEN NOTES

To capture a handwritten note in the Whitelines notebook, follow these steps:

1. Take a picture of the note from the mobile link app and be sure to get all four corners of the page. The registration marks in the corner tell the camera to capture everything on the page within those marks.

2. There are three boxes at the bottom of the page to indicate where you want the captured image sent. You can send it to an email address like your personal Springpad account (you can find your Springpad email address in Settings, Services), your Evernote account, or Dropbox. Just click to put an x in the box of your choice.

3. Send the note to the notebook of your choice.

Figure 25.14 shows the note I sent from my phone to my account on Springpad.

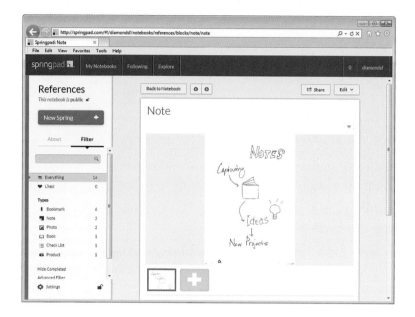

FIGURE 25.14

Note sent from my iPhone.

SOCIAL MEDIA SHARING

Don't limit yourself to creating notebooks that can only be used for just you or your staff. You also can do the following:

- **Create private notebooks to share with customers:** These can include meeting notes, pictures of planning diagrams, or images of product literature. Customers can add to the notebooks with their ideas.

- **Capture bar codes of books:** Make a collection of your books so that you can share them with your audience.

- **Create audio notes:** Give your customers tips or instructions in private notebooks.

- **Take photos of events:** Either share the photos privately with customers or make them public.

- **Share the links:** Use the social-platform links to make your customers aware of new deals and discounts.

- **Let customers share your content:** Put Spring It buttons on your website and blog.

After you get started, you'll probably think of many more ways to market your content using Springpad. Using the notebook helps you capture visual content you create yourself.

TIP   Also, remember that you can take a picture of any notes you write. You don't need a special notebook. You just won't have the automatic send features you get when you use the Whitelines notebook.

IDEAS TO USE

Consider what your audience wants, and create a mobile strategy that will position you to grow as mobile goes mainstream.

Choose mobile apps that use visual techniques like those recommended to increase your staff and your own productivity.

Use mobile apps that enable you to create unique visual displays so that your content can stand out. If you don't, you will look as though you aren't aware of new techniques.

IDEA MAP

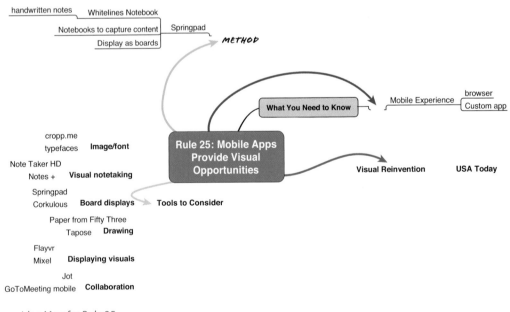

Idea Map for Rule 25

ENDNOTES

Chaffey, Dave. "Understanding Consumer Mobile Usage." Smart Insights, December 2011. http://www.smartinsights.com/mobile-marketing/app-marketing/consumer-mobile-usage/. Data source: Royal Pingdom, Yahoo "Mobile Modes" White paper, August, 2011.

Smith, Kevin. "The 25 Most Disruptive Apps of 2012." http://www.businessinsider.com/the-top-25-most-disruptive-apps-2012-12?op=1.

Google, "Understanding Mobile Users." Google Insights. http://www.thinkwithgoogle.com/insights/featured/understanding-mobile-users/.

You can get the Whitelines/ Springpad app at https://itunes.apple.com/se/app/whitelines-link/id552914549?mt=8.

To purchase a Whitelines notebook, visit http://www.whitelinesshop.se/link-a4-lined/340-0.

YOUTUBE IS THE PLACE TO VIEW VIDEOS

In Rule 26, we look at YouTube, the largest video site on the Web. We also discuss what to consider when choosing a tool to create company videos.

WHAT YOU NEED TO KNOW

You already know that online videos are a huge phenomenon. I'm sure you've watched videos sent to you by your family, friends, and colleagues. Oddly, because of the popularity of videos, some social media marketers are reluctant to dive in and upload their own company videos, fearing that they won't measure up.

The good news is that if you think through the issues surrounding video development, you might feel more confident about sharing your own content.

YouTube was launched in 2005. It is now second only to Facebook in number of unique visitors. Its content database is enormous. Nearly 8 years

YouTube was launched in 2005. It is now second only to Facebook in number of unique visitors. Its content database is enormous. Nearly 8 years of content is uploaded every day, according to YouTube's own statistics.

FIGURE 26.2
YouTube Show and Tell.

FIGURE 26.3
Mashable on YouTube.

UPLOAD VIDEOS

There are no major restrictions on uploading YouTube content other than the obvious ones about public decency and safety. This gives you the opportunity to showcase your business in any way that makes sense to you. You don't need permission to discuss a product or service. The only concerns you should have are whether the video connects with your target audience and whether they believe it is valuable. As a businessperson, you know what your parameters are.

ANALYZE BUILT-IN ANALYTICS

You can determine how well you are connecting with others by looking at the analytics that are part of the service. You'll be able to see such things as how many people are watching and which videos are the most popular.

WHY YOUTUBE IS GREAT FOR SOCIAL MEDIA

As we've done with other social media platforms, let's look at why YouTube is great for social media:

- **Built-in audience:** There are 800 million unique visitors on YouTube, which makes it second only to Facebook.

- **Content management:** One of the valuable aspects of YouTube is that it is a content management system for your videos. That means that you can upload your videos and be able to show them without dealing with hosting fees on another site. This is significant. After you have a link to your YouTube video, you can place that link on all your social media channels.

- **Storytelling:** The secret to great social media content is that it tells a story. If you can create videos that engage your viewer, you can hold their attention. That's not a small feat. Beware of creating a video that drones on about your company and never gives the viewer a reason to find out more about you and your products. (See Rule 3, "Social Media Is Storytelling, So Tell Stories," for more on storytelling.)

- **Search Engine Optimization (SEO) structure:** YouTube is structured so that the information you provide is properly sent to Google Search. (Remember that YouTube is owned by Google.) The work you have to do is provide the right keywords and think through the ways people will find you.

- **Free:** As with other social media platforms, YouTube is free. That's key because if you choose to host videos on your own site or on a different hosting site, there will be fees.

- **Apps:** There are YouTube apps for Android devices, iPhones, and the iPad. Your customers will be able to watch your videos while on the go.

- **Community features:** I've consolidated the features you need to look at to build your community. The first three are numbered as shown in Figure 26.4, and descriptions of them follow:

Share ——
Likes ——
Favorites ——

FIGURE 26.4

Malcolm Gladwell on YouTube.

1. *Likes:* This is a good measure of topics that stand out and really resonate, so look at your likes regularly. Also note if you get a thumbs down on a video and see whether you can determine why.

2. *Share button:* There is a Share button under every video. Click on that and select from the options. They include linking to social networks, creating a link to embed on your website or blog, and sending an email.

3. *Favorites:* If someone wants to bookmark the video, she can add it to her favorites by clicking the Add To button. Obviously, this indicates that you've interested someone in your content enough to have her watch it more than once.

- **Subscribers:** People who like your content can subscribe to your channel, as shown on Chris Brogan's channel in Figure 26.5. Obviously, getting people to subscribe is a goal. Just as with any other social platform, you want to have a dedicated audience who cares about your content and looks to you for something valuable.

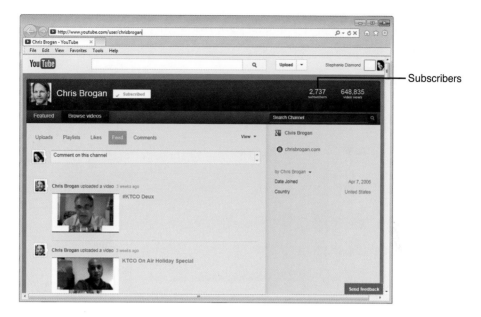

FIGURE 26.5

Chris Brogan on YouTube.

- **Commenting:** People can comment on your videos, as shown in Figure 26.6. They can also comment on your channel if you allow it. Remember that responding to people who comment is a good way to engage your viewers. If you are concerned about the kind of comments you might get, you can choose a setting that allows you to moderate the comments. You can also delete comments after the fact. Also, just as you would like to get comments, remember to comment on videos you find useful.

PROMOTION

Want to make it more likely that people will watch your videos? Consider the following tips:

- **Brand your content every time.**

   Make sure that every video you create has your branding. Don't think that just creating *channel* branding is enough. People need to see your branding many times before it registers. Reinforce it every time you send something out.

- **Develop brief videos.**

   Keep it short! Have you thought twice about watching something that was even five minutes long? Unless you are presenting a webinar you recorded, be brief. You want your audience to come back for more so respect their time.

Comments ——

FIGURE 26.6

Comments on YouTube.

- **Share your videos everywhere.**

  Don't forget to share your video links on all your channels. This includes email newsletters and blogs.

- **Consider sending bulletins and/or private messages.**

  You can send your subscribers something YouTube calls a "bulletin" if you want to alert them that you've posted something new. It's like an email blast. You can also send a private message to someone if warranted.

- **Pay for advertising.**

  Consider paying for advertising. But before you do, think through what you want to accomplish by spending this money. You need to know what your success metrics are so that you are not just doing it because your competitors are.

- **Include a call to action.**

  Every video should have a call to action. For example, you want to let your viewers know what to do next: how they can get your product, interact with your company, or sign up for your newsletter. Don't think it's obvious to them. Viewers aren't going to give it that much thought. They have too much to do. If it's important enough to create a video, it's important enough to set up a path for them to follow.

TIP Want private hosting? YouTube allows you to set up private videos that can be seen by up to 50 people. If you want to control your videos beyond this or have some specific need, there are other hosting services you can use, including these:

Vimeo: http://vimeo.com

Viddler: http://www.viddler.com/

Dailymotion: http://www.dailymotion.com/us

Wistia: http://wistia.com

TOOLS TO CONSIDER

Generally, the greatest stumbling block in creating company videos is lack of professional expertise. If you have the budget to get a professional video team, it is likely you have created at least a few videos. But what about those who don't have a budget or the approval of management to spend time creating videos?

One way to dip your toe in is to use an online tool and create a few "test" videos. Here are a few you might want to consider. (In the section "A Visual Marketing Method" we talk about collecting the content you need.)

SCREEN RECORDERS

Let's start with something very simple, a free screen recorder. Using one of these tools, you can easily develop a short tutorial or demonstrate your product. Then promote it and let your customers know that you have posted it on YouTube. Look at the feedback you get.

Here are some screen-recorder tools to consider:

- **Jing:** http://www.techsmith.com/jing.html

- **Screenr:** http://www.screenr.com/

- **BB FlashBack Express:** http://www.bbsoftware.co.uk/BBFlashBack_FreePlayer.aspx

- **Ezvid:** http://www.ezvid.com/

ADVANCED SOFTWARE

If you want to jump in a bit further, consider creating a test video with advanced screen-recording software. You need to have someone learn the software (or hire someone for an added fee), and then prepare some content to put in the video.

Here are some advanced software tools to consider:

- **ScreenFlow:** http://www.telestream.net/screenflow/overview.htm; fee

- **Camtasia:** http://www.techsmith.com/camtasia.html; fee

- **Storytelling Machines:** http://storytellingmachines.com, as shown in Figure 26.7; free

FIGURE 26.7
Storytelling Machines.

ANIMATED VIDEOS

Creating an animated video can be done with some of the tools listed in this section. The cost is moderate. It takes more time and effort to get the video done, but for these types of marketing videos, it can be effective.

Here are some animated-video tools to consider:

- **Sparkol VideoScribe:** http://www.sparkol.com/home.php

- **GoAnimate:** http://goanimate.com/

- **Powtoon:** http://www.powtoon.com, as shown in Figure 26.8

The goal of test videos is to help you get over the fear and confusion of starting to create videos. These tools can help.

FIGURE 26.8

Powtoon.

 # A VISUAL MARKETING METHOD

Method: What content can you repurpose to make creating videos easy?

If you find it hard to think of content to create for your videos, the first thing you should do is look at the content you already have.

> **TIP** If you haven't done a content inventory as suggested in Rule 7, "Know Your Content," you might want to go back over that rule now.

When it comes to video, we suggest that you look for the following "raw material" for repurposing:

- **Podcasts:** Look at the topics for which you created podcasts. This tells you that there is a need or an opportunity that you or staff responded to. Perhaps you interviewed an expert or answered some questions about a product launch. To capture the audio, you could take notes, have the audio transcribed, or use pieces of the audio as part of a video.

Good for: Training and tutorials, launches, interviews, and case studies

- **Product photos:** If you have good-looking product photos (and if you don't, you should), you can use them as part of your new video.

  Good for: Product demos, webinars, sales and marketing videos, in-store kiosk videos, and advertising

- **Testimonials:** Audio testimonials can always be repurposed if you don't have video. You can take a photo and put a voice-over of the client speaking.

  Good for: Social proof pages on your website and other social channels and emailed newsletter content

- **Video taken at events and trade shows:** You might have this already posted online, but that doesn't mean it couldn't be put in your video in a different context.

  Good for: Training and tutorials, sales and marketing videos

- **Questions asked on your support site:** This is valuable content. Not only should you use these questions to write articles for your channels, but you also should also use them to create little tutorials that can be placed on your support site.

  Good for: Training and tutorials, product demos, webinars, and launches

- **Information collected about customers you've served:** It is likely that you have created some form of case study or collected information on successful projects. These can be used to create showcase videos.

  Good for: Case studies, product demos, webinars, and advertising

- **Questions asked of your salespeople:** When you are considering product demos, don't forget to gather the questions most asked of your salespeople. Put these in videos that can be sent to all your channels to help boost leads.

  Good for: Sales and marketing videos, webinars, emailed newsletter video, and kiosks

 # IDEAS TO USE

YouTube's audience is second only to Facebook. If you are looking for a built-in audience to promote to, you should consider testing YouTube.

If you or your team is fearful about creating videos for your company, consider creating test videos with the tools recommended. If the result is not satisfactory, you have not have wasted your time. You'll know what you need to do to create better ones the next time.

Before you start creating new content for your videos, look at the content you already have that can be repurposed.

 IDEA MAP

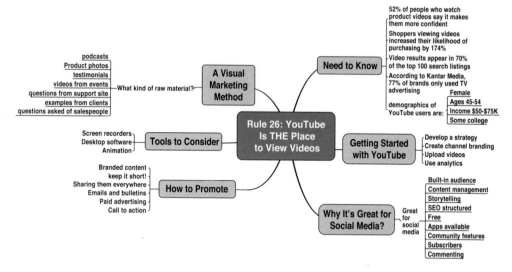

Idea Map for Rule 26

ENDNOTES

Chappell, Brian. "2012 Social Network Analysis Report." Ignite Social Media, July 2012. YouTube. http://www.ignitesocialmedia.com/social-media-stats/2012-social-network-analysis-report/#Youtube.

Kantar Media, "Kantar Media Finds Nearly a Quarter of Top Brands Are Using Online Video Advertising." http://kantarmediana.com/intelligence/press/nearly-quarter-top-brands-are-using-online-video-advertising.

"Video statistics: The Impact of Video." Invodo. http://www.invodo.com/html/resources/video-statistics/.

YouTube Statistics: http://www.youtube.com/t/press_statistics.

INDEX

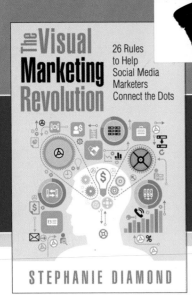

26 Rules to Help Social Media Marketers Connect the Dots

STEPHANIE DIAMOND

FREE
Online Edition

Your purchase of **The Visual Marketing Revolution** includes access to a free online edition for 45 days through the **Safari Books Online** subscription service. Nearly every Que book is available online through **Safari Books Online**, along with thousands of books and videos from publishers such as Addison-Wesley Professional, Cisco Press, Exam Cram, IBM Press, O'Reilly Media, Prentice Hall, Sams, and VMware Press.

Safari Books Online is a digital library providing searchable, on-demand access to thousands of technology, digital media, and professional development books and videos from leading publishers. With one monthly or yearly subscription price, you get unlimited access to learning tools and information on topics including mobile app and software development, tips and tricks on using your favorite gadgets, networking, project management, graphic design, and much more.

Activate your FREE Online Edition at
informit.com/safarifree

STEP 1: Enter the coupon code: RBDCUWA.

STEP 2: New Safari users, complete the brief regi
Safari subscribers, just log in.

If you have difficulty registering on Safari or accessing the onlin
please e-mail customer-service@safaribooksonline.com